Designs and their Consequences

Designs and their Consequences

Architecture and Aesthetics

Richard Hill

Yale University Press

New Haven and London

Printed in Singapore

Library of Congress Cataloging-in-Publication Data

Hill, Richard, 1948–
Designs and their consequences / Richard Hill,
p.   cm.
Includes bibliographical references and index.
ISBN 0-300-07948-6 (cloth: alk. paper)
1. Architecture – Philosophy.   2. Architecture – Aesthetics.
I. Title.
NA2500.H55   1999
720′.1 – dc21   98-50530
                                      CIP

A catalogue record for this book is available from
The British Library

Contents

'See what a difference it makes to the appearance of a room when the windows have the right proportion. – You think philosophy is difficult enough but I can tell you it is nothing to the difficulty of being a good architect. When I was building the house for my sister in Vienna I was so completely exhausted at the end of the day that all I could do was to go to a "flic" every night.'

Ludwig Wittgenstein,
quoted in *Ludwig Wittgenstein: Personal Recollections*,
ed. Rush Rhees, Oxford (Basil Blackwell),
1981, pp. 121–22.

Acknowledgements

I wish to thank the following people who have read drafts of part of the book, or helped with advice on specific topics: Jon Broome, Stuart Burchell, Louise Campbell, Philip Christou, Jane Darke, the late Robin Evans, Benedicte Foo, Michael Hatchett, Jill Hodges, Francis M. Jones, Michael Jones, Rodney Mace, David Medd, Andrew Peckham, Tim Ronalds, Robert Thorne, Steve Walker, Paul Williams, Ed Winters, Ken Worpole, Larraine Worpole.

Adrian Forty has been generous with comments, advice and encouragement; the latter has been particularly important, and I am most grateful to him. Peter Howard made it possible for me to begin work in earnest on the book while I was employed at Howard and Constable Ltd. He and his colleagues created a setting where debate about architecture and building was taken seriously. I, like many others, greatly value the experience of having worked for the company.

Katharine Ridler edited, and considerably improved, the text. Philippa Lewis, with the assistance of Tessa Gibson, took on the task of finding pictures and dealt with my queries with great patience and good humour. I am grateful to Laura Church of Yale University Press who helped me through the early stages of production. Gillian Malpass at Yale led me step by step through the business of making the book real. My heartfelt thanks are due for making the process such a pleasure.

My wife, Tanis Hinchcliffe, introduced me to a number of the topics that are discussed in the book, and I am indebted to her for the improvement they brought. But there is also a more private matter, which the reader cannot share, and I can only report, namely the marvellous gifts of patience and support that Tanis lavished on me. Between the lines, as it were, the reader might note my returning love and thanks.

Introduction

Aesthetics has the reputation of snuffing out the object it studies. Wordsworth's phrase was 'we murder to dissect'. Aesthetic theory, it is suggested, turns architectural pleasures, the human life in buildings and the lives of buildings themselves into dusty abstractions. As the avant-garde well knows, the arrival of the aesthetic theorist is a sign that it is time to move on to something new. My main reason for writing this book is to sketch out an opposite viewpoint: that learning about aesthetics can make the pleasures of architecture sharper, and our understanding of it keener. I should explain how this idea arose.

Some years ago I taught an adult education course entitled 'housing standards and aesthetics'. The idea behind it was that the design of housing embraces more than just the decisions of the architect. He or she works within a network of regulations, social norms, commercial decisions, technical choices, and each of these has an aesthetic dimension. It was interesting to prepare the course, and it was politely received, but at the end I had to admit that 'aesthetics' was as obscure a notion as it had been at the beginning. I then re-read Richard Wollheim's introduction to aesthetic theory *Art and its Objects*, hoping that it would illuminate the problem. It began to do this, but to my surprise and delight it began also to make sense of the day-to-day issues that I was facing at the time in running building jobs on site. In fact, it was one of the driest topics in aesthetics — the ontology of artworks — that seemed to have most resonance, since it connected with that gruelling and intriguing process in which designs are made into real buildings.

Wollheim's work on aesthetics is a prominent part of the Anglo-American or analytical stream of philosophical aesthetics. Such remarks touch a rather tender spot, since although I cannot claim any adequate grasp of that philosophical outlook, I am aware that it is the context in which I found myself. Essentially, this book records an attempt to relate my own understanding of architecture — formed in architectural training and experience — to my understanding of that kind of aesthetic enquiry. Metaphors about journeys, routes, landscapes have made their way into the writing, and this is unsurprising since it is exploratory. This also means that the reader is asked to hike through the same territory, not with the promise of reaching an exotic place, but with the more modest hope that they too will find the journey interesting.

The geographical metaphor does have limitations. I doubt that aesthetics is a single territory criss-crossed by paths made by different schools of aesthetic theory. It may be that particular outlooks define their own themes, which are of little interest to contending viewpoints. The argument of the book centres on three such themes, which are important to the analytical approach to aesthetics. The first asks what kinds of things works of art are: are they primarily ideas that find homes in physical objects, or are they the physical objects themselves? The second theme deals with the question of whether there is a distinctive kind of 'aesthetic experience' and, if so, how it relates to our ordinary perception of objects, and our ordinary emotional responses. The third asks why the arts are divided up in a particular way: what gives arts their individuality and what do they have in common? These are very general issues and their significance for architecture will emerge only as the arguments of the book develop.

The reader might object and ask on what grounds architecture is construed as an art, and might expect some kind of answer before spending time on following the twists and turns of a discussion that is based on that proposition. The short answer is that architecture is an art by virtue of being classed among the visual arts, belonging in turn to a larger system of the arts. This is a fact about the way that contemporary culture is structured and it connects with a great range of institutional features of training, patronage, criticism, curating which architecture shares with the other arts. But of course this might be just the point that the objector has in mind: architecture is an art, but only because it is put into that category. Since anything can be given the status of an art, merely by being put in a pigeonhole, there is nothing to be learnt from investigating such a category. Aesthetics cannot expect to learn much of interest by investigating the individual arts, architecture included: they are arts not because of what they are but because of what they have been called.

I cannot suggest a simple solution to this problem, and I shall have to depend on the reader's patience and to trust that the arguments that follow will address it from a number of standpoints, giving reasons to think that architecture's status as an art is not merely a matter of naming. The objector might wish to make an additional point, perhaps accepting that architecture is an art but going on to say that this in itself is a problem, since the fact that architecture is an art is a flaw in our culture. In other words, architecture is an art but it should not be. This idea gets support from many directions, from conservatives and radicals in politics and culture alike. Often it is based on the view that the art of architecture is superficial compared with the products of vernacular building, and moreover that it gets more superficial as time goes by. Architecture construed as an art allows the avant-garde to express their individual ideas, but this is an indulgence. This outlook holds that architecture properly construed engages practice and skill, within a visual tradition, but not the egotism of the artist. In short, it argues that architecture should forthwith cease to be an art, and so its discussions about the relationship between architecture and aesthetics are affected by that aim.

It may be impossible to achieve the aim, precisely because architecture is so deeply entrenched among the arts and in the culture generally, but even so I do not believe it is desirable that architecture should cease to be an art. Architecture's status as an art is indeed riven with difficulties, and among them the relationship between the artistic egotism of the architect and his or her social responsibilities looms large. But I do not believe that the fact that architecture is an art is in itself a problem. On the contrary, I believe that the arguments of this book put us in an affirmative mood, since, in helping to explain architecture's status as an art, we are able to say something interesting about an important project in which practical objects are given human significance.

I have pointed out that the book divides into three according to broad themes in aesthetic theory, but there is also another way of seeing the division. The first two chapters, which deal with the nature of architectural works, focus on the working practices of architects and their relationships with builders. As I have already suggested, the apparently dry topic of the ontology of architectural works must take its material from the day-to-day activities of the architect and builder. The second section of the book, running from Chapters Three to Six, deals with 'architectural experience' and its relationship to perception and feeling. Here I constantly refer to 'the spectator'. This is a simplification because the spectator will also perceive buildings using senses other than sight. However, since I argue that sight is by far the most important sense that we need to consider, it does not distort the issue. A further meaning of 'the spectator' alludes to the fact that we can experience buildings without using them. In an urban world we are spectators all the time as we go past buildings and see them in the distance; and a tourist, or anyone who visits buildings for pleasure, may be considered a spectator.

In the third section of the book another kind of actor appears, the user. For much of Chapters Seven and Eight users are shadowy figures, partly because the notion of use is surprisingly elusive. In turn, 'usefulness' comes to dominate the discussion, a looser category that suits the difficulties of definition, but the users are still there in the background. The question of usefulness, its general relationship to aesthetics, and the particular claim of architecture to be distinctively a useful art, raises theoretical problems as tricky as any in the aesthetics of architecture. However, there is no doubt that architecture derives from practical human needs. The theoretical difficulties should not obscure the basic hierarchy in which the building .of useful objects becomes the origin of a complex cultural project.

The arrangement of the chapters of the book appears to reverse this priority: it does not begin by examining the origins of architecture in usefulness, but with the fact that buildings are always preceded by designs. This means that we immediately have to face complex issues that arise from the historical development of architecture as an art. I believe that it is more appropriate to discuss aesthetic issues this way – to attempt to unpack the complexity of cultural objects rather than to hazard explanations of how their origins gave rise to such complexity. Chapter One therefore opens the discussion of ontological questions – those that ask what kind of thing architecture is – with a historical sketch of the idea that architecture is an art of design. I suggest that we can explore this idea in two ways. For theorists of architecture it has been used as a definition of what is essential to architecture as an art, placing the emphasis on the design for the building rather than the building as a physical object. We may also pursue the idea in another sense: namely that the practical activity of architects is dominated by the design process, separately from the process of building. In this sense architecture is an art of design because designing is what architects do. These two senses of 'the art of design' are related in complex ways.

The notion that architecture is primarily about design is important to the history of its development as an art in the post-Renaissance period. It does not, however, enable us to distinguish between designs which are considered to be at the centre of artistic developments and those that emulate, borrow from or vulgarise those designs, which makes it a blunt instrument for the purpose of aesthetic argument. But it is helpful in setting a broader context for questions of ontology. These are as relevant to understanding the design of the mass of building projects that are produced away from the artistic centre of architecture, as they are to understanding those central works. Chapter

One therefore provides a background against which the relationship of ideas, designs and buildings can be discussed in more detail, in the knowledge that these discussions are based on artistic definitions and on the practical organisation of building production.

Chapter Two begins by investigating the relationship between drawings and designs. I suggest that drawings are essentially pictures of buildings, although they may employ specialised forms of projection. The point is important in understanding the role of the builder: in order to organise the logistics of production the builder must have access to drawings which will enable him or her to visualise the completed object. Drawings are both physical objects in their own right and representations of other physical objects, namely buildings. I argue that it is more fruitful to consider proposed buildings in this light, so that the proposal is a representation of a physical object, than to consider that a proposed building is an idea which will later be made real.

Buildings are made in accordance with the numerous representations that are comprised in a set of drawings, but the drawings are not exhaustive of the aesthetic significance of a building. Two sets of issues are involved. The first revolves around the fact that many buildings can, in principle, be produced from a single design. In some cases this is important to the aesthetic identity of buildings, since we approach them as members of a larger class of objects. In other cases our aesthetic response to buildings is based on their uniqueness: accordingly, we need to have an explanation of how uniqueness can be imposed on the replicability of designs. The second kind of issue arises in both of these cases, and centres on the fact that the architect may continue to make decisions about the design of a building long after the drawings are finished. The chapter concludes by suggesting that in many cases the drawings for a building fail to specify aesthetically important aspects: the only sure criterion for the aesthetic identity of the building is the building itself.

Chapter Three opens the central part of the book, which focuses on the spectator's responses. My aim is to sketch an account of 'architectural experience' that follows from the physical identity of the building that is stressed in the previous chapter. I begin by criticising a view of architectural experience that was influentially expressed by Sigfried Giedion. It derived part of its force from modernist views of painting and sculpture, but I point out that it had roots in an older tradition of thinking about the relationship of the senses. In place of this view of architectural experience which assumes the fragmentariness of perception, the integration of the senses of touch and vision, and the importance of movement, I suggest an account that is based on the constancy of our perception of real objects, the importance of our knowledge of them as whole objects and the primacy of vision over the other senses.

The next chapter asks whether there is such a thing as the 'aesthetic experience' of architecture distinct from the ordinary kind of experience discussed in Chapter Three, because if there were, the study of aesthetics could be the study of that distinctive kind of experience. I begin by examining the idea that there is a kind of seeing that naturally brings emotion with it, that could be considered as distinctively aesthetic. Again, the idea has a long history, but it finds expression in the tradition of 'empathy theory' that flourished at the end of the nineteenth century and is still influential. The difficulty is that these arguments tend to be too blunt and generalised to give direct access to a special kind of 'aesthetic experience' but they do help to extend our understanding of the everyday raw material of experience, which an architect may then choose to dispose in pursuit of aesthetic effect.

The second type of candidate for 'aesthetic experience' arises from the distinction between realistic and non-realistic perception of objects. In the former case we see a building as it really is – a physical object of a certain kind – but in the case of non-realistic perception we are freed from realism. So, for example, in some lights we may see an opera house as sails over the waters of a harbour. However, there are cases where it is difficult to make a clear distinction between realistic and non-realistic perception: the pleasures that come from perceiving and contemplating the materials of buildings, or light in the interiors of buildings, or simple constructional forms, may have claims to being placed in both categories. Nevertheless, the notion of non-realistic seeing is a powerful one and it is the basis of the discussion of meaning and expression in the following two chapters.

The main thrust of Chapter Five is that an account of architectural meaning needs to be based on architecture's visual character, rather than analogies to language. I discuss some of the difficulties of the language analogy and in particular the temptation to think that because architecture has orderliness it therefore has a grammatical structure. I argue that architecture's orderliness takes many forms and has many charms, but that it is not grammatical. The task then is to develop an argument in favour of distinctively visual meaning. Architecture shares the type of iconic meaning that is central to painting and sculpture and this enables us to understand some of the aesthetic effect of architecture.

Our hope, furthermore, is to show that architecture has its own distinctive kind of visual meaning which is independent of the other visual arts. In the last section of Chapter Five I suggest that architecture delivers meaning in its own special way by encouraging us to see realistic aspects of buildings operating in quite unrealistic ways. So, to take a typical modern example, we may see a roof as hovering but also know that it is not really hovering at all. The argument rests on the proposition made by Wollheim about the 'twofoldness' of pictorial seeing, and it aims to find a distinctive place for twofoldness within architectural meaning.

Chapter Six carries the idea of non-realistic seeing into the field of expression. I begin by outlining R. G. Collingwood's influential theory of artistic expression and discuss some of its implications for architecture. However, the central aim of the chapter is to suggest a mechanism that will explain the fact that buildings can express human feelings and virtues. This suggestion is based on the idea that we see buildings as expressive because, at some level, we treat them as if they had the human facial and bodily characteristics that are appropriate to certain inner states. Chapters Five and Six so far employ somewhat specialist definitions of meaning and expression and at this point I make the more speculative suggestion that we endow buildings with varying kinds of significance out of an impulse to humanise the world of objects.

I begin Chapter Seven by discussing the idea that architecture is distinguished from the other arts by the fact that the use of buildings entails a distinctive kind of experience. There are difficulties with the proposition. It is true that users experience buildings differently from spectators but I do not believe that this difference points to a specifically architectural form of experience. In fact, users differ from spectators by virtue of the kind of attention that they engage, and these forms of attention are habitually in use in other areas of daily life and aesthetic experience.

I then turn to another kind of argument for architecture's special character as an art of usefulness, which can be found in Kant's account of the distinctions between the fine arts. The core of his argument is that the detailed aesthetic treatment of a building can give depth and complexity of meaning to a building's use. However, his idea of a building's use rests on a notion of building types and this in turn is a descriptive kind of endeavour – putting buildings into various categories. I believe that our expectations for the relationship between aesthetics and usefulness go deeper than that, and that we want aesthetics to respond to our sense of the purposiveness of use, to our sense that buildings are for something. This is the issue that dominates the second part of Chapter Seven, which proceeds by discussing in some detail the terms 'purpose', 'function' and 'use' that we habitually employ in attempting to relate the design and usefulness of buildings. The discussion suggests that we cannot take these terms and simply put them in the place of Kant's descriptive categories. The reason is that they do not enable us to specify usefulness in isolation from its physical settings: they entail interactive relationships between usefulness and designs.

Chapter Eight examines the response that modern architecture offered to this problem. The discussion about the relationship between aesthetics and usefulness found a new kind of focus in the intimacies of the design process. A 'sustaining outlook' developed, under the influence of Romanticism, which emphasised the sense that designing involved searching rather than making, and that this took place in a world of designs that already had a quasi-biological coherence. I suggest that this outlook is a way of responding to the kind of perplexities involved in notions of design, function and use that were discussed in the previous chapter. It does not solve these perplexities, but it enables us to think through them in a way that makes possible the production of new designs.

I then discuss the influential critique of modernist thinking that has been developed by Peter Eisenman. He has pointed to the logical difficulties that are entailed in trying to derive designs from statements about use or function. The argument was generalised in a series of essays and projects that successively aimed to show the arbitrariness of any kind of thematic basis to architecture. It in turn posed a challenge to the idea, central to the history of aesthetics, that the arts have features in common but they also have their own justification for being a particular art. Eisenman's work points us towards the possibility that architecture could be an art in general but that it need not be an art in particular. My own view is that this is untenable, and that an art without some particularity of theme will slide away into a kind of philosophical speculation. The chapter ends by admitting the great difficulties of making usefulness thematic. The fact that usefulness is fundamental to architecture does not mean that its relationship to aesthetics is simple.

Chapter 1

An Art of Design

1   Let us begin by discussing designs: they are, after all, where build-ings begin. In the mid-sixteenth century Giorgio Vasari put architec-ture alongside painting and sculpture, calling them the 'arts of design', and this grouping commonly came to be described as the 'fine arts'. We might today call them the visual arts, but it is important to note that Vasari stressed their design aspect rather than their visual aspect. *Disegno* is ambiguous in Vasari's meaning, just as it is in English: it can mean drawing and it can mean also the form or the scheme for an object. The latter meaning is significant for Vasari because it enables him to distinguish the arts of design from other traditional crafts which involve direct manual production. Patricia Lee Rubin points out that *disegno* brought together both Platonic and Aristotelian outlooks, the former in the notion of an ideal object which was to be depicted, the latter in the role of the artist's hand in mediating between the sense of sight and the world of abstract universals. Rubin notes also that the prestige of *disegno* already had a considerable history, especially in Florence, which took patriotic pride in its skill in *disegno*. Official support for the founding of the Accademia del Disegno in 1563 for-malised the connection.[1]

Vasari's stress on the design of painting or sculpture does not chime with present usage: that the painter or sculptor works by hand in the medium is now a sign of artistic prestige, not an aspect of artisan status to be put aside. For architecture, the point is still an essential one: architects draw and they make designs but they are not engaged in manual work on site. Vasari's definition therefore seems to offer something more than an arbitrary naming of architecture as an art: it seems to have roots in the developing practice of architecture.

By Vasari's time what architects did increasingly, though not universally, was to design one building after another, for others to build. The activity was learnt by practice, through familiarity with historical precedents and through knowledge of written texts and drawn exemplars. The model for architectural activity was to design a whole building, not merely to participate in a campaign constructing one element of a building that might take decades to complete. The paradigm came to include the design of both the interior and the exterior of the building, although in practice designing facades or interiors, or re-modelling existing buildings, were tasks that occupied much of architects' careers. We might contrast this working life with that of the master mason in charge of a project in a medieval setting. He was immersed in administrative, practical and financial tasks, as well as the design process, and the building rose around him. The fine art architect is immersed in the activity of design, but the purpose of that activity is always that an object will be produced at a distance, out of a separate building process.

The greater significance and prestige given to design in Italy, in comparison with the management of the whole building process, has a number of aspects. Few of the leading Florentine architects of the fifteenth century were recruited from the building trades: they came from among goldsmiths, cabinetmakers, sculptors and stonecutters, intarsia workers. Goldsmiths, for instance, had experience of making shrines and reliquaries in miniature architectural form, they made drawings and worked from them and had a practical knowledge of proportion and geometry and of decorative details. They and other craftworkers had well-developed design skills that were already linked to architectural forms.[2]

Early Renaissance architecture involved new forms of decoration and the application of new proportional and compositional systems. It did not as a rule involve new spatial arrangements and so did not pose technical challenges that would require experienced builders to stretch their existing skills. Architecture could become partly separate from building, since it was the application or ordering of decoration and embellishment to fairly conventional building volumes.[3]

Alberti's summary of the architect's position is written against such a background:

> Before I go any further, however, I should explain exactly whom I mean by an architect; for it is no carpenter that I would have you compare to the greatest exponents of other disciplines: the carpenter is but an instrument in the hands of the architect. Him I consider an architect, who by sure and wonderful reason and method, knows both how to devise through his own mind and energy and to realise by construction, whatever can be most beautifully fitted out for the noble needs of man, by the movement of weights and the joining and massing of bodies. To do this he must have an understanding and knowledge of all the highest and most noble disciplines. This then is the architect.[4]

Alberti forcefully expresses the separation between the architect and the manual trades. His view of the architect's role suggests that changes in the pattern of architectural practice were reflected back onto architects' perceptions of their own individuality. The size of architectural projects is relevant here. Architects increasingly made their living from selling design services for buildings commissioned by individual secular clients, and became less dependent on large church building projects.[5] But as important as the change in patronage was the fact that the architect was not expected to manage the whole construction project itself. Such arrangements hardly existed before the middle of the fifteenth century: an architect would not have been able to make a living out of design work on its own and would have had to take on the overall site management as well. This restricted the number of jobs that an architect could handle over the length of a career.

The change to a new pattern of practice developed first not in the Renaissance heartland of central Italy, but in northern Italy – Genoa, Vicenza, Verona – and in France. An example can be found in the work of Galeazzo Alessi, who prepared outline designs for numerous *palazzi* 'by remote control', with no detailed involvement in work on site. We can see in the careers of Philibert de l'Orme and Palladio the gradual development of a new pattern of architectural work. De l'Orme writes of some of the difficulties involved in the architect's new role, pointing out that since architects were not protected by a guild they had to be willing to take on a wide variety of work and to take on smaller commissions. He nevertheless advised that architects should supervise work on site, and had to face retaliation from masons and master builders who saw supervision as their role, and who claimed the status of architect but without the proper knowledge and training.

Palladio operated in a variety of ways in different jobs, sometimes involved in site management, sometimes going so far as to buy the stonemason's sharpening stones. Normally, he was employed for general site supervision, again an economic necessity since payments for the design stage were so meagre. His duties during the course of construction included making full-scale drawings of the masonry profiles. But there were occasions when his duties ended with the preparation of the design and the job was carried out on site under the supervision of another architect.[6] Changes in the way architects worked were interlinked with the capabilities of the building industry itself. Richard Goldthwaite points out that the growing independence and mobility of Florentine architects from job to job was made possible by the existence of a building industry comprised of stable and reliable groups of highly skilled tradespeople. The growing separation of architects from on-site production control was not necessarily related to the degradation or de-skilling of the building industry, as a Ruskinian might have us believe.

By being responsible for numerous varied and small jobs over a lifetime, rather than staying as designer, project manager and administrator in one place and perhaps for one large building over a lifetime, an architect could create a body of work – an 'oeuvre' – and could develop stylistically as an individual. Changes also took place in the fifteenth and sixteenth centuries in the running of larger projects. Although such projects retained much of the collective, consensual way of working that had characterised large religious building projects in the Middle Ages, there was a shift towards the dominance of an architectural director, with supporting advice from technical and constructional experts. That this could upset the traditional building industry is evident from the backlash that Sforza's architect Filarete experienced when he was appointed by the Duke as architectural director in Milan. When Philip II of Spain put Herrera in charge of the Escorial he did so outside the chain of command of the site staff, so that they could not sabotage Herrera's design from within and so that it could be implemented without modification.[7] The organisation of St Peter's, Rome, entailed a separation of architectural control from financial management and labour supervision. Individual architects benefited in cases where they were given untramelled control over a project, but they were themselves dependent on the recruitment decisions of their patrons who might decide on a joint directorship, as in the case of Fra Giocondo and Giuliano da Sangallo at St Peter's, in order to obtain both the artistic and complementary technical skills.[8]

Long-term projects were centres of training, as they had always been. Bramante's Vatican studio was a training ground for Raphael, Peruzzi and Michelangelo. But James Ackerman remarks that unlike the painters' workshops of the High Renaissance in which styles were continued and developed by many hands through a consistent organisation and practice, the architectural offices were ad hoc organisations with little stylistic cohesion. Their contribution was not the creation of a style but something more long-lasting, what Ackerman calls 'a rugged individualism', which set the tone for subsequent notions of the architect as an artistic personality.[9]

We can look at the stress on design, and the extension of individual architects' oeuvres, from a different viewpoint. Architects began to design buildings far away from their studios, working at a distance from the site, which they might see at only a few key stages in construction. Perhaps they were also becoming metaphorically distanced from their employers, who increasingly became clients, encountered once for a specific project, rather than patrons over a period of time. Working at a distance always puts a strain on the relationship between the architect and the building project. Brunelleschi found that work on the Foundling Hospital had not proceeded as he had anticipated in his absence,[10] and similar anecdotes are reported of both Vignola and Michelangelo. Architects had to learn new techniques of drawing, and develop new kinds of inspection routines on site. As architects' individuality and the newness of particular designs grew, so did the significance of drawings, since architects had to communicate their new ideas to builders trained in a traditional manner. The possibility could arise in architects' minds that drawings could be exhaustive of the aesthetic significance of the actual building. From there it is a short step to seeing the drawing as the special activity of the architect, emphasising their essentially private and individual relationship to architectural projects.

We could press this point further by considering the increase in texts of practical advice and example, substituting to a certain extent for the experience and skills learnt in a workshop group. Theoretical texts such as those of Alberti were initially of less significance than the manuscript pattern books that circulated among architects, but with Serlio in 1540, Delorme in 1568 and Palladio in 1570, architectural books embedded drawn examples and precedents of buildings into a setting of theory and explanation that was useful and accessible to practising architects (fig. 1). Architectural prints and their assembly into albums, such as those of du Cerceau (1576–79), had also developed by this time. Architects were no longer dependent for precedent, advice, example on their patrons and on their own practical experience but became part of an international culture of architectural style, which both extended the possibilities of an architect's range and also made the range available to all.

The authority of books was an important part of the claim of architects to high social status. Their claim was made easier by the fact that architecture became a subject in which princes and nobles took an interest. It was not necessarily disinterested knowledge: nobles could take advantage of the distinction between *disegno* and the practical execution of building to set the overall design of a building for others to execute. For example, Alberti, writing to his representative on site at S. Francesco, Rimini, chides him for doubting the practicality of his design of the cupola, based as it is on Roman models, and refuses to let him alter the positions of pilasters which had been set up for proportional reasons. He is ambivalent, however, on other structural matters, advising his representative to get specialist advice. One of the masons asks Alberti if he can visit him in Rome to discuss what he considers is an impractical suggestion for the vaulting of the nave. The relationship between the Duke of Urbino and his architect Laurana is also instructive. The Duke, it seems, decided the overall design and proportions of the palace, leaving Laurana in a mainly administrative and executive role. A most striking example is that of Cosimo de' Medici, who was said to have laid out the plan of the Badia at Fiesole himself, walking about the site, describing his wishes, tracing an outline in the ground. In attendance was a skilled master who noted it all down on paper.[11]

Nobles who became architects in this way were acting out a fantasy of the architect's developing role: that the architect should be all-powerful but should have no practical connection with the process of building on site. Biblical analogies of the role of architects therefore had to make nice distinctions. In describing Nicholas V's plans for refurbishing Rome, it was the Pope who was compared with King Solomon. Hiram of Tyre had not been the actual architect of the Temple, but only a highly skilled supervisor of works, and it was with him that Bernardo Rossellino, the architect, was compared.[12]

The important point is that architects became makers, albeit not of things, but of designs. They gradually lost their direct administrative contact with the process of making on site and with the immediate organisation of labour, materials and the logistics of construction. In return, they gained their own distinct mode of making things, but this time imagined things, future objects. The idea that architecture is an art of design captures this sense that architects are making things in their own right. It brings together a definition of architecture as an art, a body of aesthetic ideas, and alludes to developments in the working practices of architects.

2   We can see that two sets of issues are running closely parallel to one another. Vasari tells us that what is important about architecture is the design and that this enables architecture to take its place among the other arts of design. Then, looking at the development of architectural practice and its relation to building and clients, we have another reason to assert the importance of design. Here the stress is on the process of designing, whereas in Vasari's definition the emphasis looks inward to the nature of architecture. Although the two definitions run in parallel, the second has important implications that reach far beyond the central ground of artistic activity that Vasari wished to identify. In this part of the chapter I shall examine these implications.

The second type of interest in *disegno*, although it may have developed in inter-relationship with fine art architecture, is an issue that vastly exceeds the boundaries of that architecture. What I have in mind is that with the transition to modern types of urbanised economies and their vast demands for building, the separation between design and building becomes the typical case. In Vasari's time that idea of separation may still have served to distinguish artistic from vernacular production, but in an urbanising economy this could no longer be the case. A connected point is equally important. The expansion of the practical relations of *disegno* also brought with it a multiplication of versions of the designs that originated in the artistic centre of the building culture. The Vasarian impulse is now put under a great deal of pressure, since there is a real difficulty in distinguishing the works of fine art from those of the mass emulation of fine art designs.

Focusing on the origins of architecture as a fine art may induce the feeling that on the one hand there is architecture – what architects do – and on the other hand there is building. Since only a tiny minority of buildings has ever fallen into the category of works of art, it appears logical to confine discussion of the question of works of art merely to them. The vast mass of buildings which were never designed as works of art would then be discussed in some other context. This line of argument would neglect the fact that works of art became the object of emulation on a vast scale throughout the building culture: there may have been very few buildings that were designed as works of art, but there are very many which look like them. A myriad of buildings, not works of art themselves, is influenced by those which are. Fine art architecture is not only part of a wider field of architectural and building activity, but it is also indissolubly linked to the rest of that wider field.

The urbanisation of eighteenth-century England provides an insight into this process of the diffusion of art into everyday production. The proportion of the population living in the larger towns doubled over the century; an entirely new hierarchy of urban centres developed, with towns such as Birmingham, Liverpool, Manchester and Leeds taking over from the county towns. Towns developed new specialised identities, as ports, manufacturing centres, dockyards and resorts; and a new kind of urbanised countryside developed in manufacturing districts. All this involved the construction of houses in prodigious quantities across a range of prices, as well as more almshouses, hospitals, workhouses, charity schools, chapels, churches, town halls, exchanges, assembly rooms, theatres, factory buildings, warehouses and canal installations.

Such a volume of construction work entailed the expansion of the building industry, and the way in which it occurred is of great interest. The tasks involved in building – detailed design, supervision, surveying, management – as well as the actual building trades, were carried out by tradespeople working independently or in small groups in constantly shifting alliances. Knowledge of the techniques involved in all these tasks had to be widely dispersed. In conditions of expanding demand the building trade could therefore be a route for economic and social upward mobility, with self-education a principal vehicle along it. Trained carpenters could go on to learn about the essentials of other trades through their partners in small development ventures, but they might then be hungry for knowledge and information from books. They would need to pore over and understand examples of complex roof constructions and joinery detailing that they had not yet encountered in practice. They would need to be adept at arithmetic for pricing, surveying, measuring, buying materials, and would devour ready reckoners, price books and arithmetic primers. They would be interested in texts that set out standard designs for cottages, houses and agricultural buildings. They would need to know how to decorate a building, how to design a doorcase, how to choose an appropriate moulding. And thus they would need to know the Orders and all the associated rules for classical architecture.

This created a programme for architectural publishing driven from below rather than from the patrician viewpoint of earlier texts. Its origins have been traced to the sixteenth century, through the popularity of classical primers such as Hans Blum's *Quinque Columnarum*, Shute's *The First and Chief Groundes of Architecture* and Billingsley's *Euclid*.[13] The striking point is that by the eighteenth century technical and stylistic advice are not seen as two separate compartments deserving two sorts of books. Textbooks of building typically unite technical information with advice on architectural style. 'Useful propositions in geometry' may be the prelude to more specific instruction in carpentry; or guidance on arithmetic and geometry, or on the making of scales. Plain trigonometry, mensuration, mechanics and hydrostatics might be interspersed among other chapters on design, mouldings and building construction.

The two largest books of instruction, Isaac Ware's *A Complete Body of Architecture* of 1756 (running to 748 pages) and Batty Langley's *Ancient Masonry* (1736; 934 pages), each have extensive sections on mathematics. In Ware's case it forms Book 10 of his giant volume, dealing with 'the sciences and arts subservient to architecture' and comprises a system of arithmetic; the rule of 3; geometry; perspective and mensuration. The book ends with a complete worked example of a priced bill of quantities. The first 428 pages of Langley's are taken up with arithmetical and geometrical lectures. Only then does he begin his exhaustive depiction of alternative treatments of the orders.

Books of instruction varied in size, from these vast compilations to pocket books a few inches square, thus suiting a range of budgets. At the modest end of the scale Francis Price's *The British Carpenter* (1759), after sections on geometry and the techniques of carpentry, moves on to Palladio's orders of architecture, with the appropriate ornaments of doors and windows. William Pain's *The Builder's Pocket-Treasure or Palladio delineated and explained* (1763) combines, as its title implies, instruction in carpentry with instruction in the orders (figs 2 and 3).

Batty Langley is the most famous of these publishers. His numerous volumes of technical and aesthetic advice, whether in sumptuous or modest formats, were collages of examples generated elsewhere in an energetic and profitable process of recycling. An academy supplemented the publishing programme, one which we might nowadays describe as a distance learning system. Langley offered access to technical and aesthetic skills, and the possibility of social and economic advancement.

The territory of *disegno* was vastly more extensive than that occupied by the leading artist architects who were the focus of Vasari's attention. It was not only fine art architects who used drawings, and it was not only in the context of the fine arts that designs took on lives of their own. It seems rather that the distinctive kind of work that architects did, centred on drawings, was greatly generalised across the building industry. It is possible that Vasari wished to distinguish the work of the finest architects from the world of artisan building. The distinction may still have been meaningful in his day, with artisan building proceeding on the basis of custom and practical knowledge, and fine art architecture becoming reliant on drawings. But by the eighteenth century this split was no longer significant. The entire design and building culture was imbued with the use of drawings and these made it possible for the modes of fine art architecture to replace an artisan culture of design.[14]

Designs can be disseminated in other ways than the publication of drawings. Consider the striking example of the production of artificial stone in the second half of the eighteenth century. Although a market had previously existed for this material, it was the establishment of Eleanor Coade's Manufactory in 1769 that marked the beginning of large-scale reliable production.[15] The first step in the process was to sculpt a clay model; a reverse plaster mould was made of this. The final material, a mixture of clay, crushed stoneware, flint, fine sand and a

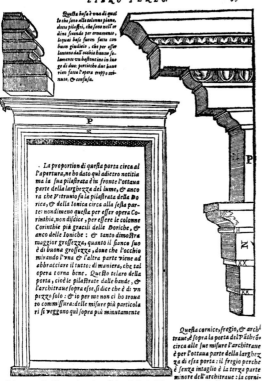

Questa base è una di quel le che sono alle colonne piane, dette pilastri, che sono nell' or dine secondo per ornamento, lequai base furon fatte con buon giudicio, che per esser lontane dall'occhio hanno so lamento un bastone ino in luo go di dua: perciochè due haue rien fatta l'opera troppo mi nuta, & confusa.

. La proportion di questa porta circa al l'apertura, ne ho dato quì adietro notitia ma la sua pilastrata è in fronte l'ottaua parte della larghezza del lume, & anco ra che Vitruuio fa la pilastrata della Do rica, & della Ionica circa la sesta par te: nondimeno questa per esser opera Co rinthia, non disdice , per essere le colonne Corinthie più gracili delle Doriche, & anco delle Ioniche :   & tanto dimostra maggior grossezza, quanto il fianco suo è di buona grossezza, done che l'occhio mirando l'una & l'altra parte viene ad abbracciare il tutto: di maniera, che tal opera torna bene. Questo telaro della porta, cioè le pilastrate dalle bande , & l'architraue sopra esse, si dice che è di un pezzo solo : & io per me non ci ho trova to commissura: delle misure più particola ri si veggono quì sopra più minutamente

Questa cornice, fregio, & archi traue, è sopra la porta del Pãtheõ, circa alle sue misure l'architraue è per l'ottaua parte della larghez za di essa porta : il fregio perche è senza intaglio è la terza parte minore dell'architraue : la corni ce è alta quanto l'architraue circa a i membri particolari egli sono proportionati all'opera grande doue col compasso si potrà trouare tutte le parti .

1   Details of the interior of the Pantheon, Rome, from Sebastiano Serlio, *Tutte l'Opere d'Architettura et Prospetiva*, Book Three (1540).

3 (*facing page*)   Setting out a staircase, from William Pain, *The Builder's Pocket-Treasure*.

2 (*below*)   Instruction in the classical orders, from William Pain, *The Builder's Pocket-Treasure or Palladio delineated and explained* (1763).

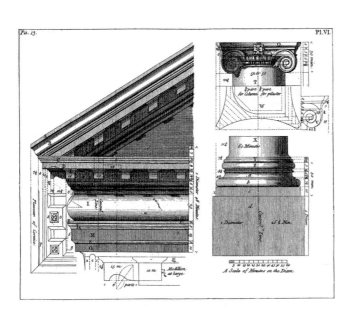

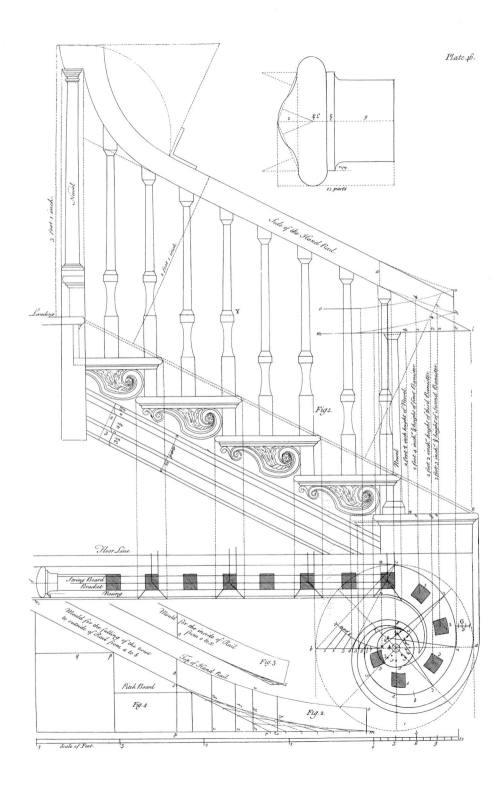

Plate 46.

Side of the Hand Rail.

Fig. 1.

Newel

3 feet 1 inch.

2 feet 1 inch.

Y

Newel

Landing

3 feet 4 inch height of Newel.

2 feet 4 inch Height of First Baluster.

2 feet 2 inch height of Third Baluster.

3 feet 3 inch Height of Second Baluster.

12 parts

Floor Line

String Board
Bracket
Nosing

Mould for the falling of the twist
to outside of Rail from a to b

Mould for the inside of Rail
from o to x

Fig. 3

Top of Hand Rail

Pitch Board

Fig. 4

Fig. 2

Scale of Feet.

vitrifying agent, was then pushed into the mould. After removal from the mould the items were left to dry before being fired at a high temperature. The process was technically advanced and could produce sculptural objects up to nine feet (nearly 3 m) in length.

Coade's approach to marketing bore some similarities to Wedgwood's system of showrooms and catalogues.[16] She set up a gallery, carefully designed as an architectural ensemble using Coade products and, of course, a catalogue, which in 1784 contained no fewer than 700 designs. Items could be ordered by post and would be delivered directly to the customer, in the later period by means of Pickford's canal transport. Small items were made for stock, and some popular items may also have been made in batches, but it appears that most production was carried out on the basis of individual orders, either from the catalogue or as single commissions.

The range of products was extraordinary – garden ornaments; individual building components ranging from columns to balustrades; external decorations for buildings, such as paterae and medallions; tripods and pedestals for furniture; small ornaments which could be used both inside and outside buildings; unique productions that ranged from the enormous sculptural ensemble at Greenwich Hospital to the strongly authentic-seeming Gothic screen at St George's Chapel, Windsor. The partial records of the firm that are still available name 148 architects who used Coade stone.

The Coade catalogue could be thought of as the mid-point in a chain of draughting and production processes. Beyond the catalogue lie the stages of production, sales and distribution. Preceding it is the process of accumulating designs. Coade bought plaster casts of classical sculptures and authoritative volumes of reproductions of classical sculptures and architectural elements. Effort was devoted to ensuring the greatest possible fidelity of reproduction. In an older architectural culture an element, passed on by example from one craftworker to another with only poor or rudimentary drawn examples to go on, would have mutated as it went from hand to hand. The Coade system aimed to avoid contamination by the intermediate processes of production. Ionic and Doric columns, for example, were updated to take advantage of the latest archaeological research as soon as it was published.

Along with this fidelity of reproduction went the possibility of re-combinations of primary elements into new ensembles. An important feature of the production process was that pieces from a number of moulds could be joined together after moulding but before they dried and were fired in the kiln. On completion they would appear as a single object. One of the most charming of these transmutations is the set of Ionic capitals at All Souls Langham Place, London, where winged cherubs nestle within the volutes (fig. 4). The cherubs come from one mould, the capitals from another, and they were joined together before being sent to the kiln. These mutations of designs which started life with strict Classical pedigrees opened up a world quite different from that of craft production, where mutations bear the imprint of a particular maker. Aspects of the original design remain perfectly intact within the mutation and form part of a new whole.

The history of moulding planes provides a further example of the force of 'mechanical' imitation.[17] Up to the mid-seventeenth century carpenters and joiners made their own planes. After that, when a wider range of classical mouldings became general, special planes began to be manufactured, the cutting edges of which were ground to the shape of a given moulding (fig. 5). A surviving example of a cabinetmaker's tool chest contains 75 planes. Up to about 1840 firms making moulding planes were family concerns headed by a master craftworker, becoming factory-type businesses after that date. In order to make a number of planes of a standard profile, it was necessary to have a 'mother plane'. This incorporated the moulding in reverse and was used to make the moulded underside of each individual plane. The moulding was transmitted from the mother plane to a multiplicity of individual moulding planes and then, over a multiplicity of craft careers, to a myriad pieces of finished joinery. Before factory production, moulding planes were made on a piecework basis within the master's workshop. The mother plane, however, remained the property of the master. A mother plane is merely a shape, a design or, more specifically, a means of enforcing a shape on another piece of material. It is an abstract shape, and it is a physical thing in the world, a hard cutting edge; but it is also an economic entity, part of the means of production for the master of a small workshop.

These kinds of developments suggest that the notion of *disegno* can usefully be extended from its origins in fine art architecture to a much larger view of the building process. Then there are further ramifications for fine art architects themselves, since the projects that they designed were also influenced by wider changes in the building process. The work of the Adam brothers provides examples of the ways that the newly independent lives of designs could form a crucial part of a new pattern of architectural practice.

The key innovation in plastering in eighteenth-century Britain was the use of 'composition' for the production of the repetitive enrichments which were an essential part of decorative ensembles. Composition was in use in France from the time of Louis XIV but its importation into Britain is generally associated with the Adam brothers.[18] Along with the wide use of composition enrichments came an extension in the types of moulds that were used – sulphur and metal as well as boxwood and pearwood. In a typical Adam design the plane of the ceiling is left flat or in simple coved shapes. There are no heavy mouldings projecting deep below the ceiling, as would have been the case with earlier styles. Panels of very low-relief sculpture are introduced in places, many carried out with great virtuosity by Joseph Rose and his nephew. However, the bulk of the plasterer's work was now of two kinds: the broad expanses of smooth planes which, though requiring consummate skill to achieve a perfect finish, do not require any aesthetic interpretation; and the applied 'enrichments', made of composition paste pressed into wood or metal moulds. The moulds themselves are works of great skill in carving, but the process of applying the warm pieces of composition that were removed from them to the prepared flat and curved panels of the ceilings needed care, dexterity and accuracy, rather than a sculptor's eye (fig. 6). The overall process economised on sculptural work, devising a style which combined a large quantity of less skilled work in applying the enrichments with much very high-quality, but not imaginatively conceived, broad work.

4 (*left*) Capitals at All Souls' church, Langham Place, London, supplied by Coade's Manufactory (1824).

5 Examples of moulding planes, from the Building of Bath Museum.

6 Samples of composition decorations at George Jackson and Sons, produced from carved wooden moulds. Many date from the origins of the firm (in which the Adams participated) in the 1780s.

The economic and logistical implications of the Adam style of plastering are striking, but need to be considered in the context of the
way that their entire architectural office was run. One of the distinguishing features of the practice was a higher level of fees than the 5%
typical at the time. This made it possible to have a large office staff
producing highly detailed drawings of each decorated surface of a
project, complete with furniture, providing an unusually comprehensive interior design. Robert Adam would produce a charcoal or pencil
outline drawing and give it to the draughtsmen to work up in suc-
cessive levels of detail, concluding with a final working drawing rendered in the intended colours.[19] Comparisons of the drawings with the
actual projects show that the plasterers and other trades executed the
work exactly in accordance with the working drawings, having little
scope for exercising their own aesthetic choices (figs 7–9). The clients,
however, could be confident that they would get exactly what the
architect had promised – in fact, a largely two-dimensional, but full-
size, version of the architects' final scale drawings.

One consequence of this pattern of work was that not only did the
balance of site work change from *in situ* to moulded and applied work,
but the overall balance of site work and office work changed. Inputs
of skilled labour on site were substituted by a greater level of detail of
working drawings, prepared in the office according to a standard procedure, by draughtsmen who were highly experienced and productive.
The centre of gravity of the design process was moving closer to the
architect, away from the craftworker and the site.

It was the Adams' fate that imitators could take any or all of the elements and reproduce them at will. The two-dimensionality of the style
certainly assisted this: it provided a repertoire of elements that could
be disposed in a new design on the drawing board. Whereas a Baroque
ceiling might need a sculptural skill in order to fit it to a particular
site, the appropriation of an Adam design could be done on paper, as
pattern-making. George Richardson, who had worked for the Adams
and subsequently published his book of ceiling designs based on that
experience, put it like this:

From this collection, the nobility and gentry may not only make a choice and have it executed, but by blending particular parts, with others, may form new designs according to their fancy. The architect may also occasionally find assistance from this work, by altering the arrangement of the different compartments, as they admit of almost infinite variation . . . It may also be serviceable to several professions for other purposes, as the figures, the ornaments and the enrichments can be introduced with propriety in other subjects that require embellishment.[20]

The work of the Adam brothers exemplifies the changing relationships of architect, builder, craftworkers and client. The individual architect, now at a distance from the project, produced detailed designs for the work. They were his designs not the craftworker's, and this strengthened the sense that architects produced complete and controlled works of art, although in the medium of drawing and therefore separately from the actual building process. But precisely because they had become merely designs, 'pieces of human invention',[21] they could be reproduced, borrowed, vulgarised. They were both the architect's private productions and part of the public world of artistic emulation, and its counterpart world of plagiarism.

3   Vasari's proposition that architecture is an art of design has proved to be fertile in unexpected ways. Firstly, we began to see that the term 'art of design' could have two kinds of meanings. The distinction is not easy to capture concisely. One kind of meaning looks towards the nature of architecture as an art, inwards towards what is essential about it as an art. This is the way in which Vasari uses the term. In the other sense, architecture is an art of design when seen in the context of activities and practices that link it with the outer world of builders, producers of building elements, clients, books. This ambiguity could be taken as an instance of the principle that we can observe a cultural phenomenon from a number of viewpoints. So we can look at the idea of architecture being an 'art of design' in the context of the history

Ceiling for the Saloon at N dele

7 (*facing page top*)   Sketch design for the ceiling of the Saloon at Nostell Priory, Yorkshire, in the hand of Robert Adam.

8 (*facing page bottom*)   Working drawing for the ceiling of the Saloon at Nostell Priory.

9   The Saloon at Nostell Priory (1765–75).

of ideas on the one hand, and the history of cultural practices on the other. But the issue is more complicated and interesting than that, because ideas and cultural practices do affect each other: they are not just two viewpoints from which we can choose to look at the development of architecture, but two aspects of reality. Theories about architecture as an art of design affected the ways that architects worked; and, conversely, institutional changes in the demand for buildings, the organisation of the profession and the scale and technical complexity of the building industry affected the way that architecture was construed as an art of design. Issues of ontology, of what the architectural object is, arise in both these relations: viewpoints affect practice and practice influences viewpoints.

Secondly, we found that if we enquired about the definition of an art we might find ourselves coming across a much broader field of cultural activity than we had expected. The fine arts had centres, in which new kinds of works were generated, and extensive peripheries in which those works were emulated, imitated, reproduced. Perhaps our expectation was that definitions of the fine arts would point to that centre of artistic activity, and would provide a means of distinguishing it from the periphery of everyday cultural activity. However, when we hauled in its catch, the idea that architecture is an art of design brought with it not only the prized creatures at the centre of the art, but also a vast number of lesser fish. It is not simply that the idea of an 'art of design' is too crude a concept to distinguish central products of art from peripheral ones, but that the relation of peripheral to central designs involves exactly that *disegno*-like split between designs and production which we are attempting to use to define the centre of the art itself. The implications of the 'art of design' appear everywhere and not just at the centre of the art: they also provide the mechanism which makes possible the vast multiplication of designs originating at the centre.

In the next chapter I shall accept that discussions of ontology – of the nature of architectural objects – are likely to lead us into a much wider cultural field than the central canon of architectural works. This does not mean that discussions of art need to be abandoned for a broader category, for example of cultural production, for the important reason that we have learnt just how difficult it is to make a clear distinction between the centre of art and its periphery, and how pervasive artistic questions are across the whole cultural field. But the argument will move away from the kind of question that opened this chapter, 'what constitutes architecture as an art?', and that proposed the answer 'that it is an art of design'. Instead, I shall focus in more detail on the inter-relations of ideas, designs and drawings in the following chapters. To conclude this chapter, I shall briefly comment on the further history of how the question was answered, since that will provide more evidence of the centrality of questions of ontology in the aesthetics of architecture.

4   Architecture was the last art to join 'the modern system of the arts', as Paul Kristeller has pointed out. He had in mind the grouping that comprised music, poetry, painting, sculpture and, from 1751 onwards, architecture. The significance of the date is that in 1751, in the 'Discours Préliminaire' of his and Diderot's *Encyclopédie*, d'Alembert was the first to put architecture alongside those other fine arts.[22] Kristeller's remark is an arresting one partly because it jolts our sense that architecture has a long history as an art. It does, but his point suggests that the status of architecture before 1751, and the company it kept among other human activities, might be strange and unfamiliar to us. The remark is also striking because it carries the sense of a cultural edifice being completed. The process of construction of 'the modern system of the arts' had begun in earnest in the Renaissance and went through many stages of trial and error but finally it was finished in 1751. The structure has been robust in the succeeding years: architecture still maintains its prestige in the company of music, poetry, painting and sculpture. It is true that we no longer use the term 'the fine arts' but we capture the same idea with the shorter usage 'the arts'.[23] It is also true that the constellation of the arts has changed: the novel in the nineteenth and the movies in the twentieth century have been the most obvious additions. The date 1751 is striking for a further reason, which is that the mid-eighteenth century is often seen as a watershed in architecture, broadly, as the beginning of the modern architectural world.[24] It is an interesting thought that architecture becomes a fine art just at the moment when it is becoming modern.

The way in which architecture was treated in the *Encyclopédie* has been investigated by Kevin Harrington in some detail. Entries on particular aspects of architecture were largely contributed by the architect and theorist J.-F. Blondel, whereas the 'Discours Préliminaire' was written by d'Alembert, who together with Diderot was joint editor of the whole enterprise. Harrington suggests that two approaches to the definition of the fine arts can be discerned. In other writings Blondel had described architecture as a fine art but clearly he had something quite different in mind from the kind of system that Kristeller describes, since he considered architecture an art on which the fine arts of agriculture, painting and sculpture are dependent. Harrington proposes that Blondel, as a professional architect and specialist educator, was not much concerned with the relationship of architecture to non-visual arts: that tended to be a question that interested amateurs and theorists.[25]

The latter role was taken by Diderot and d'Alembert. Neither was an expert on architecture, and it appears that it was the process of compiling the structure of the *Encyclopédie*, in the 'Prospectus' and the 'Discours Préliminaire', that helped them to develop their views on the subject. In fact, the place of architecture shifts significantly in the short period between the production of the 'Prospectus' in 1750 and the 'Discours Préliminaire' of the following year. In the earlier publication Diderot placed architecture in the sphere of reason and among 'the science of the needs of man' or 'natural jurisprudence'; it found its location among the other fine arts, in the sphere of imagination, only in 1751. The difference between these approaches and that of Blondel suggests that the place of architecture among the other arts can be discussed from the top down, in the manner of Diderot and d'Alembert's proposals, or from the bottom up, as the theorist-practitioner Blondel attempted. In the former case the setting is the entire geography of human knowledge and action, and in the latter it is the more modest territory of the organisation of practical trades, professions and callings.

For d'Alembert, architecture takes its place among the fine arts because it is an art of imitation. Here is another kind of answer to the question of what constitutes architecture as an art. The prevailing view at the time, derived (and greatly generalised) from Aristotle's *Poetics*, was that the concept of imitation provided the defining feature of the fine arts. Architecture had not conventionally fitted into a theory of imitation. Kristeller points out that Batteux, writing an influential treatise on the division of the arts shortly before the *Encyclopédie*, had not included architecture among the imitative arts,[26] and it was d'Alembert's innovation to do so in the 'Discours Préliminaire'. His argument was that architecture imitates nature because its interplay of structural similarity with the contingencies of particular designs imitates the way that nature combines structural similarity with variety.[27]

The question of imitation had often been discussed in relation to architecture before the mid-eighteenth century. The significance of the *Encyclopédie*'s definition is that architecture becomes an art of imitation at the strategic rather than the tactical level. The decision was necessary if architecture was to take its place among the other arts, since imitation was the concept that was believed to unify the arts. This view was powerful for a period, but its dominance eventually began to be eroded and by the 1830s other views of the unity of the arts, derived from Romanticism, were commonplace. The shift in attitudes left architecture's status as an art untouched, and may indeed have strengthened it. However, I want to make a suggestion about the weakness of the *Encyclopédie*'s definition, namely that it grated against aspects of the practice of architecture.

Consider the notion of imitation in a much wider sense than d'Alembert's. Coade's moulds and a joiner's moulding planes can form the basis of mechanical imitation; books can provide sample designs and architectural details; casts derived from actual classical buildings can provide examples to copy; the principles of the classical Orders can be codified in writing and in drawings, to be learnt and reproduced; and at the most abstract end of this process we return to d'Alembert who asserts that most elevated responsibility of the architect, to imitate the structure of nature herself.

Venetian Windows of the Tuscan Order whose Members are described at large in Plates I. II.   Plate XI.

Batty Langley Invent and Delin. 1739.   Thos. Langley Sculp.

10   Imitation disapproved: a plate from Batty Langley, *The City and Country Builder's and Workman's Treasury of Designs* (1745).

11   Imitation approved: measuring antiquities on site. An illustration from Sir John Soane's Royal Academy Lectures.

12 (*facing page*)   From A. W. N. Pugin, *Contrasts* (1836).

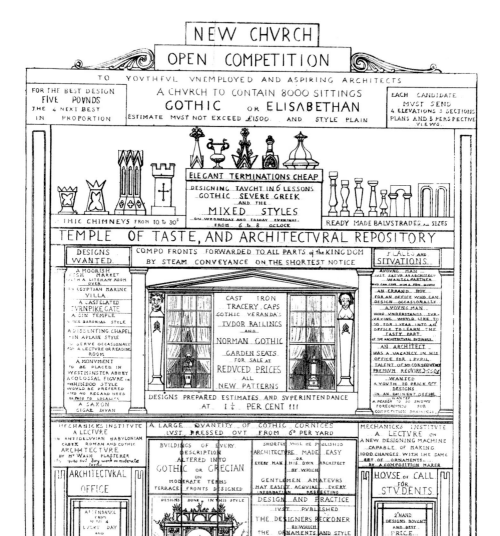

The point is not merely a play on words. The existence of a spectrum of possibilities for imitation caused intense anxiety at the end of the eighteenth century and the beginning of the nineteenth. Students of architecture at the Royal Academy in London were forbidden to copy from Batty Langley's useful compilations and were required to study authentic casts and fragments (figs 10 and 11). David Watkin points out that Sir John Soane, that most assiduous collector of architectural fragments, saw Langley as part of the cause of the low level of current architecture, where 'everything seems to threaten us with an entire decay'.[28] Behind the lament is the fact that a process of copying was centrally involved in both the formation of fine art architects and in the formation of the carpenter who became a surveyor and an architect. Perhaps the worry was that architecture's social status would be eroded: the mass reproduction of designs would vulgarise architecture, vulgarise it in the dictionary sense, of spoiling it by 'making too common or frequented or well known'.

To sustain imitation as the founding aesthetic principle for architecture required the most subtle reasoning that the Neo-classical movement could muster, and it always had to remain at a high level of abstraction in order to keep architecture safe from the tide of vulgarisation. By the early nineteenth century the role of imitation could no longer be sustained and Romanticism offered its own pole of attraction. Accompanying this shift in sensibility was the wholesale rejection of the practice of copying. In *Contrasts* Pugin viciously satirised the 'new improved and cheap principles' that the nineteenth century acquired out of the profusion of imitative practices: the gimcrack reproductions, the riotous profusions of styles, the promise that architecture could be learnt from ready reckoners or in six lessons. He illustrated a spoof poster to support his point – 'Mechanicks Institute: A lecture on a new designing machine capable of making 1000 changes with the same set of ornaments. By a composition maker' (fig. 12).[29] Pugin had originally made his living as a pattern-designer, illustrator, seller of designs, so it is the more touching when he later remarked that he wished to produce a treatise on 'Natural Architecture'[30] that would assert the virtues of simple practical design as it is practised by artisan builders.

My suggestion is that the definition of architecture as an art of imitation runs into trouble because imitation – taken in a broad sense – gradually came to be seen both as the origin of architecture and also the cause of its decline and degradation. The attempts to insulate special kinds of imitation and to cast out others could not prevent this. The situation is not dissimilar to that of Vasari's definition, which could not separate the core of an art from a vast periphery. Building everywhere became an art of imitation, just as building everywhere took on the characteristics of an 'art of design'. The view of architecture's artistic nature that derived from Romanticism (discussed in Chapter Eight) responded to this difficulty by making its defining feature an approach to design so dependent on personal outlook and sensibility that only those who had been inculcated with that outlook in formal training could profess it. Romanticism saved architecture from imitation by turning it inward, so that the definition of a true architect became not the kind of objects that were designed but the kind of creative life that was led. It seems that theorists are not free to define the art of architecture just as they wish. The real relationships between design and building, set in the larger culture and economy, may make such a definition unstable and, in the end, untenable. Those real conditions of building will press against the definition and make it blunt.

Chapter 2

Designs and Buildings

1   What is the relationship between designs and real buildings? In the previous chapter I assumed that designs and drawings were intimately linked but the connection needs to be set out in more detail. The first task is to revise the notion of a design, recognising that the design of a whole building will be too complex to be captured in a single drawing. Buildings require multitudes of drawings and an Adam ceiling design on a single sheet is a misleading simplification of what is involved. The design of the building as a whole is in that set of drawings, but it is also important to note that it is unified in the architect's mind. This mental construction unifies the fragmentary content of the drawings into a single object. Architects know buildings off by heart and with a level of complexity and detail that could never be achieved in a single drawing. This knowledge, whether of a real or imagined building, remains in the mind when the architect is unaware of it, as knowledge does.

We can, on demand, form mental images of those aspects of real or imagined buildings of which we have knowledge, and architects do so with vividness and accuracy. The limitations on forming such mental images are similar to those that apply to ordinary seeing. For example, we cannot see part of the outside of a building and the corresponding inner face at the same time, and nor can we imagine an interior and a facade simultaneously. It could be objected that many forms of drawings do precisely this, presenting a number of aspects of a building on a single sheet (fig. 13). We can see this as a single drawing, and we may be able to memorise the layout of the whole drawing, but we cannot really look at two or more of the component views simultaneously: at best we can attend to one view and have in mind its relation to others on the sheet. But it is difficult to divide attention equally between two images.

Some clarification of terms may help us here. A drawing is a physical object, a piece of paper. It can contain a number of images, each with distinctive content – perhaps a plan and an elevation side by side. The plan and elevation comprise distinct views of the building: thus each is both a separate image and a separate view. However, cases where different views are assembled into a single image are not uncommon, as in the eighteenth-century convention in which a plan of a room and its surrounding walls were flattened out like a cardboard box, or the yet more ingenious projections devised by El Lissitzky (figs 14 and 15). It is very difficult to attend to two of the constituent views simultaneously, just as it is difficult to attend to two separated views at once. The scope of our attention to the views that comprise a drawing is broadly the same as the scope of our attention to views of a building in reality. Drawings and mental images offer freedom to conceive of buildings that do not exist, but we imagine them in the ways that we see real buildings.

The second point I wish to stress is that the views which comprise an architectural drawing are pictures. A good deal hangs on our accepting this: otherwise basic aspects of the production process are incomprehensible. If we look at a real building or landscape what we see is contained in our view; the corresponding representation in a drawing is a picture. This is obvious and unobjectionable for perspective views of buildings: they are no different from the projections that the painter commonly employs. However, there are two difficulties with perspective views. The first is that they are specific to a single viewing position. This has to be chosen in order to make the drawing but to do so runs counter to the fact that we can have many viewing positions in a real building, and can imagine many viewing positions in an imagined building. The second difficulty is that the elements of an object in a perspective picture cannot be drawn to a common scale, for obvious reasons. 'Orthographic' projections get round these two difficulties.[1] They allow us to imagine any viewing position in a plane parallel to the picture; and they allow the drawing to be done true to scale. Plans, elevations and sectional elevations capture a scene in two dimensions only, by reducing pictorial depth to zero (figs 16 and 17). Consequently, views have to be multiplied, with one orthographic projection of each relevant surface, but in exchange for tolerating a plethora of views we get accuracy of dimensions and freedom of viewpoint.

This is easy to accept for elevations, which are simply views of building surfaces drawn according to an orthographic projection. Sectional elevations are slightly more difficult to construe as pictures, because we have to accept a convention in which part of the construction directly facing us has been shown as cut through.[2] For an unbuilt building there is a double imaginative task. We have to imagine the building and also imagine it in an unreal state, sliced through like an anatomical specimen. But we are familiar with such demands in paintings: for instance, to imagine a real woodland clearing where the unreal mythical activities of satyrs and nymphs are acted out.

We could say that plans are pictures of the floor, with the construction sawn through horizontally. Some plans do depict a floor in detail, perhaps showing a pattern of tiles, but this is not generally why we look at floor plans and it does not explain why they have such significance. More important is the fact that a plan view shows the shape of the building on the ground, the arrangement of its spaces, the disposition and thickness of structural members, and the positions of doors and windows. The plan, combined with an assumption (derived in turn from sections and elevations) about ceiling heights enables the viewer to imagine aspects of the building that are not depicted: the skilled interpreter will be able to imagine the play of light and shadow, the sense of transition from one room to another. Again, such interpretation is within the scope of pictures. We can see the horror or joy of an event, shown in a picture, yet these are emotional states not physical objects, which in themselves can neither be seen nor pictured.

It could be argued that a plan is really only a diagram from which we can interpret aspects of the building, just as we can make interpretations from a diagram of changes in the Dow Jones Index over time. The argument might stress that a diagram is a simplification of a real situation, concentrating on some salient features. An electrical wiring diagram is an example, showing how a number of outlets are linked up but not the length of the cables or the routes that they take. But it is difficult to accept that a plan must be a simplification since at sufficiently large scale it can represent every configuration of the objects that can be seen on a given plane, if necessary down to the profiles of built-in joinery, window mouldings, architraves and so on. In fact, the purpose of selecting a particular scale is precisely to allow chosen aspects of the building to be discerned without simplification.

It could also be argued that a plan is like a diagram because its interpretation is a skill that depends on understanding a conventional code. The follower of the changes in the Dow Jones Index must at some time have been schooled in the idea that a graph has two axes, that one represents time, the other quantities. It is true that in order to interpret plans we need to understand the convention of projection that is being used, but once we have got the hang of the projection we do not have to 'read off' the data, as we must always do in the Dow Jones Index case. Plans engage a form of pictorial seeing, diagrams do not. Within the constraints of the projective convention we see a building.[3] When we become adept at interpreting graphs we are not able to see the Dow Jones Index, for the obvious reason that the Dow Jones Index is not a visible object but a series of numbers appropriate to certain dates.

That outlines the situation after designing has taken place. If we took it as a description of the process of designing itself – that an architect has a series of mental images of what the building will be like and proceeds to draw them – we would go seriously adrift. So the third

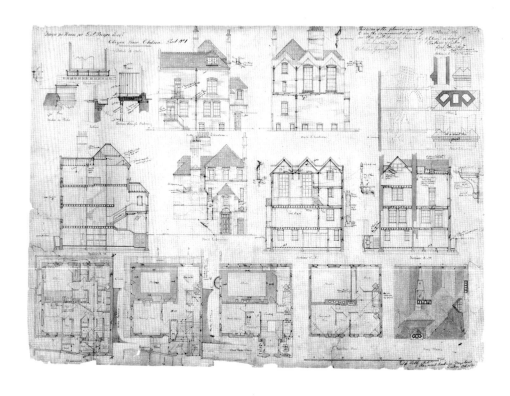

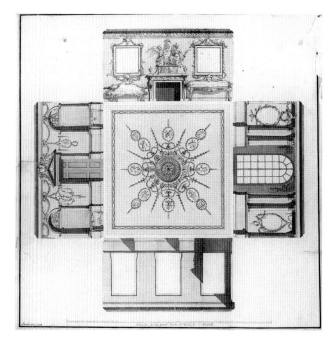

13 (*above*) Multiple images on a single sheet. A drawing by Philip Webb's office for a house at Glebe Place, Chelsea, London (1868).

14 Views of walls and plan combined in a single image. A design for the Great Room at Kimberley Hall, Norfolk, by John Sanderson.

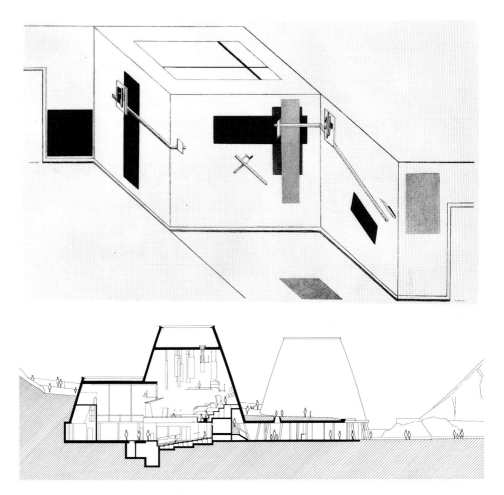

15 (*top*) A form of projection devised by El Lissitzky, allowing multiple axonometric views (1923).

16 Sectional elevation of the Landmark Theatre showing that multiple viewing positions, parallel to the picture, are possible.

17 (*right*) Perspective sketch (by John Hinton), true for only one viewing position, of the Landmark Theatre, Ilfracombe, England, designed by Tim Ronalds (1998).

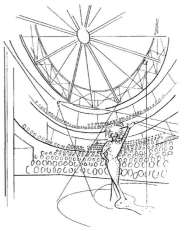

basic point is that the process of drawing is interactive, at least for part of the time: the architect finds that having drawn a particular view a previously unknown aspect of the design is revealed. As we have seen, Vasari captured something of this complex relationship between idea and drawing in the notion of *disegno*. Once a building has been designed there is no doubt that it can form an object in the mind, memorised in some detail. The process of design, on the other hand, depends to a degree on interaction with the process of drawing, in which pictorial seeing feeds off the marked surface of the paper.[4]

2   In the previous chapter I remarked on the consequences of the fact that designs could be copied, and the sense that designs take on lives of their own, getting out of the control of their originators. We can now apply this idea to the design for a whole building, as sets of drawings are printed and published, enabling imagined and unbuilt designs for buildings to become influential at a high level of detail and completeness. Copies of drawings are central to the process of producing real buildings, going in numerous directions to consultants, specialists, sub-contractors, public authorities, as well as to the client and the builder. Having given some attention to the nature of the link between drawings and designs, we can now see more clearly what happens when the builder takes delivery of a set of drawings.[5]

For example, we can correct a common misunderstanding, one that was expressed by Alberti when he stated that the builder was 'but an instrument in the hands of the architect'. The set of drawings given to the builder is often thought of as an instruction, and this would fit with Alberti's view of the process. Instructions could be fed to a builder in the same way that they can be fed to a machine. The implication is that the relationship is quite asymmetrical: the architect does the devising — a thoughtful and imaginative activity — and the builder, in Alberti's words, 'moves weights and joins and masses bodies'. A building contract at some point will indeed say 'build what is shown in the drawings' and that will be the key instruction to the builder.

Obviously, the builder is expected to make a physical object. How does he or she know what kind of physical object to make? By looking at the drawings, where he or she will find a building represented. That is the thing to build, the object pictured there in the drawings. The builder examines these pictures in detail, in conjunction with the schedules and specifications. Two kinds of imaginative work are involved. The finished building has to be constructed in the mind, as a three-dimensional object. It then has to be constructed in the mind a second time, now stage by stage, so that the logistics can be understood. Can it be built at all? Can it be built safely? How much will it cost to build? How long will it take to build? An instrument cannot do this kind of thinking.

The only way in which the builder could be given a set of instructions would be in the unlikely event that a comprehensive notation could be devised for all the actions and materials involved in building, and their placing on spatial co-ordinates.[6] Note that this would dramatically change the architect's role. He or she would have to do exactly what the builder normally does: imagine the building in various stages of construction and imagine in intimate detail the setting of one component on another. Only then could the list of instructions be compiled. Recall that the architect in the post-Renaissance period was defined precisely in opposition to this intimate involvement in the on-site construction process. In freeing themselves from the mason's yard, architects also absented themselves from this kind of detailed understanding of the logistics of construction.

The contradiction within Alberti's approach is that if he wishes the builder to be an instrument, a mechanic, he must also accept that the architect reverts to an archaic role as the detailed organiser of on-site production, precisely so that he or she can formulate those detailed instructions. If, on the other hand, the architect is to fulfil the post-Renaissance role, devising the project at a distance from the production process, it follows that the builder must have all the drawings that are necessary for picturing the building, so that the logistics of building it can also be imagined.

3   That, in a very schematic form, is how drawings, ideas and buildings are related. A kind of pictorial seeing is involved, by necessity.
Designs for buildings comprise sets of drawings; drawings comprise sets
of views; and those views, taken together, are of a complex physical
object. The implication is that long before construction starts on site
we need to construe an architectural work as a physical object. It is
true that it is an imagined one, but there is no difficulty in conceiv-
ing of such a thing. It follows that we also need to construe the world
of independent designs, the practical world of *disegno* that I described
in the previous chapter, as comprising physical objects – ceilings of
certain designs and configurations, standard runs of classical decoration,
a type of column, and so on.

The interactivity of the process of drawing is significant. A design
emerges partly from the physical process of drawing, from seeing what
the hand has drawn on the page and grasping its implications – that
a physical object, namely the building, is depicted. But interactivity
between drawing and design is not essential. Frank Lloyd Wright said
of Fallingwater that he 'shook the design out of his sleeve', meaning
that the design of the building had developed in its entirety in his
mind. Eventually – when the client's patience had started to wear thin
– he drew it up, but before he did so it was just an idea (figs 18 and
19).

This could be the basis of an alternative view of the chain that links
designs and buildings. Wright had an idea for a building, which he
drew up. Eventually the builder produced an object which corresponded with what was shown in the drawings, thereby making an idea
real. On this view, architectural designs would represent ideas and
buildings would be the means of making the idea real. However I
believe that the argument rests on a confusion between the content of
the design process and the type of mental or practical activity of which
it is the object. Drawings do not give us access to the architect's ideas
in the sense that they enable us to share his or her inner world: they
give access to representations of physical objects, just as a painting
of Snowdon is a representation of a mountain, not a representation of
the part of Richard Wilson's mind that was occupied in making the

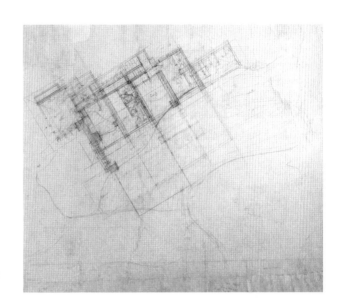

18   Early design drawing of Fallingwater by Frank Lloyd Wright: ground floor (1935).

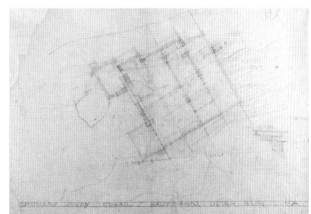

19   Fallingwater: first-floor plan.

20   *Snowdon from Llyn Nantlle* by Richard Wilson (c.1765).

painting (fig. 20). The drawings of Fallingwater do not give us entry to Wright's mind: they give us access to the design of Fallingwater.

The point can usefully be linked to the previous discussion. Drawings are physical objects and the views they depict represent physical objects – buildings or parts of buildings. The builder sees those depicted physical objects in the drawings and organises a logistical process accordingly. Seeing something in a drawing and seeing it in reality are obviously two different things. It is the builder's task to make real what he or she sees in pictures. But nowhere do we need to suggest that the architect draws ideas, that the client sees ideas, that the builder sees ideas, or that the builder builds ideas. The object of everyone's attention is always a physical building, at first as the content of varieties of picturing and then made real and accessible to the senses.

4   So far I have emphasised the apparent continuity between designs and buildings. I want now to point to some obstacles to this continuity. There is an interesting asymmetry between buildings and the designs that are reproduced in drawings. Designs can be reproduced again and again, with no apparent limit. In the process they lose nothing of their authenticity. The hundred thousandth paper copy of the plan of James Stirling's Stuttgart Museum is as valid as the first or the hundredth, its ontology unaffected by the process of reproduction. The situation with buildings is different. They divide into two categories. The first comprises buildings whose identity as architectural works is unaffected by the number that are built. For example, when J. J. P. Oud designed a standard house type for the Weissenhof exhibition in Stuttgart, every house that was built was an authentic version of that design (fig. 21). The second category comprises buildings whose identity as an architectural work seems to depend on their being unique. If a copy of Fallingwater were to be built on another site, we would consider it to be a copy of the original, not an equally valid second version. In the former category, drawings and buildings can each multiply at will, but in the latter we need some explanation for the uniqueness of the produced building.

Some types of art works are produced in multiples and we accept that this is part of their nature. Works of literature, films and performances of most plays and music fall into this category. Other types of works are produced singly and we accept that this too is in their nature. Much of the visual arts, especially painting, falls into this category (though prints and other multiples have their own more complex rules). Of course, copies can be made of paintings, sculptures and buildings, just as they can of books or musical works, and they can be made with or without the permission of their originators. The difference is that whereas we normally pay little attention to the question of the original manuscript of a work of literature or the original print of a film, we always pay attention to the fact that a painting, sculpture or work of architecture is a copy. The presumption for paintings is that only the original is authentic and has the identity of the work of art in question. So, for example, a photographic reproduction of a painting is a copy of that art work but not an art work in itself. By contrast, the literary work that is Eliot's *Middlemarch* is equally accessible in each and every printed copy.

This likening of the multiplication of designs to the reproduction of books can be taken through to the building process: if a building can be produced from one copy of a design, thousands of buildings could be produced from thousands of copies of that design. On these rather abstract grounds we might then conclude that the aesthetic identity of works of architecture lies in their being copies, just like books. So how can we explain the fact that a large proportion of architectural works seem better suited to the category of painting? For example, would another, later version of Scharoun's Berlin Philharmonie building be a copy of that original work, and open to all the doubts about identity that we have in the face of a copy of a painting?

Some buildings are unique because they are devised to fit a particular site or use, but this practical constraint is not decisive. A copy of the Philharmonie building could be built on many other sites and would presumably be as good a concert hall as the original. Indeed, a number of alternative sites were considered for the building, using the same basic plan configuration.[7] There are many woodland streams where a rich man might choose to build a copy of Fallingwater, once copyright clearance had been given. If practicality were the only issue, the individuality or uniqueness of architectural works would be insecure, always a matter of chance rather than necessity. It fails to account for our conviction that individuality of this kind is intrinsic, not accidental, and we seek a better explanation.

I suggest that the main reason why some buildings have the status of individual works rather than multiples is that the architect and client wished them so, and that this wish became intrinsic to the design process. Individuality thus becomes a feature of the building, but it is not a visible one. The point needs some explanation. One way of looking at the design process is that a client sets a problem and the design of a building offers a solution to that problem. Problem and solution are conceptually quite separate. In this case, the design can be repeated in any circumstance where it provides an acceptable solution to another problem. But this might be a misleading way of thinking about the design process and in particular about the relationship between the client's wants and a design. The situation I have in mind is where a design makes a problem coherent: that it is only the existence of a design that makes it possible to articulate a problem. In such a context the division into problem and solution distorts the nature of the design process. There is a difference between the client's wants being considered as the cause of a design, and the notion that those wants are part of the nature of a design.

An analogy, which might at first seem far-fetched, is with a sea creature and its shell. The living creature makes the shell, just as a client's wants make a building. But the shell is also part of the creature, just as the design makes the client's wants coherent. The shell alone is a mere shell, and a design which is repeated in a different context from its living origin is a mere copy of one that originally had individual significance. In Chapter Eight I shall describe in more detail the outlook within which ideas of this kind develop. I do not believe they are fanciful, though they are often given poetic or elliptical expression; in fact, they arise from real conceptual difficulties within the design process. For the moment, the point to note is that the constraint imposed by the request to build only one, unique architectural work can be an important aspect of a design. It is not a visible feature, it is true, but a feature of the history of its production. Designs embody pictures of proposed buildings, and it may not be just the content of the pictures that determines the identity of any resulting building, but also the history of that design in the particular circumstances of the project.

This is the first clear indication that the aesthetic identity of a building resides in something more than the fact that it was built in accordance with a given set of drawings. It may also be essential to its identity that it conforms to a notion of uniqueness that is inscribed in the design process – inscribed in the history of the project but not directly visible in the resulting drawings.[8]

5   When we turn our attention back to the other way of linking designs and buildings, in which multiple instances can be produced, another difficulty emerges. More precisely, the question re-emerges of whether the architectural work is a physical or an ideal object. The question is not unique to architecture and arises in all those arts that are comprised of multiple instances. Typically, there is a set of physical objects – actual performances of a piece of music or a play, or multiple instances of a building design – each distinct and real yet having the given work in common between them. The obvious conclusion to draw is that the work – the play or piece of music or design – has now become an idea, one to which the physical instances bear some relation. On the face of it, how could it be otherwise? How could those multiple instances possess both their own individual physicality and share physicality with the design? The performances come to be considered as physical carriers for an ideal object rather than as physical pieces of music or design.

The difficulty is that the logic goes against our intuition that an art work such as a musical performance, or a building that is produced in multiples, somehow fuses the design and the physical instance. Shunting off the design, and thus the aesthetic identity of the work, into the ideal realm and away from the physical offends this intuition. Richard Wollheim has proposed a solution to this problem, which hinges on adopting a specific logical form in which the multiple cases are termed 'tokens' and the work at a generic level is termed a 'type'.[9] The idea of a 'type' contrasts with the more familiar logical form of a 'class'. The class of performances of a piece of music simply gathers together those performances, but the class itself does not have the characteristics of those performances. The point about a type, however, is that relevant features of the multiple tokens are transmitted to the type.

The consequence for our purposes is that physical features can be transmitted to the type, for example the texture of instrumentation, the timbre of the instruments, the frequencies and loudness of sounds that are part of the character of a musical work. These are features of tokens, but they may equally be described as characteristics of the type. Then the problem of separating a physical work from the ideal object that lies behind it can be avoided. Our original intuition – that each separate work can fuse its physicality with the design generically considered – can be logically supported, and the generic work can also be considered as having physicality.

That is the main point about the type–token idea, although much else hangs on it, as we shall see. It is not difficult to apply the idea to architecture. Take the celebrated apartments that Le Corbusier repeated as multiples within a number of his 'Unités d'Habitation'. If we think of them as the class of the Unité apartments, each one physically distinct, we would then have to put the design that they share at a different level, as an ideal object. If we consider them as tokens, then the type of the apartment would possess all those physical qualities of light and spaciousness, that is possessed by each token in turn. This is satisfactory, because the alternative, that a physical building is the means by which ideas of lightness, space, texture, are communicated, is implausible. Each token apartment has those physical features, and that is sufficient: we do not need to assume that the physicality of each apartment is being used in a paradoxical fashion to communicate ideas of physicality which reside only in the design.

6   If we stopped here we would have a reasonably tidy arrangement from the ontological point of view. Architectural works are physical objects. Unique buildings have the reasons for their singularity as a property of their design, part of the history of their production. Multiples are also physical objects. This is congruent with their being tokens of the type-design, since a type can also have physical properties. But let us continue and look in more detail at the implications of the distinction between types and tokens. Antonio Gramsci suggested an analogy between architectural production and the production of books:

> The special objective character of architecture. In reality, the 'work of art' is the 'project' (the sum total of the designs and plans and calculations with which people other than the architect, the 'artist-planner', produce the building): an architect can be judged a great artist on the basis of his plans even without having materially built anything. The relation between the project and the material building is the same as that between the 'manuscript' and the printed book. The building is the social objectification of the art, its 'diffusion', the chance given to the public to participate in its beauty (when it is such), just like the printed book.[10]

Gramsci's argument is that all the aesthetically significant aspects of a literary work that are in the manuscript are faithfully transmitted via the process of printing to the reader. Then the analogy suggests that the same is true of architecture, and that the production process faithfully 'objectifies' what is in the architect's drawings and other documents.

The production of prefabricated buildings might be thought analogous to the production of literary works. Take the example of the 38,859 Arcon bungalows (one of the celebrated models of 'prefabs') that were built in Britain as part of the post-war emergency housing programme (fig. 22).[11] On Gramsci's argument, we could make as many new Arcon bungalows as we wished provided that we could refer to the orginal sets of drawings, schedules, calculations and so on. Everything of practical and aesthetic significance would be included in those

21 View of terrace houses at the Weissenhofsiedlung, Stuttgart,
Germany, designed by J. J. P. Oud (1927).

22 An example of the Arcon bungalow (c.1945).

drawings and could be transferred to a new batch of actual buildings. Just as a reprint of a 1940s novel would be identical, in literary aesthetic terms, to the first printing, so a new batch of Arcon bungalows built according to the original designs would be valid tokens of the Arcon type.

It is almost certain, however, that details of the new batch would differ from the original production run of the 1940s. The materials and details used might conform to the original drawings and specifications and yet differ in their texture, sheen and accuracy of fit, and standards of finish and assembly might also be noticeably different. The exact tactile and visual character of the original buildings might have been consequences of the way that the original production line was organised, with its tooling and chains of component and subcontractor supplies, and of the skills and techniques that were used by the site assembly teams. The thought would develop that an authentic new batch of Arcon bungalows would entail recreating a part of the 1940s' building and engineering industry, and the more the thought came into focus the more impossible it would seem.

More questions would follow. Production runs of complex artefacts are subject to constant modification: the challenge for production engineers is not only to maintain the identity of the product in relation to the original drawings but also to control the impact of continual modifications.[12] So before we could make a new Arcon bungalow we would have to ask on which batch, comprising which modifications, it was to be based. The defender of Gramsci's viewpoint could say that all this is interesting but misses the point of the analogy between the production of books and buildings. The claim is not that the original drawings, schedules and so on are able to specify every aspect of the building but that they specify those that are relevant to its identity as a token of a given design type. Thus, to say that the texture of the materials and the feel of the workmanship in a new batch of Arcon bungalows differ from those in the original batches is irrelevant: it would be as irrelevant as saying that a new printing of a novel is not the same literary work because it is not printed on the same kind of paper as the first.

Once again a difference arises between a theory of the identity of art works and our own sense of what is important to them. Our intuition is that details of texture, finish, accuracy – details that are bound to vary during the production process – are aesthetically important, and yet Gramsci's suggestion offers no way of accommodating this intuition. Perhaps the problem is easier for books because we can think of them in two ways, on the one hand as literary works and on the other as products of the art and craft of book production. But there is no such simple division for buildings: they are works of visual interest and that interest is continuous from the outlines of design to the smallest detail.

In fact, the ethos of prefabrication as it developed in modernism embraced this difficulty, stressing the potential it offered for evolutionary change rather than book-like repetition. An exclusive stress on drawings would overlook the role of the prototype and the cycles of trial, modification and re-trial that are essential to industrial production. It was just this kind of practical cyclical improvement that architects of the British post-war prefabricated schools programme saw as essentially modern, not an idea of relentless printing of identical tokens.[13] Part of the background to this outlook was Le Corbusier's presentation of the dialectic between the industrially produced 'type' and its step-by-step evolutionary improvement in *Vers une architecture* (1923). The identity of a work of architecture thus became a rather subtle matter, in which both the overall type and the particular evolutionary stage in the development of the type needed to be taken into account.

By contrast, it is instructive to consider the case of the architect Walter Segal, who did implicitly put into practice the literary analogy, along the lines that Gramsci describes.[14] Segal ran a small architectural practice, initially employing assistants but gradually turning into a one-man operation. This was a way of exerting tight control over the process of realising a design, doing away with the difficulties that delegation brings. He developed an extraordinarily disciplined approach to producing working drawings, structural drawings and quantities before a job started, and once a job began on site he kept conversations and meetings with the builder to the bare minimum. These decisions in turn restricted the size and volume of the work that he could handle and also led him to avoid rehabilitation work, because of the difficulty of controlling and predicting it. The desire to predict the on-site process also led him increasingly to design with standard component and material sizes. The builder would then order a certain quantity of manufactured or machined components: again, the uncertainties entailed in asking the builder to shape and machine materials were reduced.

Segal's methods led to forms of construction and detailing of the simplest and most conservative kind. It amused him that the *Architectural Review* described the flats he designed for Ovington Square, London, as 'a textbook of bad manners'. It delighted him to invent methods of construction that were even more simple and banal than those of everyday builders. Gramsci's thoughts are peculiarly apt for Segal's approach to architecture. The drawings, calculations, quantities and specifications and the explanatory manual for each of his later projects were bound together into an A4 book for the builder's use (figs 23–5). The contents of the book were intended to be exhaustive of the aesthetic effect of the finished building.[15]

An extraordinary by-product of Segal's powerful desire to control the design and building process in its entirety was that the constructional system, and his approach to contracts, were of great value to people building their own homes. What had begun as a means of avoiding interaction with the builder and of enforcing certainty at a distance developed into a simple constructional system that unskilled people could use. Segal is now remembered as the guiding force of a self-build movement in Britain, not as the architect of ill-mannered blocks of flats. He reduced the scope for interpretation by the builder, initially to satisfy his own desire for control of the entire production process; but reducing the builder's scope for interpretation was achieved by simplicity of construction and this in turn was helpful to self-builders with few conventional trade skills.

The obsessive desire for architectural control meant that Segal could work only on a small scale and within a very narrow stylistic range.

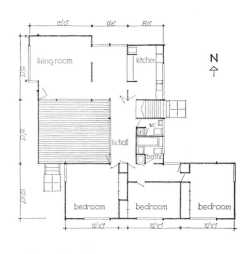

23 Part of the specification for the house at Yelling, Huntingdonshire designed by Walter Segal (1970).

24 Plan of Yelling house.

25 Interior view of the Yelling house.

The analogy of literary production that Gramsci used is appropriate to the way that he attempted to organise the process of designing and building. The paradox is that his method of work led to a severe restriction of the scale of operation rather than a truly book-like process of reproduction. This points us back to the thought that the production of multiple tokens of a design requires an explanation of the aesthetic significance that tokens have in their own right, as well as the significance that they derive from the type.

Gramsci's suggestion would enable us to maintain a tidy relationship between the ontology of designs and that of built architectural works: the aesthetic identity of a building is the same as the aesthetic identity of the type-design. But it is inadequate for our intuition of what is important about buildings.

7   The next step in the argument has perhaps already occurred to the reader: that we can turn again to the performing arts, this time noting analogies at the level of tokens rather than of types. The performance analogy recognises a two-stage process of production, and thus makes room for the fact that specific tokens have aesthetic characteristics in excess of those of the type. An interpretation of a symphony, for example, is arrived at in rehearsal, out of the directions, intentions and outlook of the conductor and the capabilities of the orchestra. Musicians might make notes on their scores to remind themselves of points of emphasis, but there is no overall notation. Each member of the orchestra must internalise the conductor's interpretation. Theatrical performances may have more written instructions, for example lighting schedules and other staging details, but the actors, like musicians, internalise the director's interpretation.[16]

There is no difficulty in accepting the usefulness of the performance analogy where buildings are produced as multiple cases of a given design. Any batch of Arcon bungalows bears the marks of the particular state of the production and assembly set-up, the exact types of materials used, the current state of modifications in force. Some of these features may have been recorded and are comparable with staging details. But any particular batch would also have a distinctive character that arose simply from the way that the complexities of production interacted at that moment, just like a performance. Our sense that the newly minted batch of Arcons may not be authentic tokens of the architectural work can now be clarified. What is at issue here is not an anxiety about their authenticity as versions of the Arcon type, which is assured by their conforming to the type drawings, but a concern that they are not authentic performances.

The idea of authentic performance points once again towards the idea that a work is inextricably connected with the historical circumstances in which it was made. I have already suggested that this can help to explain why some works have a strong individual identity. The point may also apply to types: the Arcon bungalow is as intimately a product of the social and productive conditions of 1940s Britain as Fallingwater is a product of its time and site.

The performance analogy also helps us come to terms with the ontology of architectural works that are individuals. At first sight this is curious, since the notion of performance was called in to help us explain the characteristics of multiple works. Applying the performance analogy to individual cases involves treating them as unique performances and this seems somewhat forced. Perhaps it will seem more natural as we examine the detailed level of decisions that still have to be made in order to produce a building in all its actuality.

Why do the drawings and other documents fall short of an exhaustive specification? Two kinds of situation arise. Firstly, some decisions about a building can only be made in conjunction with the builder. Secondly, some decisions can only be made once a certain stage of construction has been reached. The architect issues a set of working drawings. The builder pores over them, going through the kind of imaginative process that I have already described, making sense of what is represented. There will be errors in the drawings and the builder will note these. Dimensions may be wrong, so that something that is drawn is unbuildable. There will be ambiguities, and the builder will ask the architect which of two possible interpretations is correct. There will be omissions which the architect will have to put right. In some cases, corrected drawings will be issued but often a site drawing will be amended and sometimes the correction will simply be kept in people's heads. The builder might go further than this detailed scrutiny, and point out that a certain form of construction is contrary to the building codes, or that a detail will be troublesome to build or that a finish will be hard to achieve. The architect may take some of these comments into account and may issue revised drawings, or again the revision may be understood tacitly.

Once on site, working drawings are written over many times with amendments, notes, sketches. Important aspects of the architectural performance are contained in these amendments. At the end of the job the drawings are thrown away, if they have not already deteriorated with use. Collections of architectural drawings tend to lack precisely those drawings that were used on site in the construction process, for the reason that they were destroyed in it.

Some working drawings can only be done once a building is under construction. Actual structural dimensions have to be checked before built-in joinery can be ordered or before complex architectural metalwork can be fabricated. The builder may need to make full-size templates. Many important aesthetic decisions can be made only on the basis of samples. Brickwork pointing is a clear example, and one which highlights the interplay between judgements of taste by the architect and judgements of quality of work; at the margin, taste and quality cannot be distinguished. Often, these have to be judgements against the background of a range. The high-tech architect choosing the exact sheen or dullness of stainless steel has to show the builder both the chosen sample and also an unacceptable one, to indicate where the threshold of discrimination lies. In some cases the actual batches of a material must be shown to the architect, and no specification or sample will suffice. This is so with timber and stone used for decorative effect, but the point might extend across to fabricated items, where the architect insists on checking standards in an off-site factory. The architect may leave the choice of paint colours until samples can be done on the surfaces and in the light conditions of the completed building.

There are no fixed rules of which kinds of decisions are interactive and which are not. For example, ductwork is generally hidden in buildings and the architect is uninterested in its standard of finish. But if the architect decides that the ducting is to be exposed, then samples will be needed. Contrary cases occur: the architect may want exposed structural timber to be left rough, against the builder's first inclination. Or the architect may want the concrete to be left with the imprint of the wooden shuttering – exquisitely so – as Louis Kahn did at the Yale University art gallery in New Haven (fig. 26).[17]

The drawings and other documents used during the project are therefore insufficient to determine the exact course of the architectural performance: much of it takes place in the flux of activity on site. Furthermore, the drawings that do exist are highly redundant and repetitive. Redundancy is a virtue in detailed architectural drawings, as it is in all communications systems. The architect needs it constantly to cross-check the result of earlier design decisions and the builder needs it to cross-check the practicality of what is shown. But they may need different kinds of redundancy. So, to the great irritation of the architect, the builder may ignore many of the drawings, since the information nested in them has already been absorbed. There is no means of defining which drawings out of this over-determined set will be the ones to affect the building process.

In summary, there is no set of drawings or documents that could specify the exact final character of the building. There is no other criterion of the building in its final and detailed state than the building itself, and this is a consequence of that complex and lengthy performance process on site. Therefore, we need to add further revisions to the idea of a simple linear relationship between designs and buildings. Design in itself is inadequate as a means of accounting for the aesthetic effect of an architectural work, and the point is true both for those which are individuals and those which are types. Detailed implementation, beyond the reach of design features that are shown in drawings, will be significant in all cases to the identity of the work.

In his treatise on architecture published in 1567, Philibert de l'Orme illustrates the qualities of the good and the bad architect (fig. 27).[18] The bad architect is depicted without eyes, hands, ears and nose, to show that he cannot perceive truth, can execute nothing, cannot listen to the advice of others and cannot even sense what is good. He does have a mouth, however, 'with which he can babble and speak evil'. The good architect has three eyes, four ears, and four hands. The multiple eyes and ears are so that he can contemplate the past, present and future and the four ears show that he must listen more than he must speak. The image derives from earlier Classical representations of Wisdom: the four hands are so that the architect can study more effectively and control the project more effectively. The image fleshes out the Albertian conception of the architect, and those multiple hands remind us of the onerous responsibilities that the architect can acquire in order to control the details of work on site. But the hands are for devising and controlling, not for building.

8   The two kinds of design decisions – those that could in principle be implemented in multiple projects and those made on site – can have varying importance, according to the architect's outlook. If site decisions assume great importance a further type of analogy suggests itself, that between architecture and painting. Take, for example, the commission given in 1963 to the Swedish architect Sigurd Lewerentz to design and supervise the construction of a new church at Klippan.[19] When construction began, only the most basic sketches had been done, showing the overall dimensions of the building. There had been no clear brief and what there was Lewerentz had changed. It was only the construction of a large wooden model showing the relationship of the various rooms that reassured the clients about the proposed design. Lewerentz had hardly visited the site before the foundations were dug, but after that (his health permitting) he was on site for three days a week and worked through many evenings, planning the next day's work with the foreman, Carl Sjöholm. He was involved in minute detail with the setting out of the brickwork, imposing the most stringent rules: that bricks were to be used for all purposes – walls, floors, vaults, rooflights, altar, pulpit, seat; that only standard full-size bricks were to be used and no specials; that no bricks were to be cut (fig. 28). The bricklayers were forbidden to use plumb lines or spirit levels and had to work entirely by eye. Variations in the planned grid for the

26   Exposed concrete finish
at the Yale Art Gallery,
designed by Louis Kahn
(1950–54).

27   Detail of Philibert de
l'Orme's image of the good
architect, from *Le Premier
Tome de l'Architecture* (1567).

28   Window detail at St Peter's church, Klippan, Sweden, designed by Sigurd Lewerentz (1962–65).

29   The Farnsworth House, Plano, Illinois, designed by Mies van der Rohe (1945–51).

30   The Farnsworth House, detail of steelwork junction.

brickwork were taken up by wider joints in the flush mortar. The floor tiles, which were never cut, were chosen from piles varying in colour and size – gold tiles in the wet coatroom and light ones under the coat rail to relieve the shadow. Throughout the job there were endless alterations and on-site revisions, not just to matters of detail but also to the visual relationships of spaces.

In discussing Klippan Colin St John Wilson has quoted the painter Michael Andrews: 'Painting is the most marvelous, elaborate and complete way of making up my mind.' He continues: 'At Klippan we become witnesses of the extraordinary process by which Lewerentz, at the age of 80, slowly made up his mind.'[20] The comparison with painting is apt, since Lewerentz was getting as close as he could to working directly in the medium of building itself, like the artist manipulating paint. We also sense an obsessive desire for control over the outcome of the building and this points back to a comparison with Segal. Evidently, both men shared an obsessive desire for control of their buildings, but whereas Segal was making architecture as much like writing a book as possible, Lewerentz was making it as much like painting as possible.

9   I have attempted to trace the consequences of the incompleteness of design drawings and the ways in which additional decisions are made in order to specify a more complete object. Now that the incompleteness has become more evident, it may rekindle interest in the question of whether designs represent physical objects or whether they are ideas. If the former is the case, it is certain that they do not represent them in their entirety, since many physical attributes remain to be decided interactively during the construction process. Then it might be asked whether it is possible to conceive of an only partly physical object. The idea that something should be partly, but not entirely, a physical object is awkward and it nudges us back towards the opposing view, that a design comprises merely an idea of some of the features of the building. The features specified in this ideal object, together with others decided on site, are made physical only when the design is built.

It is true that a real building cannot be only partly physical, but it would be wrong to conclude that in order to conceive of a physical object we must do so in all its completeness. For example, it is possible to make a line drawing of a building without indicating the colour or texture of its facades; indeed, a large category of influential drawings is just like this. It would hardly be plausible to say that line drawings only gave us access to ideas, whereas drawings which rendered the textures and colours of walls were representations of physical objects. Our ability to see a physical building pictured in a drawing is not dependent on a certain degree of detail being portrayed: a meticulous rendering of brickwork might even make a building seem less real than a skilled and allusive sketch. The question is whether the process of pictorial seeing delivers a representation of a physical building.

Designs cannot represent all the aesthetically significant aspects of a building and therefore some decisions are dealt with interactively while the building is in various stages of construction. Thus, the only sure criterion of the identity of the completed architectural work is the building itself. In fact, two processes go on side by side. In the process of building, the builder makes a physical object; in the decision process, step-by-step the architect elaborates the detailed characteristics of the object. It would be a mistake to think that the architect progressively makes the building more real. Only the builder can do that, but they do it in accordance with the architect's decisions as to exactly how it will be real. That is a very schematic way of describing the division of labour between architect and builder. Of course, the builder will also take decisions about the building's outcome, for example in the minutiae of standards and practices involved in skilled work and often in larger-scale decisions about detailing. But the builder's special contribution is to make a physical object and the architect is not involved in this. The object is then directly accessible to the senses and we enter a new territory of aesthetic issues.

We can only discern the architectural work's new status, its physicality, through the channels of our senses; we cannot experience physicality as a general category. At a conceptual level, all real buildings share the same property of physicality but this is accessible to us only through the particularities of our senses. Yet some buildings seem to defy the fact and are more vividly physical than others: is this not the point about Lewerentz's Klippan, that it gives us access to physicality in a way that few buildings do? But in fact, Klippan has the same amount of physicality as any other building, no more and no less. The fact that it seems more physically present than others is a consequence of the particular way that it was designed. It is a result of the gruelling process by which Lewerentz endowed every inch of the building with the sense that a decision lay behind the moving and placing of objects – Alberti's 'movement of weights and the joining and massing of bodies'. Physicality, in this sense, is an aesthetic choice, not an index of how much physicality a building possesses.

The point still holds for buildings of minimal physicality. When we see Mies van der Rohe's Farnsworth House we see less physicality than a steel frame normally possesses (figs 29 and 30). This is because Mies devised the assembly to hide the welds and bolted connections which typically would have given us the sense of the weightiness of a steel building; the horizontal emphasis runs counter to the normal box-like physicality of steel structures; and the meticulous control over finishes and jointing makes the building seem crafted by cabinetmakers rather than builders. Conceptually, the Farnsworth House has no less physicality than Klippan – they both have an equal share – but the two buildings indicate in their different ways that physicality itself can be a theme manipulated by the architect for aesthetic effect.

The issue will receive further attention in Chapter Five. For the moment, we need to turn our attention towards the new topic, that buildings as physical objects are accessible to us through the senses.

Chapter 3

Encounters with Buildings

I This chapter is about architectural experience. I begin by describing key aspects of a modernist view of architectural experience, of the kind that was canvassed by Sigfried Giedion and Bruno Zevi, among others. My main purpose is to fix a starting point for the discussion and so I give these influential ideas much simpler shapes than they had in reality. In the second section of the chapter I discuss their limitations and then suggest an alternative framework for considering architectural experience. To begin with, this stresses the constancy of the objects of architectural experience, rather than the dynamism that intrigued Giedion and Zevi. A host of problems then needs to be addressed to enable this schematic view to accommodate the complexities of actual experience. What emerges is a provisional definition, with many rough edges.

I wish to sketch three sets of ideas that can be found in modernist views of architectural experience. The first is that spatial experience involves an integration of the senses of touch and vision; the second is that the object of attention consists of fragmentary perceptions, not a building as a whole; and the third is that architecture is primarily experienced in movement. Let us begin with 'spatial experience', the kind of experience that is considered distinctively architectural. By this is meant not the ability to see the shape of objects or their colour or texture, but an apprehension of them as three-dimensional. Coupled with this is the ability to see the extent of what lies between objects in that third dimension, the space that separates them. The orthodox modern view is that this kind of perception is a compound of seeing and touch. It derives from George Berkeley's classic formulation of the problems of visual perception in *A New Theory of Vision*, published in 1709.[1]

Berkeley argued that we see things in only two out of three dimensions, those of the plane that faces us. Strictly speaking, we do not see the third dimension, 'outness' as he describes it, at all. We only know of its existence through the sense of touch, by bodily movement into space and by reaching out and touching objects. We learn to associate these tactile experiences with the flat objects we see. As these associations gather strength, the memory of the tactile experiences recedes and we are left with the idea that we truly see the third dimension. However, properly understood, a perception in the third dimension brings together what Berkeley calls a 'visible idea' and a 'tangible idea'. Seeing the third dimension is thus an achievement of infant development, not an innate ability.[2]

J. S. Mill, writing in 1842, described Berkeley's doctrine as 'one of the least disputed doctrines in the most disputed and most disputable of all sciences – the science of man. This is the more remarkable, as no doctrine in mental philosophy is more at variance with first appearances, more contradictory to the natural prejudices of mankind'.[3] From the second part of the nineteenth century onwards it has also been one of the least disputed doctrines in the theory and criticism of architecture. Here, for example, is a statement of the idea from 1979:

> One of the magical things about our senses is that they do not function in isolation. Each sense contributes to the fuller comprehension of other sensory information . . . In order to learn to see three dimensionally one must touch, rotate, walk around things. By associating sight with bodily movement and touch, the brain begins to perceive form and depth and perspective.[4]

A striking passage in Steen Eiler Rasmussen's *Experiencing Architecture* (1959) is testimony to the power of the idea. Rasmussen describes watching a group of boys playing football against the curved wall of S. Maria Maggiore in Rome:

> It was apparently a kind of football but they also utilized the wall in the game, as in squash – a curved wall, which they played against with great virtuosity. When the ball was out it was most decidedly out, bouncing down all the steps and rolling several hundred feet further on with an eager boy rushing after it, in and out among motor cars and Vespas down near the great obelisk.

The boys' game becomes a metaphor for the process of learning spatial seeing:

> I do not claim that these Italian youngsters learned more about architecture than the tourists did. But quite unconsciously they experienced certain basic elements of architecture: the horizontal planes and the vertical walls above the slopes. And they learned to play on these elements. As I sat watching them, I sensed the whole three-dimensional composition as never before. At a quarter past eleven the boys dashed off, shouting and laughing. The great basilica stood once more in silent grandeur.[5]

Berkeley's doctrine was firmly embedded in theories of the visual arts in the 1890s, and this was probably the route by which it entered the mainstream of modernism. August Schmarsow put it thus: 'The intuited form of space . . . consists of the residues of sensory experience to which the muscular sensations of our body, the sensitivity of our skin and the structure of our body all contribute'. The sense of space in turn seeks satisfaction in art: 'We call this architecture; in plain words it is the creatress of space'.[6]

In Heinrich Wölfflin's *Principles of Art History* (1915), the Berkeleyan theme has a complex role to play in the distinction between the 'linear' and 'painterly' styles of art. In the linear style, 'The evenly firm and clear boundaries of solid objects give the spectator a feeling of security, as if he could move along them with his fingers'. A painterly representation, by contrast, 'has its roots only in the eye, and just as the child ceases to take hold of things in order to "grasp" them, so mankind has ceased to test the picture for its tactile values. A more developed art has learned to surrender itself to mere appearance.'[7] The distinction, derived from the actual perception of space, can then be put to a secondary use in architecture, so that the tangibility of the linear architecture of the Renaissance is in turn imagined, as are the 'painterly' effects of the Baroque.

These ideas can be found in simpler forms in earlier theorists of the visual arts, for example in Robert Vischer, writing in 1873: 'The child learns to see by touching, and indeed we should not disregard the fact that this invariably entails not only skin and nerve functions but also muscle movements'.[8] They would also have been the shared property of scientists, philosophers and aesthetes: Adolf Hildebrand, whose *The Problem of Form in the Fine Arts* of 1893 applies the visual–kinaesthetic distinction to painting, sculpture and architecture, was cautioned that in publishing his views on perception he would merely be repeating what the great scientist Hermann Helmholtz had already touched on.[9]

Wölfflin's remarks alert us to an extension of the idea that seeing in three dimensions is a learnt, not an innate ability, namely its transfer from the realm of the individual infant's development to that of historical change. Alois Riegl and Wilhelm Worringer, writing in the 1900s, suggested that in earlier phases of human culture, artistic forms are simplified and objects are clearly distinguished in linear formats.[10] This linear simplicity, and the comforting presence of an armature of lines that can be grasped, is a response to a threatening and uncomprehended outer world. In later phases of architecture, interlinked and complex spaces can be designed, as testimony to the culture's achievement in making more confident explorations into the outer world.

This mode of theorising, was continued on a grand scale by Sigfried Giedion: his last book, *Architecture and the Phenomenon of Transition*, divides architectural history into three epochs, each based on a distinctive 'space-conception'. Modern architecture stands at the beginning of the third space-conception, which is of architecture as both volume and interior space. His earlier *Space, Time and Architecture* then takes its place as a detailed study of the transition to this third space-conception.[11] *Space, Time and Architecture* also serves as a guide to the other key aspects of the modernist outlook: that architectural experience takes place in movement, not from the position of a static observer, and that the objects of experience are essentially fragmentary. Giedion brings these two ideas together under the larger concept of 'space-time', for example in his celebrated (or infamous) statement that it is impossible to comprehend Le Corbusier's Villa Savoie 'from a single point; quite literally it is a construction in space-time'.[12]

Giedion has been much criticised for this mis-borrowing of scientific theory, and for yoking it together with an account of new movements in art, principally Cubism and Futurism.[13] In fact, dispensing with the references to space-time and 'the fourth dimension' does little harm to his argument: the interesting points remain. Taken step-by-step they are as follows.

We cannot see a building in its totality from a single viewpoint. This is not a peculiarity of buildings but a feature of our perception of all objects. Giedion makes the point that in its early phase Cubism brought numerous views of parts of an object together in a painting. In doing so, it exposed a truth about normal seeing and gave it artistic expression. Buildings are already seen like that, as sequences of parts, but that fact can be put to aesthetic effect and intensified if they are made more transparent and fragmented than previous styles have allowed. The Bauhaus building fits this idea:

> There is the hovering, vertical grouping of planes which satisfies our feeling for a relational space, and there is the extensive transparency that permits interior and exterior to be seen simultaneously, en face and en profile, like Picasso's 'L'Arlésienne' of 1911–12: variety of levels of reference, or of points of reference . . .'[14]

In a Cubist painting the multiple views are impacted together on the canvas: the architectural analogy is that they should be experienced sequentially. Then it is easy to see how movement through space, and over time, becomes essential to the definition of architectural experience. Giedion argues that a building which takes this as thematic – the

Villa Savoie, for example[15] – will be expressing a truth about our normal perception of buildings, just as a Cubist painting expresses a truth about our normal kind of seeing (fig. 31).

Giedion gives the argument one further turn, in asserting that not only do we see objects as sets of fragments, but that in truth they are sets of fragments. Boccioni's Futurist sculpture is brought in as a witness. Objects are in a state of movement and what we see of them is only ever a stage in their process of becoming. Boccioni's sculpture *Bottle Evolving in Space* makes thematic this fact about objects in general, by representing one of the fragmentary changing states of a particular object. The architectural analogy is less clear in this case, but my understanding of it is that when we see buildings as sets of fragments we are seeing them as they truly are: it is not just that we cannot see a building all at once, rather that there never is an 'all at once'.

2   One of the most powerful aspects of the modernist view of architectural experience that I have sketched here is that it stresses the active participation of the subject. In part this was deliberate, since modernists wished most of all to distance themselves from the idea that the key to architecture was the passive contemplation of facades. However, a deeper sense of activity goes right through the set of ideas. Berkeleyan three-dimensional seeing is based on an idea of actively touching the world and is counterposed to passive two-dimensional seeing. Architectural seeing takes place in active movement. Then it is a short step to identifying this with the use of buildings, as Bruno Zevi does: 'Organic space is rich with movement, directional invitations and illusions of perspective, lively and brilliant invention. Its movement is original in that it does not aim at dazzling visual effects, but at expressing the action itself of man's life within it.'[16] This becomes a highly integrated outlook, with notions of experience, art and use all rolled up tightly together. I would like to loosen this concentration of ideas and spread them out.

First, I wish to probe the notion of active experience that is so prominent. There is a danger of associating architectural experience in movement too closely with the use of a building. We can merely contemplate a building, with no practical purpose in mind, while we are moving: this is one of the pleasures of looking at buildings, as much a pleasure as statically contemplating facades. Conversely, for much of the time when we are using buildings we are sitting or standing in one position, so that use can bring a good deal of passive contemplation with it. It would be better to disengage the idea of architectural seeing from ideas about the practical use of buildings: use can involve both passive seeing and seeing in movement, and so can the contemplation of buildings for pleasure.

The active–passive distinction also hovers around the Berkeleyan approach to spatial seeing. The seeing of the two dimensions that face us was thought of as passive, as if images were merely registered on the retina and infiltrated the mind. Three-dimensional seeing, on the other hand, was considered to involve an active exploration of the world through touching and seeing combined. Again, we can see how passive two-dimensional seeing came to be associated with facades, with contemplation, with seeing buildings from the outside, and with a certain over-aesthetic and limited conception of architecture. Use, on the other hand, came to be associated primarily with entering and going through buildings.

There may be two misunderstandings here. One is to underestimate the extent to which all seeing is active, whether it is of a two- or a three-dimensional kind. The eye does not work like a camera, faithfully repeating a sharp image of the world on the retina. The interior of the eye comprises sets of specialist receptors that capture aspects of the visual scene – bright light and dim light, movement, colour and so on. It is the brain that makes the world visible to us and it does so by constructing it out of the specialist data contributed by the eye. The process has numerous stages and involves the co-operation of a number of brain areas.[17] Against the background of this prodigious mental activity the distinction between two- and three-dimensional seeing recedes: we should consider all kinds of seeing as essentially active and complex.

We should also ask whether Berkeley's view of infant development was correct. Research in recent years has suggested that, contrary to his assumption, very young infants have a sense of the third dimension. At the very least, if there is a Berkeleyan process of learning about space, it is built on some innate abilities.[18] If three-dimensional seeing does not depend entirely on tactile exploration, we can loosen another of the tight connections within the modernist theory of architectural seeing.

Secondly, I wish to point to a difficulty in the idea that architectural seeing consists of fragments. The starting point is the idea that all objects are necessarily seen as multiplicities of fragments, that they must be seen like that since they cannot be seen in their entirety from one viewpoint. Then it seems reasonable to say that a building which is more fragmented, which allows more interpenetrating views, will respond more acutely to this essential aspect of seeing. Thus Giedion chose the Bauhaus and the Villa Savoie.

The mistake would be to think that such a building is in some sense made out of perceptual fragments. It would be closer to the truth to say that an object of a particular kind of complexity invites or necessitates a more extensive range of fragmentary viewings. Perhaps Giedion's idea arises from the analogy with Cubist paintings. In his view, Cubist paintings represent objects and they also represent the process of seeing them. They succeed in the latter task by placing a number of fragmentary views of an object together on the canvas. But a building is neither a representation of a process nor of an object: it is itself a physical object. To design a building so that it will invite new and different fragmentary viewings is not to make it into representations or pictures of such fragments.

Behind the multiple perceptions we have of, say, the Bauhaus, there is a fixed object. The characteristics of that object, its peculiar kind of complexity, make it especially fruitful for architectural seeing. There is an object behind the appearances, so to speak. This must also be a visible object. The notion that Giedion borrows from Boccioni, that there is no fixed object behind appearances, is hard to accept. At the very least, there is one person who needs to be able to see and under-

stand the object behind the fleeting appearances, and that is the architect, since he or she needs to conceive of the design of the fixed object
that will engender the richest possible combination of fragmentary
views.

In fact, architectural objects constantly re-assert their object-ness,
despite the designer's intention that they should be seen as fragments.
The point is evident in Zaha Hadid's Vitra factory fire station. One of
Hadid's aims has been to revitalise the modernist aesthetic project,
drawing in particular on Russian Suprematism. Accordingly, the fire
station is designed as an assembly of sharply pointed fragments, allud-
ing to the idea that seeing is of multiple broken parts, not whole
objects. In reality, however, the fragments take on their own identity –
and considerable beauty – as solid objects. Fragmentary views are of
course possible, but they will be views of these whole objects (fig. 32).
An architect who persisted in trying to make a building out of fragmentary views would be trying to catch and freeze the mobile life of
seeing itself.

An agenda is beginning to develop for another kind of seeing, quite
unaffected by the dynamism of modernist theory, and yet essential to
architecture – a stable, generalised kind of seeing.

3   Here is a kind of seeing directed to objects as they really are, and
for the moment I will term it 'ordinary' seeing. At the simplest level
we need it so that we can find our way around. We do not want to
carry a ball of thread everywhere so that we can find our way back
from a sequence of fragmentary but seemingly unconnected views. We
want to see where we are going and where we have come from. So
this is practical, everyday, ordinary seeing.

Ordinary seeing is a variety of perception. It therefore involves an
'intentional object'.[19] The crucial point is that perception is of something. If we see Hadid's fire station at the Vitra factory, then that is the
'intentional object' of our seeing. A distinction can be drawn with
bodily feelings such as pains or itches, which are not perceptions of an
object but merely sensations. In everyday life this connects with

another kind of assumption, namely that our beliefs about the objects we see around us are true. I see an object as the fire station designed by Hadid and I also believe it to be so, correctly. Mistakes are possible – in evening light I could mistake a distant group of Black Houses on Skye for shaggy cattle – but in ordinary seeing we do not generally believe that a building is something other than a building.

I am also assuming 'perceptual constancy'. As we move about in the world, the basic data that we receive about the colours, shapes and sizes of objects change all the time but we are quite capable of identifying that objects are constant in reality. A rectangular building at one moment presents us with a sharp prow, as we approach it diagonally; at another moment, as we look up at the facade, it turns into a pyramid, receding upwards. The shadowed face of the building might look dark grey and the sunny facade golden yellow, although we know the brick on each side is the same. A camera registers a different shape and colour of building each time, depending on where the picture is taken from and the conditions of the moment. We know that it is the same build-ing and that these kinds of changes in appearance are just that, not changes in the object itself. Perceptual constancy also ensures that in most circumstances when we are moving through or around a build-ing we see it as fixed and understand, correctly, that we are moving. This is despite the fact that the primary visual data we receive might be said to be moving across the retina.[20]

Buildings can be designed so as to make perceptual constancy more difficult to achieve, as part of an aesthetic strategy. Peter Blundell-Jones has described the effects of the complex non-rectangular and inter-locking spaces that make up the auditorium of Hans Scharoun's Phil-harmonie building in Berlin. He points out the difficulty of estimating the shape and size of the space from any single viewpoint, and the apparent change in size of the space when the spectator moves to another viewpoint: 'Walking around the hall and watching it change its apparent size is a fascinating experience'.[21] Perceptual constancy operates satisfactorily up to a certain point but, according to Blundell-Jones, the lack of normal perspective cues make it difficult to register exact shapes and distances, and this creates the delicious ambiguities.

The aesthetic strategy trades on the normal process of attaining perceptual constancy: making it a more difficult process is precisely what creates the distinctive aesthetic effect.

Perceptual constancy normally enables us to achieve the correct perception of the world when we are moving. Despite the fact that the image of the world is moving across the retina, we perceive, correctly, that it is ourselves that move, not the world. But there are two specific circumstances in which this realism of ordinary seeing deserts us and it appears that the building itself is moving. The first is termed 'motion parallax' and occurs in circumstances where we focus on an object that has other objects in layers behind and in front of it. If we move to one side, still focusing on the intermediate object, the layer in front and the layer behind seem to move in opposite directions.[22] Motion parallax is a general feature of how we see buildings that have complex layering, whether it be the buttresses, pinnacles and complex wall planes of a Gothic cathedral, or modern buildings where layers of columns, facade skins and sunshades are disengaged from one another. It can also be a feature of interiors, vividly exploited in Jean Nouvel's version of a hypostyle hall at the Institut du Monde Arabe in Paris (fig. 33).

The second circumstance is 'motion perspective'. If I fix my gaze on a point straight ahead while I am walking forward, objects on all sides seem to move away from that point. Objects nearer to me flow past more rapidly, while those nearer the point move little, if at all. The application to our progression through long columned facades or nave-like columned spaces is obvious.

Motion parallax and motion persective are always relative to a particular viewpoint, and therefore to individual momentary views. Those views have a special character but they do not challenge our perception of the whole building as a fixed and stable object. They do pose an interesting challenge to the idea of 'ordinary seeing', however. On the face of it, they are quite outside it, since they misinform us, telling us that the building is moving when it is not. But one of the virtues of motion parallax and motion perspective is that they provide excellent cues to spatial depth.[23] In that sense they are instrumental in gaining a more realistic perception of a building, of its real dimensions

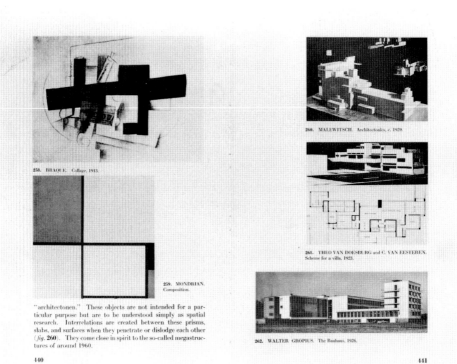

258. BRAQUE. Collage, 1913.

259. MONDRIAN. Composition.

260. MALEWITSCH. Architectonics, c. 1920.

261. THEO VAN DOESBURG and C. VAN EESTEREN. Scheme for a villa, 1923.

262. WALTER GROPIUS. The Bauhaus, 1926.

"architectonen." These objects are not intended for a particular purpose but are to be understood simply as spatial research. Interrelations are created between these prisms, slabs, and surfaces when they penetrate or dislodge each other (*fig.* **260**). They come close in spirit to the so-called megastructures of around 1960.

440   441

31   The modernist argument from painting to architecture, from Sigfried Giedion, *Space, Time and Architecture* (1941).

32 The fire station, Vitra factory, Weil-am-Rhein, Germany, designed by Zaha Hadid (1994).

33 Columned hall at the Institut du Monde Arabe, Paris, designed by Jean Nouvel (1987).

and shape. We could conclude that the peculiar phenomenology is an aid to ordinary seeing.[24]

Perceptual constancy and the fruitful joining of intention and belief form the backbone of ordinary seeing and they contribute to the achievement of seeing architecture. But this has not taken us very far into the intricacies of architectural experience. So far, 'ordinary seeing' has been a robust but extremely limited idea. I now want to build on it.

I have criticised Giedion for suggesting that a building is made out of fragments and I have stressed instead the constancy of the object that we know to exist. Furthermore, in order to see any object fully we must see it from a number of viewpoints. This is especially true for buildings which are large and multi-chambered. Giedion's argument is that we assemble a composite understanding from seeing fragmentary views, so that an understanding of the whole building is threaded along the structure of space-time. It is true that a building, by its design, might encourage this kind of journey of discovery, but I do not believe that this is how the ordinary seeing of a building works. We see part of a building, the facade say, and believe it to be the facade of a build-ing that has an interior, sides, a back, a roof, none of which we can see. Generally, such a belief is true: seeing one part of a building can be adequate evidence that a whole building, comprised of typical parts, is there.[25]

The issue is how we understand the relationship between seeing parts of a building and seeing it as a whole. Giedion suggests that seeing each fragment involves vivid shafts of attention, of concentrated seeing. The kind of seeing that he has in mind takes place at the centre of the visual field, and in quite a small area of it. It also involves rapid scanning within that small compass.[26] Surrounding it is a visual scene of which we are aware but without any sense of concentration or per-ception of detail. I might be concentrating on the lower half of the screen of my computer. I am aware of the reading lamp and the papers on my desk, but with no sense of detail or acuity, and on the very edge of my visual field I can just perceive the whiteness of the sun-light coming in through the window. No visual scene can be seen all at once with the same level of attention, and the same is true of a large object like a building that dominates the visual field. So Giedion's shafts of fragmented seeing will always be set against a background of seeing the whole scene at a different level of concentration.

That 'background seeing' of the whole visual field gives us a sense of being placed in a larger world. In the open air the issue is straightforward, but a room also creates a little perceptual world for those inside it. It is a bounded visual field within which we can explore in detail, turning around as we like, looking up and down and accumulating myriad detailed views of the larger whole. The sense that these views are set within a sustaining little visual world suggests a way in which we can develop the distinction between seeing buildings, as we might see any object, and a particular kind of architectural experience.

If I stand with my back to the statue of General Wolfe on the hill at Greenwich, London, looking towards the river, I can see The Queen's House in the middle distance. It would be a strange usage to say that I was 'experiencing' The Queen's House, just as it would be strange to say that I was 'experiencing' the other tourists who are standing nearby and admiring the view. It is enough to say that I am seeing or looking at The Queen's House. But I might say that I am 'experiencing the view', where this refers to the slope falling away in front of me, Greenwich Palace lying beyond The Queen's House, the Thames, the office blocks on the Isle of Dogs, the whole vista of London from the dome of St Paul's in the west to the Millennium Dome in the east, with the clouds above, and this phrase would capture the sense of an enclosing background seeing of a whole visible world (fig. 34).

Let us say provisionally that seeing and looking are appropriate to objects set within the visual field, when we fix them with a particular attention, and that 'visually experiencing' involves the whole visual field. We can direct concentrated attention to any point in the surrounding world, but it is also possible to relax that concentration and instead to cultivate a sense that attention is spread equally around the visible world. That is one of the pleasures of being on the hill at Greenwich, lost in contemplation of the city.

If I walk down the hill and go right up to The Queen's House, it gradually fills my field of vision, and 'architectural experience' begins to seem an apt phrase. As a building gradually dominates the field of vision, it begins to form a little visual world of its own. A facade, close-up, might be beautifully enclosing. And there is no doubt that when I go inside, through the great cube room, up the tulip stair, through the enfilade of rooms, it is experiencing that is at issue, not merely seeing or looking. It is even possible to complete the sequence in a thoroughly Corbusian way, by emerging onto the loggia, an inside-out space partly enclosed by the little world of the building and partly by the larger landscape beyond (figs 35–9).

A summary of this very schematic approach to 'ordinary seeing' would now go as follows. We see a building as a building and we do so, generally correctly, from seeing only a part, from quite restricted perceptual information. We perceive it, in the sense of perceiving an intentional object rather than by experiencing bodily sensations which are caused by it. Nor do we perceive a building as an end result of synthesising a number of partial views: the process of recognition is much more immediate than that. Then, on closer engagement with the building, we move from a shortage of visual information to plenitude. The building becomes a visual world which we explore, and we gradually perceive its parts in detail. At the heart of 'visually experiencing', contrasted with merely seeing, is the fact that there is too much to see, a surfeit of seeing. We explore within that visual world, whether it is an interior or a landscape, amplifying our background sense of its identity with detailed shafts of attention. We initially identify the whole from the part; then we become aware of the whole as an enclosing totality; then we are able step-by-step to perceive in detail the parts within the whole.

4   If seeing is to be examined then so must the other senses: it would be strange if the ordinary experience of architecture gathered nothing from them. One of the senses, taste, is irrelevant to architecture but touch (considered broadly to include sensing of temperature, humidity and air movement), smell and hearing each deliver perceptions of a building. Each sense is a distinctive mode of perception but they operate in parallel, contributing to the experience of a particular building.

Touch gives access to sensible features of a building that are first accessible to sight. We can see the shape of a handrail and we can also feel its shape; we can see its smoothness and also feel it. Shape and smoothness are therefore examples of 'common sensibles', features that can be perceived by more than one sense modality.[27] The same principle operates in the case of hardness. We can feel the hardness of building materials, particularly in the case of floors. The acuity of touch in our feet responds to the way that the floor vibrates.[28] We can also perceive the hardness of building materials by hearing the way that they reverberate. Thus hardness is another 'common sensible', accessible by more than one sense modality.

In contrast, there are other features of a building that can be perceived in no other way than by touch. Only touch can allow us to perceive how warm or cold the surfaces of a building are: seeing, hearing or smell cannot help us here. Thus, unlike shape, warmth is a 'proper sensible', accessible to only one sense modality, that of touch. Smell falls into the same category: only the nose can perceive the tang of a pine-boarded interior. The senses of smell and touch give access to other 'proper sensibles' – the smell, humidity, temperature and rate of movement of the air in the building. In practice, they are more likely to be perceived than the smell and temperature of the actual surfaces of the building. This brings an ambiguity into the discussion of architectural experience. Should the stress be on the sensible qualities of the building, considered strictly as a physical object? Or should the stress be on the totality of perceptual experiences, so that we take account not only of the sensible qualities of the building but also of the air within it?

The first option would limit what the objects of architecture are, and stipulate a division within a continuous range of experiences. For example, we would say that the coldness of a handrail was significant but not the coldness of the air. The second option – which seems the

35 The Queen's House, Greenwich,
designed by Inigo Jones (built 1616–37),
and flanking colonnades (1807–16).

36 The Queen's House.

34 (*left*) The view of London from the hill at Greenwich Park, London.

37 (*above left*) The Queen's House: Cube Room.

38 (*above right*) The Queen's House: the Tulip Stair.

39 The Queen's House: the loggia.

better choice – leads us to a baggy definition of architectural experience, and points to the idea that it comprises the whole range of perceptions within the little world of the building. We are still in the field
of ordinary perception, but the definition of the object of perception
has been widened. Ordinary architectural experience is not just about
buildings, but about the physical environment that they make and
enclose.

The question of touching buildings needs some further discussion.
We do not touch buildings very much with our hands: handrails and
door handles are the main points of contact. That would be all there
is to be said about how architecture feels to the hands. But that is too
limiting. We never touch the roofs or ceilings of buildings, and rarely
the walls, yet our knowledge of their textures is a crucial part of architectural experience. We only see what a wall is like but we say, with
confidence, that it has such and such a texture. In most cases this is a
matter of a common sensible, accessible equally by seeing as by touch:
we might talk of the roughness of a concrete wall that shows the
impression of boarded shuttering, where that roughness can be both
seen and touched. Equally, we would be right to say, from seeing only,
that the steel columns in the Barcelona Pavilion were glossy, that the
travertine was smooth but fissured, and that the onyx was polished.
Touching would merely duplicate these perceptions, although it would
add its special phenomenology.

In another kind of situation, however, feeling and touching are
related in a curious and indirect manner. Rustication in English
eighteenth-century classical architecture provides examples of what I
have in mind. The attraction of the beautifully precise incising on the
wall of Kent's Horse Guards building, London, lies not in what I would
actually feel: it is a perception of it in a miniaturised form, as if I could
feel the smoothness and the incisions in one sweep of the hand. From
photographs of the old Newgate Prison we can sense, as if via one
imagined sweep of the hand, that it is rough and knobbly (figs 40 and
41).[29] The concrete architecture of the 1950s and 1960s relied for much
of its effect on these imagined miniaturised textures. Contemplating
them involves imagining how it would be to touch them if they were

at the scale of the hand and fingers. We see part of the building as having a certain texture. It is not the texture we would feel if we were to touch the actual building, but it is the texture we would feel if the building were miniaturised (figs 42 and 43). Imagination has an essential but rather limited task: not to see the texture as something else, but merely as smaller so that the hand can pass over it.

Again we are faced with a choice of how to categorise a common feature of architectural experience. We could put 'textural seeing' of architecture under the heading of imaginative rather than ordinary experience. This would have the interesting consequence that the sense of touch through the hands would have very restricted relevance to the ordinary experience of architecture. Alternatively, we could admit textural seeing to ordinary experience, since it seems removed from it only by the intriguing matter of a change of scale. Let us adopt the more inclusive definition for the moment, accepting that the idea of ordinary architectural experience becomes baggier still.

From the sense of touch, strictly considered, we need to turn to the 'kinaesthetic' (or 'proprioceptive') sense. This sense enables us to be aware of the muscular changes that occur when we move about. The mechanisms include the central nervous system's monitoring of commands it sends to the muscles, and the operation of receptors located in muscle tissue and the tendons.[30] They do not give us information about the outer world but do provide us with a type of perception, a perception of our own movement.

The kinaesthetic sense has occupied many discussions about architecture. Goethe is quoted as writing about it as follows:

> One would think that architecture as a fine art works solely for the eyes. Instead, it should work primarily for the sense of mechanical motion in the human body — something to which scant attention is paid. When in dance we move according to definite rules, we experience a pleasant sensation. A similar sensation should be aroused in someone who is led blindfolded through a well-built house. This involves the difficult and complicated doctrine of proportions which gives the building and its various parts their character.[31]

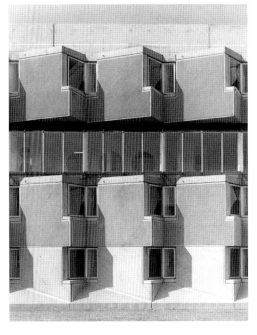

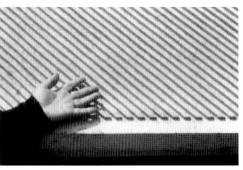

41   Newgate Prison, London, designed by George Dance the Younger (1770–80).

40 (*above left*)   Horse Guards, London, designed by William Kent (*c.*1745–8).

42   Textured concrete at student residences, St Andrew's University, Scotland, designed by James Stirling (1964).

43   The actual size of the concrete ribbing at St Andrew's, with James Stirling's hand for scale.

Goethe's interest is in the fact that the kinaesthetic sense can give access to the rules and pleasures of proportion, just as it does to the rules and pleasures of dance. If we have a sense of the repetition of footsteps as we cross and re-cross a room, this could give the same kind of knowledge of plan dimensions and shape that we can gain by sight. (If we count our paces we will probably estimate the size of the room more accurately than by guessing just from sight.) We have a perceptual procedure that gives us another kind of access to a common sensible, namely the building's shape. For the sighted and un-blindfolded person the same knowledge could be gained from the modality of sight.

5   Each time we take a pace forward we also make a footfall, and touch the floor again. Thus, in practice kinaesthetic and touch sensations are necessarily linked as we walk round a building. We could count these footfalls, just as we could count our paces, and the same argument could be made: that they provide corroboration of the shape of the building in plan. Although this would tell the sighted person nothing new about the plan shape, it would bring an additional perception of the hardness of the floor surface. A combination of the kinaesthetic and touch senses is often implied in discussions of the tactile or haptic aspects of architecture.[32] Kinaesthesia could, after all, be called a kind of touch – touch inside the body – and it is an appealing idea to conceive of the body itself, apart from its specialist organs of sense, as a means of perceiving buildings. The appeal perhaps derives from the notion that sensuous experience is our primary form of engagement with the world and that seeing and hearing are weaker and of secondary importance because they act at a distance.[33]

There is another attractive idea near the surface here, which is that if we perceive an object through a number of sense modalities we will grasp it more securely: if seeing, hearing, touch, smell and the kinaesthetic sense were all to be engaged together how powerful our grasp of the object would be! Here is Kenneth Frampton describing part of Aalto's Säynätsalo Town Hall:

Thus, from the stereotomic mass and relative darkness of the entry stair, where the feeling of enclosure is augmented by the tactility of the brick treads, one enters into the bright light of the council chamber, the timber-lined roof of which is carried on fanlike, wooden trusses that splay upward to support concealed rafters above a boarded ceiling. The sense of arrival occasioned by this tectonic display is reinforced by various nonretinal sensations, from the smell of polished wood to the floor flexing under one's weight together with the general destabilization of the body as one enters onto a highly polished surface.[34]

The idea of the integration of the senses in architectural experience involves a number of issues and it is worth trying to untangle them. How can integrating the senses make a building more real? It is true that a single sense can be deceived more easily than a combination. A person who was deaf and had no acuity of touch could not know that a *scagliola* column, grained to look like marble, was hollow. They would simply see that it looked like marble and would not be able to tap it to check whether it was a fake. Frampton suggests that there is something more at stake, namely that integrating the senses enables us to have a firmer grasp of the realness of buildings. This is of cultural and social importance, asserting realness against the capacity of money endlessly to transform one thing into another.

Achieving this sense of reality becomes an expressive aim and a criterion of judgement for the spectator and critic. Thus, in the Säynätsalo example, it is not just that a catalogue could be made of the way that the various senses are affected: this host of decisions has been made to confirm the particularity and realness of the building. The effect is a matter of artistic intention, but it is based on the potential that ordinary experience offers.

We might imagine this as the possibility of orchestrating the senses, as if each played on a separate instrument of the mind. This implies an equality among the senses and the principle that each can freely contribute to the orchestrated whole. Again, it is a comforting idea but it may lead us in the wrong direction. I would stress, in contrast, the hierarchical nature of the senses in their relation to architecture. Seeing lords it over the other senses. Unlike touch, it can operate at a distance and at fine resolution across numerous channels: form, colour, shading, texture, line, distance. Unlike sound, it can provide perceptions of great complexity which persist over time. Combining the other senses with seeing is generally a question of reinforcing a mood rather than adding distinct objects of perception. In this role the other senses provide information across a small number of variables: that the sound in a building is more or less reverberative, that the air is more or less warm or humid, that the floor is springy or hard and so on.

A mood that these variables create can be right or wrong, appropriate or inappropriate, for a particular context, but it is unlikely to be unique: moods are generic not unique. But seeing delivers the astonishing uniqueness of an object. If a detail is wrong to the eye it might be for one of innumerable reasons: it might seem clumsy or weak, too refined or too rough, or inconsistent or just dull. The moods created by the other senses are not open to such fine discriminations. For such reasons there can be no compensation for the deprivation of sight. A blind person can move through and manipulate a building using their other senses, but they cannot contemplate it visually. People who are deprived of a sense will establish a new set of hierarchical relations between the senses they do have. For example, touch and acoustic reflection can form the armature of knowledge about a building, and that knowledge can be put to more intensive use in moving around the building.[35] But the loss of sight is still absolute.

By the end of the previous chapter I had charted a route from designs to buildings. In this chapter I have outlined the main sensory aspects of our relations with those bulky and complex physical objects. It seems that the discussion of aesthetics has gone backwards. I have criticised a modernist view of architectural experience which made a claim to be central to the aesthetics of architecture and in its place I have put an account of experience which is resolutely ordinary and day-to-day. In the next chapter I will resume the discussion of aesthetics proper, hoping that the description of everyday experience will in due course prove its usefulness.

Chapter 4

Aesthetic Experience

1   In the previous chapter I outlined what is involved in 'architectural experience'. Is it possible to take a further step and distinguish aesthetic from non-aesthetic experience? If the answer is yes, we can subsequently concentrate our attention on that area of experience; if it is not possible to make a clear distinction, we will have to widen the scope of aesthetic theory beyond the fields of ontology and experience that have been discussed so far. In this chapter I will discuss a number of influential views on how the distinction beteen aesthetic and non-aesthetic can be made. They reveal much of interest about architectural experience and aesthetics, but I will argue that they do not provide us with a clear and decisive 'yes' to the basic question.

We could begin with a straightforward point, namely that aesthetic experience cannot draw on any special form of sense perception. It does not arise out of the exercise of a sixth sense and whatever distinctiveness it possesses must derive ultimately from the common stock of our engagement with the world. 'Ultimately' is vague, however, and one of the key tasks will be to chart the conceptual levels by which ordinary experience and aesthetic experience are separated. The discussion in the previous chapter lacked any reference to the fact that pleasure can accompany our perception of objects. A reference to pleasure in experience would be an appealing way of distinguishing between ordinary and aesthetic experience. This is a very broad proposition, and I shall begin by discussing one application of it, namely the idea that pleasure can be derived from the emotions. The task will be to show how particular forms of architectural experience – those that bring emotion in its train – could be considered as specifically 'aesthetic'. In the later part of this chapter I shall turn to another way of making a distinction between aesthetic and non-aesthetic. The notion of imaginative activity is crucial to this viewpoint. It argues that the aesthetic experience appropriate to architecture is not a variety of the larger category of experience that we derive from our senses. Its essential feature is that imagination puts a quite un-realistic construction on something that we perceive.

Aesthetic experience can be defined as a special variety of an ordinary kind of architectural experience, one that brings emotion with it; or it can be defined in contrast with ordinary experience, as the imagination-based theory suggests. Both kinds of argument illuminate aspects of the aesthetics of architecture. But I argue that neither of them allows us to make an exhaustive distinction between aesthetic and non-aesthetic experience.

Two strands in aesthetic theory derive a definition of aesthetic experience from the operation of the emotions. The first can be found in the work of Edmund Burke, who in 1757 published *A Philosophical Enquiry into the Origin of our Ideas of the Sublime and Beautiful.*[1] The second is the more diffuse body of work termed 'empathy theory', which was particularly influential in the period from the 1880s to the 1920s, but which is still common currency.

Burke's theory of aesthetic experience depends on twin concepts, the 'sublime' and 'beautiful' of the title of his book. He argues that we find some kinds of objects sublime and some beautiful. To put it more exactly, we shall find those objects sublime or beautiful because they have certain definite characteristics. There are three steps in the argument. The first is the idea that specific kinds of emotional response match our perception of those special characteristics of objects. Thus Burke draws the distinction between the feeling of 'delight', which he

associates with the sublime, and the feeling of 'pleasure' which is linked
to the category of the beautiful. Delight has its origins in the 'passions'
that derive from a person's instinct of self-preservation. Along with the
instinct of self-preservation go emotions of the sense of danger and the
fear of death, illness and pain. Burke makes the bold suggestion that
these emotions have a positive side which can be cultivated, on the
assumption that the actual danger is kept within bounds. Indeed, the
power that these emotions derive from their origins in real fear and
danger means that when we do enjoy them in a controlled fashion
they have a peculiar intensity. These emotions are contrasted with other
kinds of feelings which fall into the category of 'pleasure'. These derive
from an engagement with society, and the most notable instances are
love – as a social phenomenon distinguished from individual lust – and
sympathy with other persons.

In the second stage of the argument Burke turns to the characteristics of objects that make them specially sublime or beautiful and thus
suited to engender delight or pleasure. Delight can come from the
obscurity of objects, from the sense of power that they communicate,
from their vastness, from the repetition or uniformity of their constituent parts, or from their darkness and lightness. The sublime is at
work in such cases. As we shall see, the latter category is of considerable interest for discussions of architecture. Examples of sensible characteristics of objects that bring pleasure, and where beauty is at work,
are smallness, smoothness and gradual variation. The contrast between
the attributes of sublimity and beauty reinforces the sense that Burke's
'pleasure' is a milder kind of aesthetic experience than 'delight'.

Thirdly, Burke gives himself the task of making a causal explanation
of the link between beautiful and sublime characteristics of objects and
the emotions that they engender. In his account of how sublimity and
delight are connected, he points out that real terror produces a bodily
agitation or tension. Seeing sublime objects produces similar kinds of
bodily tensions.

An example of how the argument works in detail can be observed
in the case of the abrupt transition from light into darkness, which
Burke identified as an example of the sublime. He argues that the iris

of the eye undergoes muscular strain as it rapidly adapts the size of the pupil to the new light conditions. This kind of muscular strain is associated with conditions of terror, but it is also a source of delight, since stimulating exercise of the body is delightful. The strain that the eye undergoes in these conditions of sharp contrast is sufficient to activate an association with that feeling of terror, albeit in a muted and delightful form. Explanations for other emotional effects of sublime objects use similar physiologically based arguments, as do the explanations for the power of beautiful objects.

Seeing in itself may bring feeling with it, according to Burke. This notion of 'feelingful seeing' is the core of his distinctive twin version of aesthetic experience. It is apparent that it involves a quite different approach to the process of seeing from the one that I outlined in the dicussion of ordinary seeing. I gave prominence to the idea of an 'intentional object' of perception: that perception is 'about' the particular object before us, and is not just a sensation derived from it. Burke comes at the question from a quite different angle. He is interested in the sensible features of objects considered in categories: obscurity, vastness, uniformity, smoothness, littleness and so on. Particular objects are aesthetically significant as bearers of these categories, but they are of no other intrinsic interest. Then he is interested in the bodily sensations that these sensible features create in our sensory apparatus. He is not interested in the content of perceptual experiences, in the particular thing that is seen, touched or otherwise sensed. His primary interest is in the process of bodily sensation rather than perception, and the notion that such sensations can explain why it is we experience certain emotions in the presence of certain objects. The act of perception – a mode of attention to objects in the world – is being squeezed out between these two interests and instead Burke is pointing to us towards two ways of construing 'feeling'. It can mean physical sensation and it can also mean emotion or 'affect'. His argument is that feeling/sensation influences feeling/emotion, and implies that perception is a mere intermediary in this process, largely irrelevant to the nature of aesthetic experience.

A broader issue is also relevant here, and points us towards the discussion of empathy theories. Burke's twin aesthetic experiences involve distinctive emotional patterns which are activated by our seeing certain kinds of sensible features of objects. However, he assumes that unconscious processes make the link between feeling/sensation and feeling/emotion. When we see something sublime we are not aware of any of the intermediate causal links that Burke describes, for example those between real terror, the exercise of the body that is involved in terror, related forms of exercise that bring delight, and the analogous stimulation of the perceptual system.

2   'Empathy' theories are based on more elaborated ideas of unconscious processes than were available to Burke, but they share a basic dependence on the activities of the unconscious mind. I propose to sketch how empathy theories developed their own conceptions of a distinctively aesthetic form of 'feelingful seeing'.[2] Then we will be in a better position to assess whether it is plausible that there should be a distinctive form of aesthetic experience of architecture separate from the ordinary kind.

To ease ourselves into the complexities of empathy theory, it may be best to take some steps back and recall the discussion of kinaesthetic perception. In the previous chapter I examined this in the context of bodily movement and its contribution to an awareness of space. Empathy theories give a greater significance to the kinaesthetic sense and the ways that it can be engaged by the form of buildings. For example, they suggest that the regularity of the structures of buildings evokes the regularity of breathing, their symmetry evokes the symmetry in the body which makes us comfortable, and different proportions relate to different rates of breathing, so that 'narrow proportions produce the impression of an almost breathless and hurried upward striving'.[3] The examples come from Wölfflin, but the idea was common in architectural discussion by the early twentieth century. Geoffrey Scott provides the classic formulation of the idea. We look at a building and 'identify ourselves with its apparent state', but that apparent state is in turn invested with human kinaesthetic sensation. Scott points out examples in common use: that 'arches "spring", vistas "stretch", domes "swell", Greek temples are "calm", and baroque facades "restless". The whole of architecture is, in fact, unconsciously invested by us with human movement and human moods.'[4]

Many intermediate propositions and arguments are necessary to connect the initial kinaesthetic perceptions with the emotions that are invested in outer objects. It is assumed that we possess a memory of the initial bodily perceptions so that we are capable of recalling what the body felt like at a certain moment. It is also assumed that this physical memory is laid down in association with the memory of the kind of architectural configuration that caused it. Seeing a certain kind of building element evokes once again the kinaesthetic perception even if we only see it, and don't actually move through it. So we might look at a narrow entrance, like one that we had to squeeze through in the past, and we will be reminded of those bodily feelings. The argument hinges on the idea that kinaesthetic perceptions have emotional content. In Wölfflin's example, 'upward striving' becomes the emotional content associated with the physical memory of moving through narrow spaces. This is the crucial point of the argument and, just as for Burke, it involves transmuting feeling/sensation into feeling/emotion. This change of state is closely connected with the notion that we project inner states onto outer objects. We invest buildings with human feelings, both kinaesthetic and emotional. We can then identify with those feelings and in doing so we also identify ourselves with the physical 'body' of the building, the body that has the feelings.

These are the typical steps in the argument, but a considerable range of views go under the heading of 'empathy'. For readers of English, Scott's account is the most accessible and it is close to Wölfflin's. It is important to observe how two separate intellectual traditions were intermingled. One was the attempt to develop a psychology on scientific principles. This was influential in elaborating the stages of argument that I have described, with their stress on the role of memory and association. The other tradition, which originated in Romanticism, provided the basis for the view that feelings can inhabit inanimate objects. Its key feature was the idea that there is a spirit, will or idea which underlies animate life, but which also finds appropriate kinds of expression in non-animate forms. These two traditions could grate against, as well as reinforce each other: Wölfflin himself grappled with Schopenhauer and with the experimental psychologists, rejecting and accepting parts from each.[5]

Reading the empathy theorists inevitably brings Freud to mind. In one sense the connection is unwarranted, since Freud appears to have had no interest in defining areas of experience as specially aesthetic. However, he did share with the empathists the aim of understanding a certain kind of emotionally charged seeing. At the broadest level, Freud and the empathists both form part of a movement to transform the theory of the 'will' or 'spirit' of speculative philosophy into a theory of the unconscious mind.[6] Both Freud and his near-contemporary Wölfflin take the findings of modern psychological science and the tradition of speculative metaphysics as intellectual raw material. There are more direct connections, notably in the use that both the empathists and Freud made of the theory of dreams. Robert Vischer, one of the influential early theorists of the idea of empathy, drew on Karl Albert Scherner's *The Life of the Dream* of 1861, in order to explain the basic features of the empathy process. Freud also drew on Scherner, via Volkelt's *Dream-Phantasy* of 1875, in writing *The Interpretation of Dreams*.[7]

The theory of dreams is a junction at which empathists and Freud come together but it is also a point from which they take off in different directions. Vischer's interest in dreams is that they can provide a model for empathic processes during waking life. The residue of daily experience forms the material for dreams, but the narrative, as it were, is determined by the state of the body during sleep. The images in dreams have close analogies to the sleeper's bodily state. As Vischer puts it: 'If I am sleeping with my knee bent and I involuntarily stretch it out in response to a corrective muscle stimulus, I might imagine being thrown from a tower or seeing someone else being thrown.'[8] Whereas in dreams we invest an image with our bodily state, empathic states in waking life involve investing an outer object with our inner emotions. There are many steps between the two processes but the underlying structure is similar.

In *The Interpretation of Dreams*, Freud goes to some length to argue, contrary to Scherner, that the bodily state of the sleeper only explains a very limited part of what takes place in dreams. The more important part of the explanation of dreams lies in the structure of unconscious life itself. Perhaps the empathists thought of the unconscious as a medium in which the actions of the body and mind could be related, as if it were an adjunct to conscious life. Freud is much more assertive about the role of the unconscious: 'The first of these displeasing propositions of psycho-analysis is this: that mental processes are essentially unconscious, and that those which are conscious are merely isolated acts and part of the whole psychic entity.'[9]

The difference between the outlooks becomes much wider: bluntly, Freud is not much concerned with the fundamental idea of analogies of bodily and mental life, as pursued by empathists, or the idea that the emotional charge of an object is to be explained by the memory of some associated bodily state. Freud's theory of emotion is much more fine-grained, and it derives from the second 'displeasing proposition of psycho-analysis', which asserts the centrality of the sexual impulses, described in 'both the narrower and wider sense'.[10] In exchange for the fine grain of Freud's theorising, we have to accept a restriction of the scope of the loading of 'affect' onto what is seen. It centres, not on a broad category of inter-relations between bodily feelings and emotions (with the fuzziness of explanation that is often entailed), but on those cases where there is a sexual explanation for the emotional power of an object, 'in the narrower or wider sense'.

There is a delightful irony here. We raise our eyebrows when Geoffrey Scott says that architecture is 'unconsciously invested with human moods' and then talks of spires soaring, domes swelling and so on, as if these were rather chaste moods and had nothing to do with the character of the phallus-spire or the breast-dome. We might suspect that empathists are right in identifying that certain configurations of buildings have emotional power, but that they are wrong in their explanation, and that the examples they hit on are precisely those that a Freudian theory would better explain.[11]

It bears repeating that Freud considered that his version of 'feelingful seeing', with its origins in a sexual impulse, was part of quite ordinary day-to-day experience. He had no wish to identify it as peculiarly aesthetic and in fact his interests in aesthetics lay more with the activities of the artist than in analysing the experience of the spectator. Nevertheless, other writers have drawn on Freud's work in order to develop an expanded notion of the emotional content of seeing, and have done so within the context of a distinctive aesthetic experience. Scott's examples have alerted us to explanations of the erotic force behind feelingful seeing, very much in 'the narrower sense' to which Freud refers. The point I have in mind, by contrast, is the way in which writers have pursued the implications of the sexual impulses 'in the wider sense'. These take us into the question of the development of the infant and child's sexuality and from there into the parent–infant relationships which form the setting for the education of the emotions. This is the territory that Adrian Stokes explored, in a remarkable series of essays on art and architecture. He was guided by Melanie Klein's view that the early stages of infant development create distinctive emotional 'positions' which colour the infant's perception of the outer world and form part of the furniture of later life.[12]

It may be that Freudian and empathy theories alert us to examples of feelingful seeing that partly overlap and partly adjoin one another. Each outlook has cases that the other would find it difficult to account for: it is hard to imagine how Wölfflin's instances of the affective power of symmetry and regularity in buildings could be given a Freudian explanation, and it would be difficult to incorporate some of Stokes's examples into an empathy viewpoint. The area of overlap works two ways. As we have seen, Freudian theory can give plausible explanations for the effects of the kind of examples that Scott brings forward. But it is also true that the fertility of Adrian Stokes's psychoanalytic writings comes partly from his earlier immersion in the nineteenth-century aesthetic tradition.[13] It might even be said that Klein's key concept of 'projective identification' has very strong affinities with an empathy viewpoint. There is a great deal that requires further study and it is important that it is done on an inter-disciplinary basis, so that cases can be subjected to scrutiny from a number of contending viewpoints.

3   I have attempted to illustrate a tradition of thinking about architectural experience. At any particular moment it bears the imprint of the larger culture, but the common thread is the idea that a distinctively aesthetic mode of architectural experience can be identified. It may be Burkean, Wölfflinian or Stokesian but it has that feature in common. Now, suppose a reader agrees that there is evidence of a distinctive mode of experience – the feelingful mode of seeing, as I have so relentlessly put it – but parts company on the idea that it is distinctively aesthetic. What kinds of arguments might he or she bring forward to support such scepticism?

Theories of 'feelingful seeing' deal with broad categories of the 'sensible' characteristics of objects: that they are smooth, dark, constricted, centralised, phallus-like, breast-like and so on. They also deal with broad categories of emotional response such as pleasure, delight or Melanie Klein's psychological 'positions'. But we want aesthetics to deal in specificity, not broad categories. There is a mismatch between the breadth of these categories and the particularity of buildings, and indeed between their breadth and the obsessional effort that goes into making buildings particular. For example, Soane's fascination with effects of light and shadow may owe something to Burke,[14] but his work gives us the sense of an endless enquiry into the qualities and effects of light and shadow. Our feeling is that darkness and light in themselves are the raw material out of which Soane attempts to make very specific aesthetic effects, and this is some distance from Burke's proposition that darkness and light can in some elementary sense create emotional effects.

We get a similar sense of the limitations of empathy theory if we follow Geoffrey Scott's argument right to the end of *The Architecture of Humanism*. Beauty, he says, can come from the empathic states that he has described but the point does not exhaust the aesthetics of architecture: 'Mass, space, and line afford the material of individual aesthetic pleasures, of beauty isolated and detached. But architecture aims at more than isolated pleasures. It is above all an art of synthesis'. He then argues that it is style that creates a synthesis and that style 'through coherence, subordinates beauty to the pattern of the mind.'[15] It is true that Scott still sees empathic experience as distinctively aesthetic, but the suggestion is made that aesthetic experience has to be thought of as multi-levelled, and once that is done the constituent empathic experiences become raw material for a higher level of stylistic integration.

Note also the pitfalls that can lie in the way of using Klein's categories in practical architectural criticism. Colin St John Wilson uses her distinction between types of psychological 'positions' as a means of explaining the distinctive emotional effects of either being enclosed by buildings or seeing them as objects from outside.[16] In fact, Klein's distinction hardly justifies this argument. On one hand she notes the combination of intense pleasure and fierce rejection that comes from the infant's relation to a 'part-object' – primarily the mother's breast – and on the other she notes the 'depressive' position that comes with realising that the mother is a whole object and one to whom reparation for the former rage is due. Adrian Stokes's application of Klein's ideas is more apt than Wilson's, partly because it responds to the idea that architectural fragments can bring an overwhelming kind of pleasure. It is noticeable that Stokes never discusses buildings in the conventional mode of criticism adopted by Wilson. His examples, as in his remarkable book on Venice, come from the contingent fragments of a city – the meeting of the mouldings of a column and a rectangular pier; the white glare at the end of a shadowed passage; semi-circular steps that lead up to the rectangular blackness of a doorway; the exact relation of a line of washing to a window opening, of a paving texture to the wall which is built on it (figs 44 and 45).[17]

We begin to think of the kinds of seeing that are imbued with feeling as part of the architect's and spectator's raw material and it becomes difficult to separate them from other aspects of day-to-day architectural experience. In short, we are inclined to follow Freud and put feelingful seeing into the field of ordinary experience.

The emphasis of theories of feelingful seeing is on single experiences, and necessarily so, since the outlook hinges on one-to-one relationships between properties of objects and modes of feeling. But these individual pleasures of perceiving a building are not identical with a pleasure we might have in experiencing it as a whole. A Burkean might eloquently explain the individual pleasures of a building – that the bricks are this pleasing red-brown colour, that the white paintwork and the grey slate are pleasing in their special ways – but the exercise might seem deficient, as if the aesthetic experience of a building were merely a flowing stream of individual experiences.

In the previous chapter I discussed the relationship between the perceptual experience of parts of buildings, and of buildings as complex and complete objects. We want any account of architectural aesthetics to recognise both these two issues. The viewpoints that I have discussed tend to stay at the level of individual experiences, neglecting the fact that an architectural work is also a complex unity. The constituent multiple experiences of a building can form patterns and inter-relationships and it may be these that give the specifically aesthetic character to a building. Then, the thought would continue, it hardly matters whether or not those component experiences are aesthetic or non-aesthetic: the important issue to examine is how the elements are ordered and thereby given significance.

4   A quite different kind of approach to the idea of architectural experience is in prospect here. Feelingful seeing takes its place among the modes of ordinary day-to-day experience: we would concur with Freud on that. Then we have to understand and explain the ways in which that ordinary experience can be ordered and given aesthetic coherence. I wish to pursue the suggestion made by Roger Scruton in *The Aesthetics of Architecture* (1979) that the place to look for a distinctively aesthetic mode of attention is not among particular patterns of emotional response, or sensible characteristics of objects, but in the imaginative activity which gives coherence to certain complex objects.

Scruton begins with the facade of a Gothic cathedral. We can see its complex array of porches, arcades and pinnacles as a piling up of little buildings, as if they added up to a view of a heavenly city. This is imaginative seeing and it is to be contrasted with seeing the facade literally, 'as a mass of masonry', as Scruton puts it. Later on, he points out how imaginative attention can allow more than one interpretation of a given facade, and how this ambiguity can contribute to the richness of the experience. The idea of 'seeing-as' is important: we can see the columns of Peruzzi's Palazzo Massimo either as four pairs, including the pilasters on each side, or as three pairs, with each pair forming an opening (fig. 46). The former case stresses the sense of a colonnade continuous with the structure of the building above, and the latter case stresses the entrance of the building. This kind of seeing is 'a paradigm of architectural experience: the experience can never be "purer", less interpreted, than this.'[18]

These are the first of a series of examples that are delightfully dry and close in spirit to the formalist strand in modern architectural criticism. Many of the buildings that Robert Venturi studies in *Complexity and Contradiction in Architecture* (1966) encourage two kinds of 'seeing-as', and he suggests that the ambiguity is the source of the aesthetic energy in the design.[19] But Scruton takes the argument much further than formal analysis. Interpretations of column arrangements may offer a paradigm of architectural experience, but the full importance of imaginative seeing comes from our ability to see buildings as having symbolic qualities. These in turn are part of a social and moral order, so that in the end imaginative seeing gives us intimations of how we should live, morally and socially.

The distinction that Scruton makes is useful and important. There is 'realistic' seeing, of objects as they really are. What he has in mind is the core of ordinary seeing as I discussed it in Chapter Three. 'Non-realistic' seeing, by contrast, can embrace objects which are quite inaccessible to ordinary seeing. We know that ordinarily, or realistically, the facade of Amiens cathedral is not a heavenly city. The distinction gives us the starting point for understanding the ability of buildings to carry representations and expressive features (a point from which I will develop the arguments of Chapters Five and Six). It also helps us in the more modest task of understanding how sequences of ordinary architectural experience are given aesthetic coherence.

Return for a moment to the eighteenth century, to the French architect and theorist Nicolas Le Camus de Mézières. In *The Genius of Archi-*

tecture, published in 1780, Le Camus discusses the way in which individual architectural experiences can be manipulated, and does so from a theoretical viewpoint that is broadly similar to Burke's. So, 'If you wish to see gaiety unconfined, contrive to have as much daylight as possible and masses that are not too strong, so that nothing seems to engage the mind and that enjoyment may be unreflective'.[20] The bulk of Le Camus's book is about the design of grand and expensive urban houses. It contains much detailed practical advice together with recommendations on design and decoration that flesh out the architectural principles. However, Robin Middleton suggests that Le Camus's innovation was to go beyond itemising individual 'effects' and to discuss their combination in an ensemble. There is advice about the relationships between rooms, both from the point of view of practicality and of manners and custom; the emotional effects appropriate to each room are discussed; the cumulative effect of rooms is discussed, going from the entrance to the grandest space and from there to the most intimate room; and all this is brought together under the precept that the design of a house and all its detailed effects should reflect the position and status of its owner.

The outlook is basic to modern architectural thinking. An example of its application to a modern building type can be found at Clare Hall, a graduate college designed by Ralph Erskine (figs 47–9). The entrance is a cleft in a dark facade and leads into a sunlit courtyard. A sequence of common rooms, bar and dining room opens off that courtyard, rising in stages and gathered together under a continuously sloping mothering roof. The type of response that is provoked, which leads us to consider the cumulative integration of individual experiences into a satisfactory whole, would fit into the notion of 'non-realistic' seeing to which Scruton refers. Bringing experiences together into a larger whole, for example by relations of contrast and accumulation, must imply an ordering process which is not present in individual experiences or their mere co-presence. My suggestion is that once we have accepted Scruton's basic distinction between realistic and non-realistic seeing, we can put it to work in architectural areas other than the formal analysis with which Scruton begins.

44   A passageway, illustrated in Adrian Stokes, *Venice: An Aspect of Art* (1945).

45   Column details illustrated in *Venice: An Aspect of Art.*

46   The Palazzo Massimo, Rome, designed by Baldassare Peruzzi (1532–36).

47, 48 and 49   Clare Hall, Cambridge, designed by Ralph Erskine (1966–69).

5   Let us turn to some of the difficulties in Scruton's argument. First, there is a tricky question about where we should locate our pleasure in shape and pattern in architecture: does this derive from realistic or non-realistic seeing? His chosen examples convincingly come down on the side of imaginative seeing, but we might say that the outcome will vary case by case depending on the nature of the pattern. A curtain-wall grid that forms a strong rectangular pattern is both a property of the building, physically and metrically, and a pattern to be seen. There would be redundancy in describing it as an example of 'seeing-as', since we are seeing what is really there. In other cases, where a facade pattern has apparent depth, or apparent overlapping of one shape by another, we would be justified in talking of 'seeing-as', since no realistic per-ception would register that there was any depth in the overlap. There are difficult judgements to be made and they have to be made case by case. To put one case into the field of non-realistic seeing and another into realistic seeing may be strictly correct, but it does cut across our intuition that we can exercise a generalised pleasure in contemplating the surfaces of objects. We would be unwilling to put too much weight on an arbitrary division of that pleasure into realistic and non-realistic sub-categories.

A second challenge arises in considering light and shadow in build-ings. Seeing light and shadow is central to architectural pleasure and delight in the tradition that unfolds from Burke to Soane and on to Ruskin, as we shall see. But Scruton's definitions raise the question of whether the experiences involved are realistic or non-realistic. In many cases the answer is straightforward: we see a physical object and it has certain 'sensible' characteristics the seeing of which give us pleasure. For example, in illustrations of buildings designed by Eileen Gray we see surfaces illuminated by slatted patterns of bright light and shadow, or by light fading off in to an interior. In such cases we see, realisti-cally, that physical objects are in certain states and the seeing brings us pleasure (figs 50 and 51).

The problematic cases are those where it is the light in the space that attracts our attention and gives us pleasure. We attach descriptive terms to the quality of light – for example, to the calm and clarity of the light in Le Corbusier's Villa La Roche – but the object of our attention is elusive (fig. 52). Is realistic or non-realistic seeing involved? It is true that we may be able to give an explanation for why the light is a certain way. In the case of the Villa La Roche, we can point to Le Corbusier's device of ensuring that light always comes from more than one direction, and thus to the confluence of two kinds of light – from the broad expanses of the north-facing windows and the more varied, sunnier light from the smaller openings. This helps to explain the cause of the visual experience but it still leaves its status obscure.

One way round the problem would be to say that the object of our attention is not light in general but the reflectivity of the surfaces that we see, whether they are the inner surfaces of the building, or the sky and parts of the outer world seen through windows. From here we could develop an argument in favour of imaginative seeing. The first step would be to propose that those individual surfaces, each with its particular reflectivity, should be construed as the basis of ordinary realistic perceptions. Then the light in the space would be treated as an imaginative object, a consequence of the architect's skill in putting certain reflective objects together and making us see them imaginatively as a whole. This would be to follow Scruton's distinction between hearing individual sounds and hearing the flow of music. The former involves realistic, the latter non-realistic, perception.

The difficulty is that we would be happy to say that sounds in music are the raw material of our imaginative perception of the flow of music, but reluctant to apply the point to seeing light in a space. The raw material is stubbornly that we see a certain kind of light, not that we see that the reflective surfaces are in particular visible states. We might hear sounds as music, but we do not see reflective surfaces as light in a space. Another approach would be to pursue the idea that the space has characteristics, and that one of its characteristics is the quality of light. But this compounds an already existing uncertainty about what the object of spatial experience is. Let us say that our perception of space falls on the literal side: we do not imagine spatial experience or imaginatively construct spatial experience from more basic elements of ordinary seeing. Perhaps we could construe the character of the light as a 'sensible' characteristic of the space. But it is hard to accept that space has visible characteristics: could it also be coloured, for example?

We talk about a world as having visible characteristics, that it can be dark on a November afternoon or bright on a spring morning. And we can talk in a similar manner about the little world of a building. At Pitshanger Manor, Soane decorated the Breakfast Room and Library in contrasting ways: sombre for the former and light and sparkling for the latter (figs 53 and 54). The light is beautifully modulated in each case; by turning round and taking a few steps, we can, metaphorically speaking, move from autumn to spring. Soane achieved his effects by manipulating surfaces with colour, decoration and mirrors, but they are not necessarily the objects of our aesthetic attention: it is the light that moves us. And still it seems wrong to say that we have imaginatively construed the light: it is there in the space.

Consider a third type of object whose viewing defies an easy classification into realistic or non-realistic seeing. Seeing building materials can bring pleasure – the grain of wood or stone, the sheen of stainless steel or the shininess of glass, the endless pleasures of brick-work.[21] At first, any thought of seeing-as or imaginative seeing feels redundant. The veneered panels that surround the core of the Farnsworth House are beautiful to look at because of what they are: we do not see them as anything different from what realistic and ordinary seeing delivers to us. If we did, we would put them into Scruton's category of non-aesthetic, non-imaginative interest. Their relation to aesthetic pleasure would then have to be as components of an orchestrated, imagined whole.

Then another observer could point to the fact that pleasures in materials are merged with thoughts about their origins and their mode of production. The grain and texture of wood is a record of its growth and of its history; the texture of concrete is the imprint of the mould into which it is poured; the texture of stainless steel is a tribute to the laborious working of an intractable material.[22] Such thoughts, if only half-formed, accompany our pleasure in seeing building materials. Consequently, we might be inclined to treat them as a loose form of imaginative contemplation that tiptoes along beside literal seeing. But this too has its problems, for what gives significance and interest to such thoughts is that they are about the real history of the materials in question. The thoughts revolve around the real history of the production of materials in order to allow us access to the elusive sense of their authenticity.

So we return to the feeling that it is the realness of building materials, whether in terms of their 'sensible' characteristics or their histories, that lies at the back of our pleasure in them. Accordingly, following Scruton's line of argument, we should then consign the experience to literal, non-imaginative, non-aesthetic seeing. Such experiences would not be irrelevant to architecture but we would have to go back to the idea of seeing them as component parts of an imaginatively construed whole. This will be appropriate for some cases, where we have a clear sense that the pleasures of materials are the grist to a larger aesthetic experience, but not in those other cases where we have a sense that materiality is the content of the aesthetic experience. From an aesthetic point of view, a building can be *about* wood or concrete or steel (fig. 55). Then those building materials may not merely provide the framework for aesthetic experience, but may be the content of it.

6 Scruton's division of architectural seeing into realistic and non-realistic is a useful one, and I will pursue its application to questions of meaning and expression in the next two chapters. However, I do not believe that it can provide a sure way of dividing all architectural experience into aesthetic and non-aesthetic. I have illustrated a number of cases where we have a strong sense that a certain kind of experience is aesthetic, but still resolutely bound to the real. The experience is not imaginative, if by that we imply that physical objects are used merely to further non-literal thoughts. The sense is rather of a contemplative enquiry into the real, an excavation of its complexity.

In the face of this perplexing phenomenon there is a temptation to cut and run, away from an imaginative theory of aesthetic experience towards an opposite conception. We can take pleasure in the way that

50 (*above*) Interior view of house 'E1027', designed by Eileen Gray (1927–29).

51 Interior of 'Tempe a Pailla', designed by Eileen Gray (1932–34).

52 Interior of the Villa La Roche, Paris, designed by Le Corbusier (1923).

53　The Breakfast Room, Pitshanger
Manor, London, designed by Sir John
Soane (1801–03).

54　The Library, Pitshanger Manor.

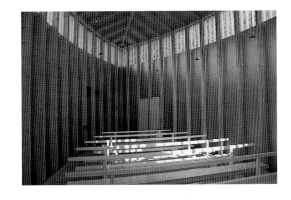

55　Sogn Benedetg Chapel,
Sumvitg, Switzerland, designed by
Peter Zumthor (1989).

things are, in the grain of wood, the chalky greyness of concrete, the light in the space. The pleasures come from real and not imagined objects. Our pleasure comes from wanting to eat them, physically incorporate them, rather than contemplate them: so imagination turns into corporeality. No one expresses this better than Adrian Stokes:

> In Italy I have been much alive to what I eat. I cannot judge how the enjoyment of food has stimulated architectural interest but I feel certain that pleasure in building broadens appetite, whether it be for the cylinders of *maccheroni* and *spaghetti*, the pilasters of *taglietelle*, the lucent golden drums of *gnocchi alla romana* or for fruit and cheese like strong-lipped apertures upon the smooth wall of wine. We partake of an inexhaustible feeding mother (a fine building announces), though we have bitten, torn, dirtied and pinched her, though we thought to have lost her utterly, to have destroyed her utterly in fantasy and act.[23]

Even so, an over-hasty explanation of elusive pleasures which resorts to the sense of touch may itself be the result of a desire for theoretical neatness.[24] There can be pleasure at a distance, and it is not necessarily merely an imagined pleasure. So I prefer to leave the matter more open. Anthony Kenny points out Aristotle's observation that 'where there is sense-perception there is also pleasure and pain'.[25] Architectural experience involves varieties of perception and these admit of pleasure and pain.

Chapter 5

Meaning

1   In this and the following chapter I shall discuss the implications of 'non-realistic' seeing. We can look at buildings and see objects or states of affairs that are not physically present. For example, we can see sunflowers represented in low-relief terracotta mouldings on buildings of the 'sweetness and light' style of the late nineteenth century. There are no actual sunflowers physically present but we see them nevertheless, via these sculptural motifs. We might see that a building is exuberant or that another is modest and know that inanimate objects cannot realistically be in these emotional states, but nevertheless see them. In this chapter I shall discuss the former kind of case and in Chapter Six I shall try to come to terms with the ability of buildings to express human feelings. In doing so I shall follow the broad distinction between the categories of 'meaning' and 'expression' in aesthetic theory.

Meaning in architecture comes from what is seen. It is an obvious point that architecture uses the visual sense to communicate meaning; music and speech, by contrast, exploit hearing. However, I wish to stress further that architecture derives very little of its meaning from the ordering or structuring of the elements within a design. Order, structure, organisation can marshall words in a manner that is productive of endless meanings, but in architecture this combinatorial process is very weak indeed. To put it another way, architecture has hardly any gramamtical structure.

The assertion needs a good deal of supporting argument. My suggestion is that architecture may seem to be grammatical but that in reality it is not. What it does possess are forms of orderliness which superficially resemble grammar. I discuss these varieties of orderliness and the different kinds of aesthetic interest that they can generate. I also aim to clarify the differences between language meaning and architectural meaning. For example, most signs in language have an arbitrary relation to their referents – the word cat does not look or sound like a cat – but this notion has hardly any application to architecture. Architectural meaning depends on individually meaningful signs and the order linking those signs makes little contribution to meaning. Language meaning, in contrast, derives from the orderly use of arbitrary signs.

In the later parts of the chapter I shall examine the ways in which this individualised kind of meaning arises from what is seen. For example, architectural meaning can employ familiar kinds of sculptural or pictorial representations in an 'iconographic' manner. However, it also extends into areas which require explanations that are special to architecture. We might say that a window seems to be cut in a wall, or that a roof is hovering. These kinds of statements engage both realistic and non-realistic seeing, in a peculiarly architectural way; they undoubtedly involve varieties of meaning; and they are of historical and theoretical importance in the development of modern architecture. In order to throw some light on these phenomena I draw once again on the work of Richard Wollheim and on his suggestions for thinking through the nature of the perceptual projects that are involved in meaningful seeing.

2   I will begin by making a distinction between two kinds of meaning, termed 'natural' and 'unnatural'. If the doctor shakes her head and says 'those spots mean measles', she does not mean that the red spots are

chattering away to one another about measles but that their existence is a sure sign of the presence of that particular infection. This is the type of case for which the term 'natural meaning' has been coined. No human intention is involved and no one, including the measles, is trying to say anything. By contrast, 'unnatural' meaning embraces all those cases where we do wish to say something. It is the ordinary kind of meaning involved in day-to-day conversation and all the other more specific uses of language.[1]

Imagine you are walking down the street and your companion points to various buildings: that one means 'offices', that one means 'school', that one means 'fire station'. Perhaps these words had been written up over each of the entrances and your friend read and correctly interpreted them and so they were responding to intended 'unnatural meanings'. More probably, he or she simply recognised these buildings as the types that they were from their overall arrangement and appearance. This is a form of 'natural meaning'. Admittedly, the connection is determined socially and historically and not with the inevitability of a disease, as is the case with spots and measles, but the connections between the use of a building and aspects of its visible form are powerful and consistent. The features in question are essential to the building type and not the result of a choice by a particular client or architect. So a fire station has to have large doors leading easily onto the street, an office block has to have multiple arrays of standardised spaces, a school has to have a mix of large and small rooms. In a given period and region these constraints mean that we will see a school as a school, an office block as an office block, a factory as a factory. These are the 'natural meanings' appropriate to an urban world and we attribute them doggedly.

As with measles and its spots, in this type of architectural meaning there has been no intention to say or depict anything: the meaning occurs 'naturally'. On the face of it, there is little of interest here for aesthetics, since the process is outside the scope of purposive human action.[2] However, it is the inevitability of natural meaning that makes it significant, since whatever meanings an architect intentionally has in mind will bear some relationship to natural meaning. It would be difficult to design a large office building so that it did not convey, via the process of natural meaning, that it is an office block. Yes, it might look like a Gothic office block, or be designed in a spectacular Expressionist style, but the passer-by will gather the natural meaning with no difficulty. Here the overlaid meanings – the natural meaning of the office block and the iconography of the Gothic decoration – can cause delight for the Post-modernist or cause the purist to wince, but the duality of meaning is inevitable.

Robert Venturi wished this duality to be astringent, and demonstrated this in his Best Catalogue Store where the iconography of the flower design wraps elegantly round the shed, leaving the meaning of 'store' to be made via natural processes, through the straightforward and conventional arrangement of the block, and its relationship to the parking lot (fig. 56). A particularly powerful natural meaning might threaten to overwhelm an initially contrasting iconography. From the 1980s, many British suburban supermarkets have been designed to look like rural farm buildings, with the result that a certain kind of bricky detailing and a large tiled roof start to become part of the natural meaning of a suburban supermarket. So the duality of natural and unnatural meaning can become complex and muddy.

A more complex view of the relationship between natural and unnatural meaning is an essential part of the functionalist outlook that I shall outline later in the book. The main point here is that the causal relationship – measles/spots or fire station/large doors – is reinterpreted as an expressive relation. One of the classic expositions of the argument can be found in Louis Sullivan's article 'The Tall Office Building Artistically Considered' of 1896.[3] Sullivan wants the architect's decisions to have the inevitability and force of natural processes and his arguments belong to a larger outlook in which the notion of expression is central. In fact, the outlook contains a rich mixture of ideas which will be better grasped once we have set out some of the basic issues involved in the concepts of meaning and expression. The point is true generally of the connections between natural and unnatural meaning: we need first to understand what is entailed in unnatural, intentional, visual meaning.

3   For the remainder of the chapter I shall discuss 'unnatural' meaning
– the devised and intended meanings that the architect wishes the spectator to grasp. First, let me explain the proposition I made earlier, that
meaning in architecture comes only from what is seen. I added that
the contribution of order or structure to architectural meaning is very
limited: it has little grammatical structure. We should note that the
comparison is with actual languages, of which English is an example,
and not with 'language' taken in a wider or metaphorical sense.[4]

Language refers outwards and enables us to make statements about
the world. It achieves this through the meanings of words and through
the way that sentences employ the rules of grammar. Both aspects are
essential. A vital consequence of the existence of grammar is that a
given group of words can create different meanings depending on their
grammatical arrangement. So the phrase 'Kate loves cats' means one
thing and the phrase 'cats love Kate' means something quite different.
These are not just different patterns of words, but because grammar is
implicated in meaning they refer to different phenomena in the world.
Now, architecture also refers outwards: for example, representations of
sunflowers on 'sweetness and light' buildings are a means of making
reference to the sunflowers. Reference to objects and events in the
world can employ visual means: this is obvious for painting and sculpture but I shall argue that it is also central to architecture's meaningfulness. But for the moment I wish to stress that architecture does not
employ grammatical structures when it refers outwards.

The proposition may be straightforward but complications arise from
the fact that architecture has many orderly features which do appear,
misleadingly, to be grammatical. Architecture, or architectural styles, is
thought of as having both vocabulary and grammar, and from there it
is implied that architecture refers to the world in a language-like way.
I believe that these views are mistaken because architecture's systematic orderliness is mis-described as grammar. Sir John Summerson
tells us of 'the grammatical workings of classical architecture – the
mechanics of it: the nature of the five orders; columns; three-quarters
and half columns: pilasters; the conjunction of columns with arches;
intercolumniation, and all that . . .'[5] in order to help us grasp the

'classical language of architecture'. Armed with this background knowledge, we can better understand the handling of architectural grammar by architects such as Bramante and Michelangelo. But although these analogies point to classical architecture's wonderful pliability, they do not give us any insight into the way that reference or meaning are constructed. When Vignola departs from the strict 'grammar' of the antique and invents a new kind of cornice at Caprarola, it is the visual and sculptural aspect which is of interest. Vignola's cornice, like Serlio's suggestion for a cornice in the Composite Order, combines architectural elements from elsewhere in the classical repertoire. But this combining does not make a new reference to the world, a new sentence. It creates a new object that has visual and sculptural attributes which can be used – as did C. R. Cockerell – as part of larger compositions (figs 57–9).[6] Summerson presents grammar as being central to an idea of architectural language, but questions of meaning and reference are not a part of that conception of the language.

A theoretically ambitious discussion of architectural grammar can be found in William Mitchell's *The Logic of Architecture*.[7] He outlines a view of grammar based on Noam Chomsky's theories of language and then aims to show that the systematic arrangement of a classical Order of architecture can be explained using the same methods that linguistic theory employs to analyse sentence structures. A sentence – his example is 'a column supports a beam' – can be divided into parts by a series of step-by-step rules. As a first stage, it can be split into a noun phrase (a column) and a verb phrase (supports the beam). Then those parts can be further subdivided into an article (a), a noun (column), a verb (supports), an article (the) and finally a noun (beam). Mitchell next turns to the conceptual structure of the classical Orders and suggests that they have a similar grammatical organisation to that of sentences in natural language. An Order divides into pedestal, column and entablature. They in turn each divide into three parts – respectively, base, dado and cap; base, shaft and capital; and architrave, frieze and cornice. At that level, various choices of designs are available which begin to differentiate the Orders one from another. These primary elements are like words in a sentence and in combination with the 'grammar' they define a particular version of the order.

On the view of the nature of language that I am suggesting, in which grammar is interlinked with reference to the world, we should expect different instances of these grammatical structures to generate distinctive references or meanings. But the grammar that Mitchell has described makes no contribution to meaning: it is merely a system of rules that determines correct and incorrect designs. If I turn the arrangement of the column upside down, so that the capital is at the bottom and the base at the top, I do not thereby make a new reference. There is merely an upside-down column, and an incorrect version of the Order. No new reference is entailed, just as no reference was entailed in the 'grammatical' structure in the first place. For example, if we took the meaning of the Doric order to be its masculinity, we would not attribute this meaning to the orderly arrangement of the parts. We would consider that the meaning derived from the iconography of the order as a whole, from the appearance of sturdiness in the proportions and the simplicity of detailing.

Someone might argue that by turning the Order on its head we could turn the meaning on its head, so the upside-down Doric would refer to the negation of masculinity. However, such a column would merely show the limitations of the language analogy. No matter how hard we tried to invert or distort an architectural element, hoping to change the meaning that derives from its iconography, we would always be tied back to that original visual meaning. Compare this outcome with a change in the arrangement of Mitchell's sample sentence by turning it round to read 'the beam supports a column', instead of 'a column supports the beam'. This refers to a different kind of event in the world: we could imagine a ground beam or a beam supporting an upper storey, a physically different matter from that referred to in the first sentence, where a column supports the beam. A change in the use of grammar has been instrumental in making a semantic change, a different reference to the world.[8]

Mitchell discusses grammar as if it were just a matter of orderliness, disconnected from questions of meaning, which are dealt with in a separate section of his book. Grammar is really used metaphorically to denote an idea of an ordering system. This becomes evident when he cites as an example of architectural grammar Bernard Tschumi's system

of pavilions at the Parc La Villette.[9] One of the guiding themes of
Tschumi's design was precisely to provide a semantically empty pattern
of architectural objects which could later be endowed with meaning
as the park developed and changed its pattern of use. The design of
La Villette has complex order but it is deliberately ungrammatical,
creating no reference to objects or events in the world.

We can begin to see that two kinds of problems arise from using
grammar as a metaphor for orderliness in architecture. First, orderliness
is a very pervasive and general aspect of architecture, one that is much
broader in scope than grammar. Second, that pervasive orderliness takes
many specific forms, each of which is of aesthetic interest, but none
of which resembles grammatical structure. Some examples will bear out
these points.

4   Here is an account by Frank Lloyd Wright of the 'grammar'
involved in the design of the 'Usonian' houses:

> Every house worth considering as a work of art must have a
> grammar of its own. 'Grammar', in this sense, means the same thing
> in any construction – whether it be of words or of stone or wood.
> It is the shape-relationship between the various elements that enter
> into the constitution of the thing. The 'grammar' of the house is its
> manifest articulation of all its parts. This will be the 'speech' it uses.
> To be achieved, construction must be grammatical. . . .[10]

Wright is concerned with a particular kind of architectural order in
which parts of the building share common features and in which these
features are also properties of the building as a whole. The idea is a
powerful one, giving recognition to the sense that architectural order
is both repetitive and hierarchical. It is a pervasive one in the modern
period, and can be found for instance in Quatremère de Quincy's Neo-
classical outlook, as cited by Sylvia Lavin: 'the essential type of carpentry, with all its constituent parts, is found imprinted in the ensemble
and in each detail of Greek architecture'.[11] Part of the idea's attraction
for nineteenth-century writers lay in its grounding in biology. Here is

the anatomist Georges Cuvier in a text published in 1812, as quoted by Philip Steadman: 'Thus, commencing our investigation by a careful survey of any one bone by itself, a person who is sufficiently master of the laws of organic structure, may, as it were, reconstruct the whole animal to which that bone had belonged.'[12]

We should note just how unlike real grammar this kind of hierarchical order is; indeed, it is tempting to call it 'false grammar'. We could take a fragment of a building and, following Cuvier or Wright, get an idea of what the whole building might be like. But we could not follow the same procedure with a sentence and hope to get access to meaning. If all we knew was the word 'Kate', it would not point us in the direction of the rest of the sentence, and of Kate's liking for cats. In that sense grammar is resolutely non-hierarchical. Whereas the point about architecture's nested hierarchies is that we can predict something of the character of the whole building from a mere part, the beauty of grammar's 'compositional' nature is that new and unexpected meanings can be created endlessly.

Let us briefly consider some alternative metaphors for particular kinds of architectural order. Music provides one source. When we look at the facade of the Villa Stein–de Monzie, designed by Le Corbusier in 1926–27, we are faced with two entrances. The axis of the drive leads towards the smaller one (which is actually just off axis and sunk slightly below the main floor), and it is only when we get close to the house that we veer to one side and find ourselves facing the large main door, squarely in the centre of its structural bay (fig. 60). Perhaps this complex play with order could be expressed in terms of grammar, but it would be very cumbersome to do so. Rather, someone could murmur, in the words of the song, 'how strange the change from major to minor' and the point would immediately be clear.[13]

In John Onians's discussion of the importance of musical order to Bramante, he points out that Bramante worked in an intellectual environment in which connections were frequently made between architecture and music. He suggests that the complex order of polyphonic music may have been in the background of Bramante's thinking when he tried new combinations of the classical Orders, creating a rich

57 (*above left*)   Serlio's suggestion for a cornice in the composite order, from Book Four of *Tutte l'Opere d'Architettura et Prospetiva* (1540).

58 (*above right*)   The cornice of the Castello Farnese, Caprarola, designed by Giacomo Vignola (1559–64).

56 (*left*) Best Products Catalog
Showroom, Oxford Valley,
Langhorne, Pennsylvania,
designed by Venturi, Scott
Brown and Associates (1978).

59 The Taylorian Institution,
Oxford, designed by C. R.
Cockerell, with its Vignolan
cornice (1841–45).

60 The entrance façade of the
Villa Stein–de Monzie, Paris,
designed by Le Corbusier
(1927).

variety of effects in a similar manner to the way a composer could combine lines of voices. This kind of superimposed order would be difficult to express and elaborate in a language analogy. Onians notes that Leonardo made the point in comparing painting with poetry. The parts of poetry come out in succession – 'the later element is not born until the earlier dies' – but in music and architecture harmonies can exist at a moment. So music is not just another way of thinking about architectural order but it may give access to aspects that are closed to language.[14]

Lutyens captured the sense of the inter-relatedness of parts within the classical Orders with another metaphor, that of a game. John Summerson quotes his remark that 'You alter one feature (which you have to, always), then every other feature has to sympathise and undergo some care and invention. Therefore it is no mean game, nor is it a game you can play lightheartedly'.[15] Each metaphor emphasises a different aspect of architectural order: that flexibility and constraint can be combined, or that numerous patterns can be superimposed at an instant, or that a theme can be presented in different modes. There are differences here, but also a strong common interest in order for its own sake, which is worth considering for a moment.

Alexander Tzonis and Liane Lefaivre have nicely referred to the 'special hedonism' that comes from contemplating the plans and elevations of classical buildings and understanding their formal structure. They also point out that this 'hedonism' can have a repressive aspect: the pleasures of order can derive from seeing the classically dressed buildings of a town in their properly regulated social stations.[16] Greek authors, as Onians has remarked, described the discipline and regularity of a row of columns as reminders of military virtues.[17] Perhaps the dialectic of pleasure and repression within classical architectural order was most passionately stated by Ruskin; and for our own age that dialectic is most evident in the beautiful works of Italian Rationalism that were produced in the service of the Fascist regime. Tschumi has discussed the matter psychologically rather than socially, suggesting that architectural games can have 'the erotic significance of bondage' and that this is a general feature of architecture's attraction rather than a distortion of it.[18]

5 There is a further contrast between architecture and language. Some words have a definite connection to their referents: for example, 'whisper' sounds a little like a whisper. However, as noted earlier, the usual case is that the relation between a word and its referent is quite arbitrary, so it is of no importance that the word 'cat' does not have any of the characteristics of a cat. Language operates by bringing these arbitrary signs together within a grammatical structure. I have stressed that architecture differs from language in its absence of grammatical structure. It is also unlike language in that its individual elements have meaning in a non-arbitrary way. The point about the sculpted brick sunflower is that it looks like a sunflower: there is nothing arbitrary about it at all.

It is difficult to imagine how an architect could successfully design a building using meanings that had only arbitrary relations to their referents. Perhaps the architect of a certain building might say that he or she has chosen – arbitrarily as it were – a round window as the sign of it being a health centre. The idea would cause some puzzlement and the obvious riposte would be that the architect misunderstood a basic point about language, namely that 'arbitrary' words are not just invented, but depend on long-term usage and public trust. It could be argued that the elements of a language go through a life cycle: that words begin by resembling their referents but use gradually wears away the resemblance so they eventually seem to be arbitrary. It is tempting to make a similar case for architecture. George Hersey has suggested that many of the details of Greek architecture had significance within the rituals of sacrifice.[19] For example, egg-and-claw mouldings depict the eggs that were commonly sacrificed and they are often shown with their shells split open revealing the soul or yolk within. Such mouldings are now simply part of the repertoire of classical architecture: we may see a line of eggs but it has no further iconographic significance for us. Thus we might think of classical architecture as comprised of 'words', the ritualistic origins of which are now lost to us, but which have left behind a resonance of arbitrary meaning. However, it would be hard to make this idea work. We might see architectural elements as representations of real objects, whether it be eggs or stylised leaves. Often, as in the capitals of the Orders, they combine with abstract shapes and profiles to make composite objects. In order to retain their place in the repertoire, such elements must stay recognisable and familiar objects, and they cannot afford to mutate, as words do, into arbitrary signs. With the aid of a historian or a copy of Vitruvius we can speculate on the iconographic significance that these elements might once have had; but we have to admit that they are now devoid of meaning and we like them for their beauty not their significance.

6   The discussion so far has circled round the comparison between language and architecture, in a critical spirit. I now wish to move towards a more constructive assessment of how architectural meaning works, rather than explaining how it does not. In fact, we have already reached a useful starting point. I have repeated the suggestion that architectural meaning operates through what is seen, and in the discussion of grammar I have attempted to justify the remark that only what is seen is meaningful. Then I noted that the elements of architectural meaning, unlike signs in language, are non-arbitrary. If we see a sculpted sunflower on a building it will not be an arbitrary sign: its reference will be to a sunflower. In architectural meaning, what is seen is what is meant. It shares this feature with the parallel kinds of meaning that arise in sculptural and pictorial representation.

A good deal of architectural meaning hinges on sculptural and pictorial representations, and for much of the remainder of this chapter I shall trace the implications of this point. I am making the assumption, which I admit I do not fully justify, that these kinds of representation do not operate via a form of language. Pictures and sulptures do not deliver meaning via a grammar of visual signs, just as architecture does not employ grammar to create meaning. The basis is resemblance rather than grammar, that a sculpture or a picture looks like the thing it represents. There are theoretical difficulties with this viewpoint and they turn into practical problems in considering some kinds of abstract art. The situation has a parallel in architecture. We can use the notion of resemblance to explain numerous cases, but after a certain point it begins to run out and we need to sketch another framework for explaining visual meaning.

Let us see how far the everyday viewpoint – that buildings, considered as physical objects, can be the bearers of both pictorial and sculptural representations – will take us. In the former case, they provide walls on which frescoes, mosaics, patterned brickwork and other kinds of two-dimensional media can be deployed. In the latter case, the building can provide the support or backing for individual sculptural objects. Perhaps the limit of pictorial representation can be seen in the Mexico City university library, which has giant pictorial representations on the four faces of a large block (fig. 61). It is obvious that the building remains only the bearer or support for pictures, and its physical form does not become part of what is represented. By contrast, the scale of sculptural representations can be increased up to the point where an entire building can become a sculpture, as in the famous restaurant made in the shape of a duckling. Given this possibility, that sculptural seeing can be of parts of buildings or entire buildings, it seems to have the edge over pictorial seeing, the scope of which is more restricted.

Ruskin invested a humble kind of sculptural representation with great significance. In the course of making the distinction between architecture and building on the grounds that the former bears features which are unnecessary for 'common use', he gave as an example of such an addition a cable moulding, a sculptural representation of a rope.[20] Such ropes still adorn the entrances and windows of countless nineteenth-century houses and sombre public buildings whose designers were anxious to make architecture rather than mere building (fig. 62). In his remarkable essay 'The Bible of Amiens', Ruskin describes the sculptural ensembles that cover the west front of the cathedral at Amiens. This vast array of statuary and low-relief sculptures depicts the apostles and prophets, illustrates their attributes and illustrates passages from the Bible (figs 63 and 66). Ruskin gives particular attention to the central porch: this is 'the bible of Amiens'. What he means by this phrase is that those persons and events described in language in the written Bible are represented here sculpturally, in the round and in low relief.

There are a number of important ideas at work here. One is that meanings which arise in language (as in the Bible) can also be represented in a manner that is appropriate to visual perception (and hence to architecture), namely in sculpture. Secondly, in case we might have been inclined to think that the west front of Amiens Cathedral was just a gallery of sculpture, Ruskin makes us see it as an architectural totality. He does this by calling it a bible, which is a kind of book, trading on the fact that books need not be of words. We are familiar with books of pictures, but Ruskin takes the thought a step further in proposing a book of sculpture, but still a book to be looked at rather than read. In ordinary usage, the meaning of a book is the meaning of what is contained in it: the meaning of the Bible is all those meanings that we read in its pages. And so it does not seem strange to say that the meaning of the building comprises those meanings that we see in the sculptures.

The idea that a building is a book, and that it is about the meanings contained in it, had been given currency by Victor Hugo in his novel *Notre-Dame of Paris* (1831), some fifty years before Ruskin's essay. Hugo suggested that architecture is a language, its sentences made up out of the elements of building construction. As we would expect from our discussion of architecture and grammar, this point was rather unproductive. In the event, the meanings that Hugo describes do not come from any architectural 'grammar' but from sculptural representations.[21] These meanings accumulate so that medieval cathedrals become, in his words, 'books known as buildings', giving expression to a living religious and social world. Then Hugo makes his famous point about the difference between the medieval and the modern age: that with the invention of printing, printed books, rather than building-books, make it possible to communicate ideas with immeasurably greater speed and reach. As he puts it, 'The book was to kill the building', meaning that the printed book kills the building-book.

Hugo contrasts stone and paper:

> In its printed form, thought is more imperishable than ever; it is volatile, elusive, indestructible. It mingles with the air. In the days of architecture, thought had turned into a mountain and taken powerful hold of a century and a place. Now it turned into a

flock of birds and was scattered on the four winds, occupying every point of air and space simultaneously.[22]

The lightness of printing is its great asset for Hugo, since it can be the means by which new ideas can fly around the world. For Ruskin, the point was precisely the opposite: he expresses a longing for an architecture of stone bibles that by their weight and permanence could instil and reinforce the authority of religion.[23]

Hugo's claim that printing would kill architecture was influential and it would be easy to take it as a general challenge to the role of representation in architecture. However, we should be careful about generalising his point too far. His central argument is that there are other and better ways of telling stories and, in particular, better ways of commenting on society than by means of architectural sculpture. Printing can disseminate these meanings more extensively and rapidly; and new meanings can constantly overtake old ones as the world changes.

Since Hugo's time architects have continued to use sculptural representation as a means of conveying meaning. When Gaudí designed the roof of the Casa Batlló as a sculptural representation of the dragon slain by Saint George, it was important that the meaning was solidly built since this asserted the resoluteness of the claims of Catalan nationalism and made a constant presence in the street (fig. 64). The result was perhaps not a book-building but a leaflet-building, which would never fade or become torn. But it is true that the general drift has been in Hugo's direction. The modern consensus is that specific commentaries about the world, of the kind that Hugo and Ruskin described as typical of medieval cathedrals, should be allowed the freedom of the mass media and not be frozen into the fabric of buildings. An example of the dominant modern approach to dealing with narrative meaning was the Vesnin brothers' design for a newspaper office, in which the building provided a supporting structure for a constantly changing display of news and information (fig. 65). The idea was an important and influential aspect of the Rogers and Piano project for the Centre Pompidou, although sadly it was not realised.

That separation between a fixed building and changeable messages

61 University Library, Mexico City, designed by Juan O'Gorman (1953).

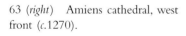

62 Cable moulding around a nineteenth-century front door, North London.

63 (*right*) Amiens cathedral, west front (*c.*1270).

66 (*facing page bottom*) Ruskin's index to the sculpture on the west front of Amiens cathedral, from *The Bible of Amiens*.

64　The Casa Batlló, Barcelona, designed by A. Gaudí (1905–07).

65　Design for offices of the *Leningradskaya Pravda*, by A. and V. Vesnin (1924).

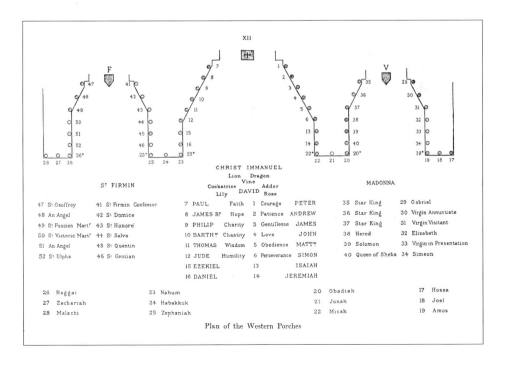

XII

F

V

CHRIST IMMANUEL
Lion　Dragon
Vine
Cockatrice　　　Adder
DAVID
Lily　　Rose

S? FIRMIN

MADONNA

47 S? Geoffroy	41 S? Firmin Confessor	7 PAUL　　Faith	1 Courage　ANDREW	35 Star King	29 Gabriel
48 An Angel	42 S? Domice	8 JAMES B?　Hope	2 Patience　ANDREW	36 Star King	30 Virgin Annuntiate
49 S? Fuscien Mart?	43 S? Honoré	9 PHILIP　Charity	3 Gentillesse　JAMES	37 Star King	31 Virgin Visitant
50 S? Victoric Mart?	44 S? Salve	10 BARTH?　Chastity	4 Love　　JOHN	38 Herod	32 Elizabeth
51 An Angel	45 S? Quentin	11 THOMAS　Wisdom	5 Obedience　MATT?	39 Solomon	33 Virgin in Presentation
52 S? Ulpha	46 S? Gentian	12 JUDE　Humility	6 Perseverance　SIMON	40 Queen of Sheba	34 Simeon
		15 EZEKIEL　　　13		ISAIAH	
		16 DANIEL　　　14		JEREMIAH	

26　Haggai	23 Nahum		20　Obadiah	17　Hosea
27　Zechariah	24 Habakkuk		21　Jonah	18　Joel
28　Malachi	25 Zephaniah		22　Micah	19　Amos

Plan of the Western Porches

should alert us to an essential point about the kind of architectural meaning that Hugo and Ruskin had in mind. They were interested in the idea that a building, via the mechanism of sculpture, could add up to a compilation of meanings, stories, social commentary. The meanings were essentially non-architectural and the sculptural ensembles were a mechanism for communicating them. Contrast this with an alternative notion in which architectural meaning refers back to the nature of the building itself rather than to narratives and propositions about the world beyond. Most commonly it is the use, purpose or function of the building that is the content of this 'internal' kind of meaning.

Is 'internal' meaning also subject to Hugo's strictures? Taking his argument too broadly would certainly lead to a bizarre conclusion: if printed books did indeed kill architectural meaning we would have to refer to books to discover the internal meaning of a particular building. The process of 'natural meaning' that I outlined earlier might save us from this difficulty, but we could not rely on it and in many cases the internal meanings of buildings would remain unexpressed. Again, it seems more useful to take a narrower view of Hugo's meaning, namely that printing threatened narrative representation in architecture, but not architectural meaning in total. Then the question arises of whether sculptural and allied forms of representation can continue to express meanings which are internal to architecture, principally about the use or purpose of buildings.

Neil Levine has used Henri Labrouste's project for the Bibliothèque Ste-Geneviève (designed in 1838–39) in order to explore just this issue.[24] A library, of course, provides a particularly complex example, since its internal meaning is bound up with writing, printing, books and the study of books. So the world of the print medium is the actual architectural content of this building type but Labrouste used sculptural and pictorial forms of representation in order to convey the content. The names of writers are inscribed on the facade of the library, in panels that resemble cases of print: names, in natural language, become the content of sculptural inscriptions. A series of busts was intended to celebrate the founders of printing. The departments of knowledge are expressed pictorially in roundels in the stair hall, and in the reading room, back-to-back with the roundels, they are named in writing. There is much else besides, including numerous sculptural references to the fact that the building would be open for readers both day and night (figs 67 and 69).

An important aspect of Labrouste's design was his rejection of the Neo-classical idea that a building type can gather internal meaning simply from the appropriate combination of classical elements. He used representations and scripts much more freely than Beaux-Arts teaching allowed, in pursuit of the aim that the internal meaning of a building should be achieved not by rote or formula but by creative invention.[25] As Levine points out, there is the seed of modernism in Labrouste's determination to make the life of the building central to its meaning, and to do so in his own way, not by using the conventions that Neo-classicism decreed. It appears that Hugo had discussed the future of architecture with Labrouste when he was writing *Notre-Dame of Paris* and this makes it the more interesting that Labrouste's design seems to straddle the new and old worlds to which Hugo alludes. He devised a celebration of the world of print, but in order to do so he used the sculptural and pictorial modes of communication that Hugo had predicted would wither away.

Hugo's prediction was only partly fulfilled: sculptural and pictorial representations are still used by architects in order to give access to the function of buildings. Note the giant sculptural object that Daniel Libeskind proposed for the Victoria and Albert Museum extension which was, originally at least, devised as a representation of the spiral development of art and knowledge. The idea was provoked by a motto inscribed on an existing part of the building (fig. 68). Libeskind's is a particularly obscure piece of iconography, and it reflects a general problem in trying to make a new visual symbol for the use of a building. The danger is that it will either go unnoticed because the symbolism is not part of the general culture or, if it is noticed, it may seem diagrammatic and simple-minded, lacking the resonances of a publicly known iconography.

67 and 69   The Bibliothèque Ste-Geneviève, Paris, designed by Henri Labrouste (1838–50), with (*below right*), a sculpted torch at the entrance.

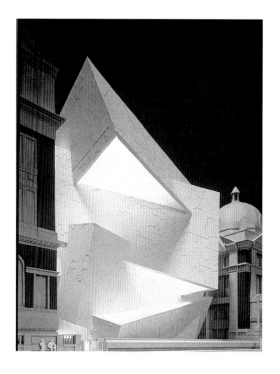

68 (*left*)   Design for an extension to the Victoria and Albert Museum, London, by Daniel Libeskind (1998).

With the Bibliothèque Ste-Geneviève Labrouste, as Levine points out, was determined to make the life of his building central to its meaning. This does indeed become one of the central aims of architecture in the nineteenth and twentieth centuries, but applying sculptural and pictorial iconographies became quite inadequate to the scale of its ambitions. Again, we are pointed in the direction of a discussion of the functionalist outlook, considered in the broadest sense, which I have already promised to discuss in a later chapter. In the meantime we need to enquire whether sculptural and pictorial representations have any further relevance to our discussion.

7   Architectural meanings may derive from sculptural representations, as we have seen, but can these include abstract compositions? How does architectural meaning operate in such cases? In fact, abstract sculptural representations are central to modern architecture. A canonical modernist instance is the house that Gerrit Rietveld designed for Mrs Schröder in 1924 (fig. 70). We see the Schröder House as an assembly of rectangular panels, aligned in each of the three dimensions and overlapping, butting against and intersecting one another. These panels, assembled rather like a house of cards, enclose an inner cuboid volume. Seeing it like this obviously involves non-realistic perception and it is not difficult to spot the ways in which Rietveld nudges us away from seeing the building, realistically, as a little box-like construction with corners. The vertical panels sail past corners and form parapets at the roof level; the horizontal ones project to form balconies and overhangs; and the panels are carefully painted in varying shades of grey to emphasise their distinctness.

But why is sculptural seeing involved? It depends on seeing the building as a physical object, but not as a house. Sculptural seeing involves some curiosity about the continuity of the surface of an object as it turns away from the viewer; it involves attention to the recession and projection of surfaces. In representational sculpture these enable us to explore the object in search of the likeness that it contains – as in the dragon contained within the configuration of the roof of the Casa

Batlló. In abstract sculpture the exploration leads us to construe the object as made up of subsidiary forms, melting, colliding or juxtaposed to one another as the sculptor's style demands. This is just what happens at the Schröder House: we construe it as an assembly of panels and this gives access to visual meaning. The building refers not to ducks, dragons, books or saints, but to those panels.

It might be objected that architecture and sculpture simply share this kind of seeing and that in essence it is neither sculptural nor architectural. I prefer to stress that sculptural seeing provides a way of gaining access to architectural meaning, but not to all architectural meaning. Its limitation of scope suggests that we should see it as a contributor to architectural meaning and in order to chart these limitations it is useful to keep it conceptually separate. Abstract sculptural representations are based on relationships between a whole object and its constituent formal elements. In the case of a building, this dual aspect will only be visible when the spectator is at a certain distance; it is lost as he or she approaches the building. It can no longer be seen as a whole, and a single element dominates the visual field. A related problem that arises with proximity to the building is that the texture and detailing of its surfaces may no longer sustain abstract seeing and instead demand realistic viewing. Proximity will also bring the realistic features of doors and windows into view and they will contend with abstract seeing. Rietveld incorporated doors and windows into his sculptural composition with great skill, so that abstract seeing could keep the upper hand. But as the visitor approaches the Schröder House a black panel must at some point turn into a door, realistically construed.

We can see this in another building that invites sculptural seeing, the Weisman Art Museum in Minneapolis, designed by Frank Gehry in 1993. From across the Mississippi we can construe the whole object as consisting of a compact group of curved forms (fig. 71). The visual meaning is that the building is made of these subsidiary objects. At a distance they seem to be lightly textured and because they are clad in steel their colours, brightness and shadows change as the sky changes. This brings a delightful variety to the sculptural ensemble which does not conflict with its abstract character: at one moment it is like polished silver and at the next it is battleship grey. Then, as we approach the building, we become aware of the large stainless steel sheets that make up each cylinder, their overlapping joints, the sense of a hard and intractable material (fig. 72). At this range, all the abstract sculptural sense is lost.

In fact, the Weisman Museum is only sculptural from one direction and the abstract composition forms the front of a large and severely rectangular brick box. This protean character is part of the charm of the building, but it does mean that its representational character is limited. Kenneth Frampton notes that Utzon recognised this issue in the design of the Sydney Opera House. At times he hoped that the building would be seen as sails over the harbour, but that at sunset it might have the glow of snowcapped mountains, and at night the floodlighting would give it a softer presence.[26] Large buildings can have a sculptural aspect but as their size increases the distance threshold for seeing their representational content will extend.

8 Sculptural representations form part of the repertoire of architectural meaning, but they have limitations. Is there a distinctively architectural form of meaning, one which exploits architecture's peculiarities rather than being constrained by them? In the remainder of the chapter I shall suggest a way that we can explore this question. In the discussion so far, sculptural and pictorial meaning have depended on the background notion of representation: that we see a building or part of a building as representing some other object. I have put this kind of representational seeing into the framework of 'non-realistic' perception. Now I wish to suggest that there can be forms of visual meaning that do not have that kind of representational character. That is, we can see a building or part of a building realistically, but we can see it as being in an unrealistic state, and it is this unrealistic state that comprises the meaning of what we see.

Consider two kinds of devices. The first operates at a fairly small scale within the overall designs of buildings and it is the device of making a window in a brick wall with no visible lintel, so that it looks as if the window opening has been cut out of the wall. It was exploited by Sullivan and Wright, and the brick houses designed by Mies van der Rohe in the 1920s and early 30s provide a store of samples. Then it entered the mainstream repertoire of modern architecture. An example can be seen in the treatment of wall openings by Van Heyningen and Haward in their design for a new building at Fitzwilliam College, Cambridge (fig. 73).

The second kind of device, at a slightly larger scale, is the cantilevered roof that seems to be hovering or floating above the ground, exemplified in some of Frank Lloyd Wright's Prairie Houses. In one sense, non-realistic seeing is at issue in these cases. We know that the windows of the Fitzwilliam building were not cut out of the wall by an eccentric builder, and we know realistically that the roof of a Prairie House is not hovering. There is visual meaning, the content of which is seeing that the window has been cut in the wall and that the roof is hovering (fig. 74).

Iconic representation or resemblance, which lay behind the earlier examples of apostles, ducks, sunflowers, dragons and so on, is not the issue here. The significance of a Wrightian hovering roof is not that it resembles another hovering roof: it is this roof, this physical object, that seems to be hovering. The task is to understand how this non-iconic process operates. We see a building or a part of a building to be in a certain state: that it hovers, or that it has had an opening cut into it. The phrases are clumsy, but behind them is the need to capture the sense that non-realistic seeing can endow building elements with dynamic attributes, seeming to do things and to have things done to them. Nevertheless, it is still the building, or part of the building, realistically seen, that is at issue: it is not a question of seeing it as something else but merely of seeing it in a non-realistic state. So realistic and unrealistic seeing are both essential parts of the process of deriving meaning.

If the building is to be seen non-realistically, aspects of its realistic state will have to be hidden or suppressed. For example, if we are to see a roof as hovering, its supports will need to be reduced to 'the minimum, pushed back as far as possible from the eaves and placed in shadow. If we are to see a window as cut into a wall, its lintel will need to be hidden, so that we get the effect of a continuous wall material running round the opening. Again, we continue to see the roof as a roof and the window as a window, and to that extent seeing remains realistic. But this is combined with the awareness that the building element is behaving in a non-realistic way.

Positive decisions of detailing must complement these negative moves. So the hovering roof must seem like a plane object and the wall around the 'cut' window must seem like a continuous surface which could be cut. Many finer points will be important in the detailing process, in order to stress the smoothness or surface continuity of the wall, the depth of the reveal and so on. The architect's task of detailing falls into two parts: suppressing aspects of the actual efficacy of the construction, and creating the conditions for a kind of speculative seeing. We can glimpse the architect working on a necessity that a building must possess, such as a window or a roof, and nudging, forming, moulding it in a certain direction, suppressing one aspect, enhancing another. And there is something of this adaptive process in the early development of modernism, as architects developed more and more audacious kinds of non-realistic construals, following on from Wright's desire to abolish the box and leading to the numerous unrealistic ways of seeing that Mies van der Rohe's 1929 Barcelona Pavilion invites.[27]

These are small examples but I believe they are characteristic of a wide range of architectural meanings. The reader might be prepared to take that on trust and find further examples in their own favourite buildings. Perhaps there is something distinctively architectural here, a particular mode in which meaning is manifested. But the difficulty now seems to be that it is too specific, a specialist form of meaning that operates alone. In finding something particular to architecture, we have lost that sense of continuity across various kinds of iconic meaning that was one of the attractions of our architectural-sculptural examples. The kind of visual meaning that we have now identified seems to feed off a much closer connection between realistic and unrealistic seeing than

70   The Schröder House, Utrecht, The Netherlands, designed by Gerrit
Rietveld (1925).

71   The Frederick R. Weisman Art
Museum, Minneapolis, designed by Frank
Gehry (1993).

72   Close-up view of the
facade of the Weisman Art
Museum.

74 (*below*) Roof of the
Cheney House, Oak Park,
Illinois, designed by Frank
Lloyd Wright (1903–04).

73   Wilson Court, Fitzwilliam College, Cambridge, designed
by Van Heyningen and Haward (1994).

those that were discussed earlier. However, this difference may seem larger than it really is. In the remaining part of the chapter I wish to develop an argument that will enable us to see the continuity between representational meaning of a straightforward sculptural kind and this peculiarly architectural kind. The argument is potentially important, since it offers the possibility of bringing a special type of visual meaning under the shelter of a larger and more general account which spans architecture and the other visual arts.

Once again I shall draw on the work of Richard Wollheim, particularly on his treatment of pictorial representation.[28] The starting point for Wollheim's discussion is the difficulty that lies within the notion of resemblance, or iconic representation, when it is applied to pictures. We may say that Goya's portrait resembles the Duke of Wellington, but we surely do not mean that a particular assemblage of canvas, wooden framework, paint and varnish resembles that particular hero. It was suggested by Richard Wollheim that we use the phrase 'seeing as' to make sense of pictorial representations: so we see the painting as a picture of the Duke of Wellington. Wollheim later adopted a slightly different formulation, that of 'seeing-in'. We see the Duke of Wellington in the picture. The difference is significant, and I shall discuss its consequences, but first we should note that Wollheim aimed to describe pictorial seeing in a way that will account for the fact that a physical object is involved – a painting – and that a quite unrealistic construal, of something not physically present, is also involved. On these accounts, architectural representations need not feel so lonely, since some kind of intimate connection between realistic and unrealistic seeing may be central to other kinds of visual meaning.

Let us see if we can trace the connections among these varieties of visual meaning. Wollheim's argument is that in order to be seen at all a pictorial representation has to be seen in a physical object, that it necessarily involves an intimacy of connection between unrealistic and realistic seeing. He describes this as the 'twofoldness' of seeing pictorial representations. There is a broader sense in which the seeing of pictures might involve our switching attention from what is depicted to the nature of the paint surface or the brushstrokes and so on: the cumulative effect of this double attention can be part of the pleasures of painting. Wollheim would accept this meaning, too, but his point is a more fundamental one: that in order to see a pictorial representation at all, what is involved is a distinctive mode of attention to the surface of a physical object. He suggests that pictorial seeing can be exercised by looking at random marks, or stains on the wall, and seeing objects or events in them, in the manner suggested by Leonardo. Then we can think of the artist as so organising and marshalling a series of marks on a canvas that we see the representation that he or she intended us to see.

How can Wollheim's argument connect with architectural representations? We could begin by translating the idea of a two-dimensional marked surface into the notion of a three-dimensional object that has been modified, adapted or moulded in any of those dimensions. This connects with my earlier hint that we could think of the work of the architect designing a 'hovering' roof or a 'cut' window as adapting the design of a realistic element of construction with the aim of fostering a particular construal. The notion of marking a surface, I suggest, has its three-dimensional equivalent in this idea that we can modify the detailed configuration of the building. The physically modified object could then invite a kind of non-realistic seeing, just as the stains that Leonardo observed invited a kind of pictorial seeing.

We engage a type of twofold seeing: we see the roof or the window realistically as roof or window (the modifications have not affected our perceptions of their basic nature), but the modifications enable us to make the unrealistic construals that the roof is hovering, and that the window is cut into the wall. Both of the two kinds of attention are essential: we need to see the objects realistically and unrealistically, acting in a certain manner. Here we should note that differences are opening up between this account and Wollheim's discussion of pictorial seeing. In our architectural examples unrealistic construals co-exist with a conceptual interest in a practical object – a roof or a window. The corresponding practical aspects of a painting – for example that it comprises a wooden frame with canvas stretched across – do not usually engage such conceptual interest.

The difference takes us back to the distinction that Wollheim makes between seeing-as and seeing-in. He considers that the latter is the characteristic mode of attention for pictorial representations. In his words, it is 'not the exercise of visual curiosity about a present object. It is the cultivation of a special kind of visual experience which fastens upon certain objects in the environment for its furtherance'.[29] In other words, we have little interest in the marked surface from a conceptual point of view, taking it as a point of departure for that distinctive visual experience. Our shared interest in both the roof and its unrealistic behaviour suggests that the kind of meaning involved would fit better in the category of seeing-as which entails 'a form of visual interest in an object present to the senses'.[30]

A further issue arises if we follow this drift and put our cases of hovering roofs and cut walls into the category of seeing-as. One of the advantages of the notion of seeing-in over seeing-as is that it accommodates a wider range of pictorial content. Seeing-as makes sense of pictures of people and things, but there are difficulties in applying it to cases where we see a state of affairs, for example a woman reading a letter. Seeing-in copes better with such cases: we can talk coherently of seeing a state of affairs in a picture, less so of seeing a picture as a state of affairs. Our hovering roof and cut window seem to involve just such states of affairs. The visual meaning involved is not of another object – we know that the objects in question are the realistically construed roof and window – but that these objects are in a certain state, just as the woman in the picture is in the state of reading a letter. On the face of it this would lead us to shift these architectural construals into the category of seeing-in. This may be unnecessary, however. On occasions it is coherent to say that an object, or part of an object, such as a building, is in a certain state and that we see it as being in that state. Thus we can see a roof as hovering or a window as having been cut in a wall. Seeing-in appears to be necessary to account for states of affairs that are depicted in two-dimensional pictures. Seeing-as suffices to deal with distinctively architectural cases, occurring in three dimensions, of the hovering and cutting variety.

9 Let us step back from these detailed considerations and review the wider issue. Distinctively architectural kinds of visual meaning do not operate exactly like pictorial seeing – which is hardly surprising – but comparing architecture and pictures does suggest that there is scope for investigating the broader strategies of visual meaning which they share. The key issue that begins to emerge is that of 'twofoldness'. A very general concept can be articulated in particular ways, and these in turn lay the basis for distinctive kinds of visual meaning. The particular kind of twofoldness involved in distinctively architectural meaning draws on the relationship between our seeing an object as a mundane element of building construction and also seeing it behaving in a quite un-mundane, unrealistic manner. It shares some of the features of pictorial seeing but not all. Note also that we do now have a framework that is large enough to accommodate the sculptural kinds of representation discussed earlier. Architectural ducks, apostles and the abstract forms of Frank Gehry entail seeing-as, a particular articulation of twofold seeing. These may not be uniquely architectural representations, but we can now see how they might form part of a larger spectrum of visual meaning. I shall sketch some of the other instances that occur on this spectrum.

We could move through a range of representational frescoes, mosaics and so on that became gradually more abstract, until we reached a case like the magnificent cliff of coloured brickwork that Ralph Erskine designed for the Byker housing project (fig. 75). This is a splendid object but we might feel that the building is the base on which a representation is placed and that this leaves the building and the representation detached from one another. In other words, pictorial representations are applied to, rather than aspects of, the building. Just as with sculptural seeing, we are left with the feeling that these kind of representations are not inherently architectural. However, there are instances on our spectrum of visual meaning where two-dimensional representations exist in more complex relationships to the physical objects that sustain them. Consider the patterned brickwork of the Brant House designed by Robert Venturi in 1970, which, seen unrealistically, makes a skipping diagonal rhythm across the facade (fig. 76).

A second example is the facades of Keble College, Oxford, designed by William Butterfield in the 1860s. There is visual meaning here too, in a repertoire that Butterfield exploited in many other buildings. Diamond patterns, typically on the upper parts of facades, seem like nets that hold roofs in place; zigzag patterns march across the middle parts of facades; and stripes predominate in lower parts, seeming to depict geological strata out of which a building has emerged (fig. 77).

On the Butterfield and Venturi buildings the pattern is much more closely implicated in the fabric of the building than is the case with Erskine's larger-scale panels of coloured brickwork. The pattern at Byker is a unique design, without repeats, that is transferred to the face of the brickwork. In the Butterfield and Venturi cases the visible patterns involve a repetition of the logistics of bricklaying, as if the building were indeed a woven or knitted fabric. The representation exploits the repetitive character of the production process and we might say that it crystallises the rhythm of building itself. So perhaps there is another kind of twofoldness here which exploits the patterning of the building and its constructional history. There is twofoldness also in the representational character of the patterns, which refer beyond themselves, to skipping rhythms in the Brant House and to nets and strata at Keble College.

These polychrome patterns have a further important feature. As they continue to flow across window and door openings and appear to continue beyond the corners of the buildings, unrealistic seeing of the pattern gets into its stride and slides over practical elements of the building as if they did not exist. It is then much easier to be nudged into making an unrealistic construal of the openings themselves, seeing them as cuts in the building; and in a similar fashion we see the block as having been cut from a larger object. It is as if the patterns infect our seeing of these other aspects of the building, making it unrealistic in turn. The counterpart is that we have a stronger sense of the flatness of the facade itself, aroused by the stubborn continuity of the pattern. And this feeds a further ambiguity in which our realistic construal of the buildings as three-dimensional blocks is held in tension with our seeing them as flat surfaces.

75 Housing at
Byker, Newcastle,
designed by Ralph
Erskine (1968–74).

76 The Brant
House, Greenwich,
Connecticut, designed
by Venturi, Scott
Brown and Associates
(1972).

77 Keble College,
Oxford, designed by
William Butterfield
(1867–83).

79   Compton Verney: stonework of main block.

80   Compton Verney: gallery extension.

78 (*left*) Compton Verney, Warwickshire, with extension by Stanton Williams (*c*.1714 and 1998).

81 Compton Verney: interior view of main block.

82 Compton Verney: interior of gallery extension.

A form of pictorial representation, which arises from the twofold relationship of realistic building and unrealistic abstract patterns, has led us into something more distinctively architectural. Surface representations have affected the way that we see three-dimensional aspects of the building, creating a new and richer sense of the relationship between block and surface, between the constructed object and what is unrealistically seen. Visual representations can refer to aspects of the very physical object that supports the representation. Again, we can glimpse the possibility that there is a great deal of continuity between different kinds of visual meaning: that twofoldness can itself make a bridge between two-dimensional and three-dimensional seeing.

Visual meaning is no longer just a matter of straightforward resemblance, whether of other objects or abstract forms, and we have the feeling that something distinctively architectural is happening when these construals bend in the direction of the real building itself. There is a sense of transition and movement between unrealistic and realistic seeing, not just an either–or choice.

I have suggested that in the case of the Schröder House we construe sculpturally the panels out of which it is made. We can make buildings out of panels that butt up to and support one another, as is the case with a certain variety of concrete panel buildings. Although the Schröder House is not made like that, and construing it as made of panels falls on the side of unrealism, an ambiguity sticks to the panels since they are both abstract and building-like.[31] For such reasons we feel that the Schröder House is more distinctively 'architectural' than the Weisman Art Museum or the Sydney Opera House. And, indeed, the argument is frequently made that the Opera House became properly architectural – rather than sculptural – precisely when the structural engineers found a way of regularising the forms in order to make them buildable in practice. The original unrealistically construed collection of forms was modified so that it gestured back in the direction of constructional realism.

10   The two sides of architectural 'twofoldness' can act on each other in different ways. A surface pattern might lead us to construe the three-dimensional character of a building more acutely; we may see a roof and also see it as hovering; or see a window and also see it as cut in a wall; or we may see a building as abstract forms and also as plausible constructional elements. Contrast these possibilities with a pervasive kind of architectural meaning that arises from emphasising or drama-tising the elements of ordinary building construction. Instead of unre-alistic and realistic combining and influencing one another, our seeing of an elaborated part of a building provokes an interest in its practical origins.

At Compton Verney, Warwickshire, a country house designed in the early eighteenth century and later extended by Robert Adam, we can observe the intensification of ordinary elements of construction. So, for example, the practical construction of strong and regular corner stonework is exaggerated to form a strong pattern of large quoins (figs 78–82). Compton Verney has recently been converted to an art gallery, to the designs of Alan Stanton and Paul Williams, and in their addi-tions we can compare that strategy of dramatising construction – one that is central to classicism – with a modern strategy for making archi-tectural meaning. Twofoldness works more ambitiously here. Large ele-ments of the building can be seen as abstractions. A wall that acts as an entrance portal is seen as a mere plane, and the large volume of the new gallery space behind it seems to hang in space. These are unreal-istic construals of practical objects (fig. 80). A similar process operates internally. In the eighteenth-century spaces the mouldings, glazing bars and panelling of practical construction are the small-scale elements out of which a larger harmony is made. In the new addition surfaces are separated and seen as self-reliant abstract elements in a larger compo-sition (figs 81 and 82).

Notions of 'seeing-as' and 'twofoldness' can enable architecture to be put into a continuum of visual meaning. This is not difficult in the case of the exaggerated quoins at Compton Verney: we can consider them as sculptural representations of an actual built corner, just as we can consider many classical mouldings as formalised sculptural versions of practical cover strips. However elsewhere in the continuum there is a more radical possibility – one that modernism may not have invented but has assiduously exploited – in which the imaginative and practical construals of buildings are stretched far apart from one another and held in acute tension.

So we hazard that this sense of connectedness between realistic and non-realistic construals, however it is articulated, is central to architectural meaning. The fluidity and musicality of architecture, we might say, comes from this movement between the real and the imagined; this is its particular kind of twofoldness. The point helps to make good the negativity of the first part of this chapter, and its denial of the role of language in giving architecture its sense of flexibility and fluidity. Now I hope it is possible to see a possible explanation, rooted in an account of visual meaning rather than language, for architecture's beautiful sense of changefulness.

Chapter 6

Expression

I In Chapter Three I made a distinction between bodily sensations and perception. In the following chapters I made a further distinction within visual perception, between realistic and non-realistic seeing, placing the discussion of meaning in the latter category. In this chapter I want to continue with that general approach, this time discussing expression in architecture. Again, my intention is to show how this elusive aspect of architecture can be related back to the processes of perceiving a physical object. This is in support of the larger project which asserts that seeing buildings in certain ways creates the possibility of meaning and expression. I hope that by the end of the chapter we shall be able to assess the strengths and weaknesses of this suggestion.

First of all I need to isolate the meaning of 'expression' that is central to the chapter. An expression can simply mean an utterance, and this is a much broader usage than the one I have in mind. Nor do I use 'expressive' in the sense that we would use of a person or an object that has a particularly striking or vivid appearance. I do not mean expression to have any special stylistic connotation: conceptual issues about expression spread much more widely than the scope of Expressionism. An example of the expression I wish to discuss is when we say that a building is exuberant or modest. In contrast we can say that a building represents exuberance, as in a similar way a building may have the capacity to represent a dragon or a series of abstract forms. The distinction is elusive at first, but the notion of expression focuses on the sense that the building itself is exuberant; and that this quality which it possesses is manifest in its appearance. Of course, this is a thoroughly unrealistic view to take of a building, and we want to know more about the process that is involved.

2   One way of making sense of this kind of unrealistic seeing is via the idea that architectural expression, in the sense that I have outlined, operates in a way analogous to facial and bodily expression. A person's actions and demeanour can be related to their inner emotional state in a number of ways. For example, we can keep feelings to ourselves, so no one knows what we are feeling; we can suppress them, pushing them away even from our own attention; our unconscious might take hold of them and repress them before we are aware of them. If we are aware of them we can talk about them; or we can express them in some form of behaviour. This latter category forms the basis of the discussion of expression that I outline later in the chapter. When we express ourselves through smiles, frowns or outbursts of anger, the emotion does its work by modifying the contours and appearance of the face, widening the mouth to raise our voice, making us red in the face, curving the mouth up or down.

A number of consequences begin to flow from this basic suggestion. One is that the spectator who sees someone with a certain kind of expression can discern the emotional state that lies behind the expression. When we see someone with a sad face we deduce, usually correctly, that they are sad. Expressiveness may mean as much to the spectator as it does to the person who is in the grip of a particular emotion. It becomes a public, shared matter, a route between the inner life and the public world of understanding, recognition and sympathy. A further point, which is crucial to artistic expression and architectural expression in particular, is that it is possible to feign bodily expressions and demeanour. The basic proposition is that inner states have distinctive ways of manifesting themselves, but we then have to account for the fact that expressions can be detached and used for effect when the inner feeling is absent.

This train of thought, which starts by considering human expression and proceeds by testing out the application of that idea to architecture, runs in a different direction to an important tradition of theorising about artistic expression. I wish to digress for a while to outline that theory; then I shall suggest that the idea of objects' being expressive in themselves fills a lack in the theory.

The influential theory of expression that I have in mind can be found in R. G. Collingwood's *The Principles of Art*, first published in 1938. It has been pointed out that Collingwood's book made a coherent philosophical argument out of ideas that were common currency in Romantic attitudes to art.[1] So along with the intrinsic interest of his arguments we can follow the implications of a much broader current of ideas, one that moves us towards the issues discussed in later chapters. Collingwood starts by making a distinction between art and craft. Craft is a process of making something to fulfil a definite objective that has been decided in advance. Means and ends can be distinguished from one another. In art it is not possible to identify an objective that a particular work fulfils. Artistic activity consists of making something in response to an unfocused impulse. Thus the term 'creating' is used in order to distinguish the activity from the 'technical' kind of making involved in crafts.[2]

There is an impulse to express an emotion but the artist is not fully aware, until he or she has created the work, what the emotion is. True artistic activity, according to Collingword, is a way in which the artist becomes aware of his or her own feelings, is able to make them explicit and to communicate them. Collingwood moves many works that we might typically describe as works of art from the category of 'art proper' to that of 'craft' or 'quasi-art', on the grounds that they involve technical rather than creative activity. The criterion is whether they are made for the purpose of creating a particular kind of effect. Works which are made for amusement, for magical purposes or as puzzles, instruction, advertisement, propaganda, exhortation are moved from art proper. Nor is representational art, so far as it has no other aim than to represent an object, to be treated as art proper. But Collingwood does accept that it is possible for works to be the means of fulfilling a specific use and to be works of art at the same time. Thus he re-casts Oscar Wilde's phrase that 'all art is quite useless' to 'what makes it art is not the same as what makes it useful.'[3] This enables buildings to be works of art, for other artistic reasons that their usefulness does not contradict.

We need to observe more closely what Collingwood means by 'expression' and 'emotion'. He takes language as a model for expression, arguing that meaning in language comes ultimately from expressive gestures. This entails a quite different assessment of the significance of grammar from that set out in the previous chapter: 'Beneath all the elaboration of specialized organisms lies the primitive life of the cell; beneath all the machinery of word and sentence lies the primitive language of mere utterance, the controlled act in which we express our emotions.'[4] By emotion Collingwood does not mean a particular set of feelings, as our normal usage would have it. His view is that all human experience is permeated by emotion, each individual 'sensum' of experience having its emotional charge. These emotional charges, arising in the primary levels of sense perception, are not lost but can be incorporated into higher mental structures. Thus, emotions that we would recognise in common usage – hatred, love, anger, shame – retain within themselves the elements of the primary experiences in which sense and feeling are combined.[5]

Collingwood suggests that painting's artistic significance comes not from mastery of depiction – that is the exercise of a craft – but from emotional expression. He rests his argument on Berenson's theory of 'tactile values'. This enables him to reach back into elementary structures of experience, namely 'The imaginary experience of certain complicated muscular movements'.[6] Such experiences, on his previous definition, would have both sensual and emotional aspects: they would ultimately rest on emotionally charged 'sensa'. We can again see the influence of ideas about empathic and spatial seeing that were described in Chapters Three and Four.

Collingwood believes that 'transmitting' emotions entails a technical process, not a creative one. It would involve making an object that somehow corresponded to the artist's feelings and handing it to the spectator, who would then have those same feelings. First, the artist would 'technically' craft an object in accordance with a preconceived plan, namely to create a certain effect in the spectator. Then, by a similar process of cause and effect, the object would manipulate the emotions of the spectator. Neither of these processes have the revelatory aspect of true creative activity, in which an impulse is made specific and coherent. It becomes evident that there is really only room for one creative activity in the truly artistic process. If, having created a work, the artist merely gives it out as an object, then the spectator is doomed to react 'technically' to it, in a process of cause and effect.

This becomes the crux of Collingwood's insistence on the ideal character of the work of art. The artist and the spectator must share the same work, the same creative experience. Considering the work of art as an ideal, imagined object, to which the physical work merely gives access, makes it possible for the same work to be experienced in different times and places. However, Collingwood recognises the problems that are raised by the dependence of the creative experience on practical experience of the medium. The problems are addressed in the remarkable final chapter of *The Principles of Art*.[7] The artist's activity now becomes a form of public labour, one that is only completed through the participation of an audience in a performance. Theatre, particularly 'group theatre' in which the work is developed by a collective, becomes the paradigm for art. In fact, this discussion is sparked off by references to Ruskin and Morris's insistence on the need for the building worker to be involved in the creative activity of design. Art in general should aspire to this intimacy between performer, artist and spectator.

3   Let us now look at how Collingwood's theory might be applied to architecture. Some of the core ideas were, and still are, widely diffused. Frank Rutter's formulation that architecture is 'Building touched

with emotion' is typical.[8] An engaging work by Bruce Allsopp gives us a more detailed attempt to apply Collingwood's ideas. Allsopp casts the distinction between art and craft as that between 'fairground architecture' and architecture proper. Fairground architecture aims to manipulate the emotions in a certain way, and its forms and designs are merely instruments to fulfil a purpose: 'We can devise decoration by arranging pleasing shapes like acanthus leaves or sprays of roses in a way which we think will be pleasing to behold. We can get an effect by means of which we have cogitated, but this is not art. It is when we devise and, so to speak, temper our device in the heat of emotion, that we produce works of art.'[9]

It is only in the latter process that architecture proper is produced. This is a striking distinction and it divides architectural sheep and goats with a high seriousness. Allsopp is building on Collingwood's point that emotional energy is locked inside a 'stimulus' and that the architect's task is to make it evident through the process of expression. Fairground architecture, although it doubtless requires skill, will not draw on that inner store of emotional energy as true art will. Allsopp then provides an attractively untidy list of the kinds of stimuli that can provide material for the architect's emotional response in architecture proper.[10] These fall into two categories. First are the conditions of an architectural problem or brief, which determine an outline design. In the second stage the architect gives expression to her or his feelings about that imaginary outline design. The stimuli here are matters of construction and practical building and the architect seeks appropriate expression for them: 'The architect, as an artist, expresses his emotions about these two groups and in the first group he will be expressing emotion stimulated by human needs and human feelings. In the second he will be expressing his emotions about building.'[11]

The division into two stages is a familiar one. Goodhart-Rendel gives an eloquent account of the second stage, and argues that architects should restrict themselves to it: 'Architecture, then, if it so choose, may run counter to the facts of building, or may simply ignore them. Normally, however, it will do best if it look among those facts for the raw material of its expression.'[12] Allsopp, though, stresses that the two stages are not separable in practice and that both are part of the total activity of designing a building. His adjustments of Collingwood's theory to the specific conditions of architecture have other implications. The first-stage stimuli come not from inside the architect but from the conditions of an architectural problem and these in turn begin with the wishes of a client. This is the origin of the stimuli to the architect's emotional response. The starting-point of architectural activity is not an unfocused desire to design a building, but a requirement that a building of a certain kind should be designed. As Suzanne Langer puts it when working through the implications of an argument similar to Collingwood's, the architect 'cannot let his inner need decide whether he will plan a cottage or a cathedral.'[13]

This involves something more than a constraint on the architect's creative freedom. The point is that the conditions of an architectural problem should be thematic to the whole design process and that in the broadest sense the design should be 'about' the conditions that the client sets. The reader will recall that in the previous chapter I briefly discussed ways in which the use of a building could be thematic to its meaning. We can now begin to contrast that approach with the outlook associated with expression. To endow a building with visual meaning about its use or purpose, the architect must devise some appropriate form of representation. This would fall into Collingwood's notion of quasi-art – the framing and execution of a deliberate intention to represent an object. The notion of expression, on the other hand, gives us a much wider range of possibilities. The architect takes the building's programme as the stimulus to a creative activity, but it is in the nature of the process that the form of the object is a result, not an intention, of that activity and could not have been known before it was embarked upon. This is the source of the great power, and theoretical elusiveness, of the Romantic conception of expression when it came into the hands of architects. Allsopp leads us to the edge of this fertile landscape of ideas and I will explore it in more detail in the following chapters. From Allsopp's point of view, and within a larger consensus of architectural ideas, it is the landscape of architecture proper.

For the moment, I wish to follow the implications of Allsopp's discussion of fairground architecture. One of the consequences of the basic division that he adopts from Collingwood is that the familiar

emotions of everyday life become the province of fairground architecture. Architecture proper deals at an abstract level with emotion, or
'affect', which is capable of attaching itself to any number of specific
objects. Our normal understanding, by contrast, is that emotions are
plural and specific. In fact, it is hard to identify what emotions have
in common: we know envy, grief and embarrassment because we have
felt them distinctly and separately, not because we have experienced
them as instances of emotion in general. If we wish to stay closer to
such emotions as we normally understand them, then we will need to
explore the fairground route.

The significance of fairground architecture is that it is designed as
a means of arousing emotion. The emotion is defined at the beginning
and the architect, like a craftworker, designs an object that delivers that
emotion. Allsopp is focusing on this means–ends relationship; consequently, the craft of creating emotional effects appropriate for law
courts or cemeteries, or other buildings that might have serious and
sombre significance, would also come under the same heading. The
term 'fairground architecture' is therefore deliberately ironic, and here
Allsopp follows Collingwood's example. It was Collingwood, after
all, who put the Aristotelian view of tragedy into the 'theory of
amusement'[14] because it involved the deliberate manipulation of the
audience's feelings of pity and fear.

4   There is an important difficulty with the notion of fairground
architecture, and consideration of it will begin to lead us back towards
the other view of expression with which I began the chapter. It can
be put as a question: are the emotions located in the building or in
the spectator? Allsopp's point is that fairground architecture – 'false art'
– manipulates our emotions. It is a mechanism whose purpose is to
create an emotion in a spectator. In an actual fairground, the spectator sees the design and decoration of the carousel and may be made
happy and carefree by seeing it. But the mechanism does not necessarily create that kind of result. Seeing an exuberant building may not
make me feel exuberant, and seeing a modest building is most unlikely

to make me feel modest. The idea that 'false art' acts as a mechanism for transmitting emotion overlooks these kinds of cases, in which we are inclined to say that the emotion is in the building. We are happy for it to remain like that, and we do not assume that the aesthetic effect of these expressive objects should depend on how contagious they are.

It is true that some buildings seem to be more manipulative than others in the way that they create architectural effects, and in these cases we might expect the expression to be contagious. The little mausoleum designed by Soane as part of the Dulwich Picture Gallery is detailed with appropriate simplicity and restraint. Above the alcove that contains the sarcophagi is a roof lantern fitted with yellow stained glass, shedding a mysterious and unearthly light. But even in this case it is the building that is made mysterious and unearthly and not the spectator.

Allsopp's idea of fairground architecture has introduced us to the idea of emotional effects, but it seems that he mistakes their target. The effects capture the building, not the spectator. 'False art' does not seem to operate in the way that Collingwood and Allsopp suggest and therefore the arguments by which it was distinguished from architecture proper seem to lose their force. Questions of value and quality, which were implied in the false art–art proper distinction, can still be posed but against a new background: that buildings themselves have the possibility of being expressive. The determined frankness is there in Michael Hopkins's Shad Thames office building; the exuberance of a Post-modernist office building like Minster Court in the City of London is there in the building (figs 83 and 84). A building can have expression without needing to earn its living by stimulating particular emotions in the spectator.

The underlying point has received a good deal of attention in discussions of expression theories of art. O. K. Bouwsma, in discussing 'sad music' concluded memorably that 'the sadness is to the music rather like the redness to the apple, than it is like the burp to the cider.'[15] Redness is part of the character of the apple, sadness is part of the character of the music and, to take an architectural example, joyfulness is part of the character of William Chambers's Casino at Marino on the outskirts of Dublin (fig. 85). The character in each case does not make us red, or make us sad, or make us joyful. Bouwsma stresses that we should begin by recognising that there there can be something about a building, or a piece of music, or a poem, that is expressive. The fact that we may be able to go further and say that the music is sad or that the building is joyful should not stop us from holding onto the idea that expression is part of the character of the building and not something that it transmits or provokes.

This seems a helpful suggestion but we might begin to suspect that Bouwsma has merely invited us to trade one mistaken view for another. We have handed in the 'contagion' view of expression and been given in exchange Ruskin's 'pathetic fallacy': that we endow inanimate objects with human feelings.[16] We can pick off part of the problem if we accept that animate objects can be expressive. Indeed, the animated body is the very paradigm of an expressive object. An animated face, a part of the body, has expression because there is life inside it: a person is animating the face. But there is nothing animating a building, it is matter without thought or feeling.

We cannot hope to breathe life into buildings and make them feel. But let us look more closely at animate expression and see if we can make a bridge that will link it with nerveless objects. I earlier alluded to the idea that the expression of our feelings in demeanour or bodily actions can form the starting point of an account of artistic expression: the emotions change the facial expression and bodily stance and move- ment. The assumption is that a process operates with great predictability and regularity. A feeling is manifested in a physical demeanour; the feeling and the demeanour are intimately connected; and a particular demeanour is invariably associated with a particular feeling. Note a further three-way division. First, there is the feeling itself in the inner life of the person. Secondly, there is the expressive demeanour of the face or the body. This is the way the face or body is, its configuration from the point of view of expression. It involves attention to certain features of the way the face lies or of the arrangement of the body. If we were not aware of the existence of human expressiveness, and did not engage this kind of attention, we would not see a demeanour. Thirdly, there is the physical body, on which all this is borne.

83 Offices at Shad Thames, London, designed by Michael Hopkins (1991).

84 Minster Court office development, London, designed by GMW (1991).

85 Casino Marino, Dublin, designed by William Chambers (1759).

An expressive demeanour or configuration is like a mask, a surface of a body.[17] Its contours are made by the feelings behind but they are also the contours of the physical object. The emotion behind the mask surface is not a physical object that stamps out the contours, but it nevertheless puts the expressive surface into just that configuration. I smile a certain way and the contours of my face change accordingly. We can attend to an expressive surface in two ways: either to the configuration, or to the feeling that gave it its shape. The object we see is the same in each case but our attention is different. When we attend to the feelings we cannot see them: they are behind the mask and there is nothing to see. We do not share them, in the literal sense that we enter the mind of the person, but we know what the feeling is. So seeing the sadness behind the expressive demeanour doesn't nec-essarily make us sad – if I had succeeded in my aim of hurting the other person I would be pleased – but we know what it is, that it is sadness.

The analogy of a mask is helpful because we know that once expres-sions have established their distinctive configurations they can then be pulled apart from their origins. In other words, as noted before, we can feign expressions, presenting the outer demeanour but not feeling what lies behind. So I might pretend to be angry in order to get my way, or pretend to smile in order to ingratiate myself with someone. Feigning expressions is part of everyday life. It may seem contradictory to the intimacy of feeling and demeanour but there is no doubt of its efficacy and its usefulness: we can seem to be in a state that we are not in.

This kind of expression works in a quite different manner from lin-guistic signs. If I use the word 'coffee' I cannot pretend to mean coffee, as I might pretend to be angry. It is true that I can make a mistake, and say something I don't mean, but otherwise whatever I say is meant. I cannot utter a word and hope that the meaning will not stick to me, in the way that I might pretend to be angry yet have no anger stick to me. Expression of the kind that I am describing makes pretence possible, signs such as words do not. The relationship of depth and surface, inner feeling and outer configuration is crucial here. An expression, in the sense that I am using the term, has depth – there is something behind it – and so there must be a surface for it to be behind or below.[18] But word signs have no depth. Coffee does not lie behind the sign 'coffee', giving the sign its surface. 'Coffee' is not the mask surface, knobbly like the beans or brown like the drink. There is nothing spatial in the relationship between the sign and the referent, so there is nothing to pull apart and form the basis of deception.

Expressions can be feigned, so that a person seems to be in a state that they are not in. These mask surfaces are also robust and transportable enough to be applied to inanimate objects. Thus a sculpted bust can have a proud expression. A building can also have a facial expression. Admittedly, it will be of a simplified kind but it is a familiar sight to see a wall where windows, or windows and a door, form eyes and mouth and look gormless or mean or coy as the case may be (figs 86–8). The physical object has a certain configuration and it is the one that attaches to a certain kind of human feeling. We see through the configuration to the feeling beneath. Faces on walls are intriguing but can they help us to make sense of architecture's ability to express a great variety of human feelings and virtues? If we wish to move the discussion onto more complex emotions we will have to try to explain formulations such as: 'Chambers's Casino at Marino has a certain configuration and it is the one that attaches to a certain kind of human feeling, namely joyfulness'.

Return for a moment to Bouwsma's stress on the central importance of identifying the work of art – music in his case, a building in ours – as 'the expressive'. We can subsequently aim to 'tag' the expression, as he puts it, but simply recognising that a work is expressive can be rewarding.[19]

There are many expressive buildings where we would have difficulty in identifying a specific feeling, but the previous discussion may make our contemplation of them more fruitful. We might say of Ronchamp that it has a certain configuration and it is the one that attaches to a certain kind of human feeling, but then be unable to proceed to naming the feeling. However, there is a great deal we can say about the expressiveness of Ronchamp merely by describing its physical

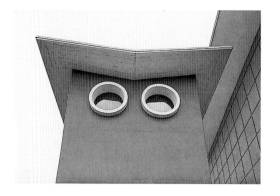

86, 87 and 88   Buildings with faces.

89   Interior of the chapel at Ronchamp, France, designed by Le Corbusier (1950–55).

90 The Mausoleum at Castle Howard, Yorkshire, designed by Nicholas Hawksmoor (1729).

91 (*above*) Housing at the Weissenhofsiedlung, Stuttgart, Germany, designed by Mart Stam (1927).

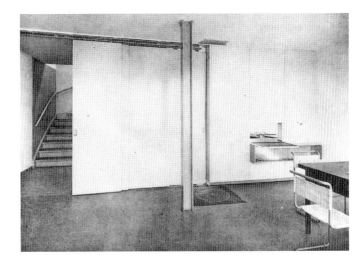

92 Interior of house by Stam at the Weissenhofsiedlung.

configuration. We could point to its soft dusky light, enlivened by the glow of the deep window reveals and the splashes of colour from the stained glass; the spiral movements into the side chapels, and up into the light coming from the towers; the roof that presses down as if the space were a cave (fig. 89). In other words, we can aim to identify what the expressive surface is and which aspects of its design, details and materials are relevant to it. The more we can describe this expressive configuration the more we come to understand the feeling of the building. In the process, the urgency of giving that feeling a name might recede.

But assume that we do eventually want to resume an attempt at explanation: where will it lead? Return to Chambers's joyful Casino near Dublin and consider its expressive configuration. Its surfaces are light. The windows are large in relation to the walls, so there is a sense of openness, connection between inner and outer. The columns are more widely spaced than usual. The sense of a walled building gives way to a playfulness between walls and columns, and a springing rhythm of projections and setbacks. Surfaces are decorated in delicate relief. Then ask: what would be the expressive configuration of a joyful person? They would be light in the way they talked. They would let us into their feelings, opening themselves up, have no sense of defensiveness, no walls around them. Their conversation would move from point to point in a springing rhythm and be delicately elaborated. Think of the Mausoleum at Castle Howard, the plodding march of its closely spaced columns, the lack of windows, the intensity and simplicity of its form, the sense of a defensive stockade (fig. 90). Then think of a sad person, moving heavily, shunning company, wrapping their grief around them, keeping the world out.

When a building expresses an emotion it has some of the characteristics that people have when they are in that emotional state. Lightness or openness or heavy rhythms or defensiveness can form part of an expressive surface. A heavy rhythm can be an aspect of the configuration of the physical building and also an aspect of the emotion of grief. If we look at the expressive surface we can see grief behind it.

5   In reality, the relationship between emotion and outer expression is not as straightforward as this argument based on human demeanour would suggest. There are difficulties in making individual examples work in this schematic manner, which I shall shortly discuss. Now I wish to discuss a question about the scope and importance of the argument. Does it engage with a merely odd or unusual aspect of architectural experience, or does it point to something of central importance? One way of opening up this question is to ask what range of human feelings can be engaged. Consider the contents of this list: 'The use of emotional terms − sad, gay, joyous, calm, restless, hopeful, playful etc. − in describing music, poems, pictures, etc., is indeed common.'[20] Most of these terms could plausibly be applied to buildings: indeed, 'calm' and 'restless' are common descriptions. But a 'hopeful' building is more tricky to imagine. Some of William James's list of primary emotions − fear, grief, love and rage − apply, but not others. A list derived from an introductory discussion of the emotions − embarrassment, envy, fear, grief, pride, remorse and shame − gives us a similar problem.[21]

The issue is made more ragged by the fact that buildings can express human virtues and vices as well as emotions. We are nearing the border between emotions and virtues when Talbot Hamlin puts it that one of the pleasures of architecture is the perception of its 'emotional tone'. He suggests that few emotions can be produced, but they are of the highest and most beneficial kind, for example the sense of power, peace, gaiety, playfulness, relaxation, and − a striking phrase − 'relaxed sociability in houses'.[22] Then if a building can have a high emotional tone surely we must allow Stanley Abercrombie to ask of an architect 'does he condescend? Does he brag? Has he provided just the degree of intellectual stimulation we are capable of appreciating, or is his building, pretending to deliver more than it can, pompous? Daring too little, is it a bore?'[23] It is indeed possible to think of expressively boastful or pompous or condescending buildings and so the question seems to be relevant. The train of thought then becomes familiar. Howard Robertson wrote about the expressive character of buildings in terms of the good qualities of human beings − nobility, generosity, refinement, neighbourliness.[24] Or take Eugene Raskin's view that honesty is an essential ingredient of architectural expression. Thus he can contrast the honesty of a New England meeting house with a European palace. In the former case 'the architect "honestly" strives to find solutions that fit the world as he sees it', and 'his sincerity will shine through irresistibly, overcoming even lack of skill'.[25]

We can hardly complain that the expressions involved in architecture come from an odd corner of human experience. On the contrary, the difficulty is in accounting for this wide-ranging and unruly catalogue of human experience. It seems also that we will need to accept that both feelings and virtues are involved. No doubt they are conceptually distinct, but they share that characteristic of linking the inner and outer worlds in which inner feelings and virtues are given bodily expression. That is a reason to incorporate virtues into our discussion, but there are still difficulties. There can be a demeanour of joy or calmness or restlessness, but where should we look for the visible surface of a virtue? Will it be the expression that the virtuous person has; or should we take it that when buildings express virtues they are expressing, in some manner, the actions of a virtuous person and not just their demeanour? We could describe someone's demeanour as honest-looking or modest, but our test of whether someone really was virtuous would be in their actions, not their demeanour. The point holds good for architectural expression. The honest or modest or generous building is more likely to have connections with those kinds of behaviour, rather than with what a virtuous person looks like.

When the term generosity is used of buildings it generally points us towards a pattern of behaviour rather than a configuration of the face or body. It carries the sense that the spaces are ample rather than minimal, that the building gives away some space beyond the required minimum. It also suggests that the transitions from one space to another are smooth and easy, so that we do not need to ask where to go next: rather, the building invites us to move forward. These are aspects of the generosity that a person might have: offering more than we have the right to expect, not counting the cost or trouble of an action done for others. There is a surface of behaviour which is analogous to the expressive surface of the building. But we have to admit that the analogy is at a very schematic level indeed.

6 Now let us turn the discussion round and consider some of the reasons why the scope of the expression of feelings and virtues in architecture might be limited. To begin with, there is likely to be a connection between an architectural style, the sensibility of a period and its expressive repertoire. The whole range of architectural expressiveness is unlikely to be available to an architect working at a particular moment and would only become visible across a wide span of time and styles. For example, the transition towards modernism in architecture could be plotted against a changing expressive repertoire. Here is Ruskin, advocating in the 1850s what architecture's prime expressive mood should be:

> As the great poem and great fiction generally affect us most by the majesty of their masses of shade, and cannot take hold upon us if they affect a continuance of lyric sprightliness, but must often be serious, and sometimes melancholy, else they do not express the truth of this wild world of ours; so there must be, in this magnificently human art of architecture, some equivalent expression for the trouble and wrath of life, for its sorrow and mystery: and this it can only give by depth or diffusion of gloom, by the frown upon its front, and the shadow of its recess.[26]

Contrast it with Lethaby, writing at the beginning of the 1890s and looking forward to a new kind of architecture:

> What, then, will this art of the future be? The message will still be of nature and man, of order and beauty, but all will be sweetness, simplicity, freedom, confidence, and light; the other is past, and well it is, for its aim was to crush life: the new, the future, is to aid life and train it, 'so that beauty may flow into the soul like a breeze'.[27]

Lethaby is predicting that future architecture will have a different kind of expressiveness from that of the past, but an expressiveness nevertheless; in the long historical perspective we can put the two kinds together as elements of a wide architectural repertoire. If we accepted this point in principle we could then turn to another view, an atemporal one, of the limitations of architectural expression. Quite simply, there may be buildings which do not have expressiveness in the sense that I have been using the term.

There is a difficulty here, in that important kinds of mental states can lead to 'unexpressive' demeanours. I might say that a person has a blank or an empty expression but still mean that the blankness or emptiness is expressive: it might be eloquent of a person numb with grief, or gripped by an examination panic. Those kinds of emotional emptiness can be among the most powerful inner states but there are duller kinds of emptiness too. Our working assumption in everyday life is that as long as people are conscious there will be some ebb and flow of expression, and so blankness can be taken to express something of a person's emotional state.

We cannot make this assumption of buildings. Their expressiveness arises because architects devise and modify designs for buildings in such a way as to encourage the spectator to see a building expressively. They can choose other ways of making a building interesting: expression, as a form of non-realistic seeing, may be quite absent. This leaves us with the difficult task of having to decide whether a particular building expresses one of those 'unexpressive' mental states or whether it is truly lacking in any expressive aspect and responsive only to realistic seeing.

The issue is important for modern architecture. It affects how we assess some of the architecture of the 1920s that goes under the heading 'New Objectivity'. In comparison with buildings designed in the 'Expressionist' style of the time, it can seem blank and undemonstrative — unexpressive in that sense. The outlook of the time was itself ambivalent as to whether the architecture was to be matter-of-fact, objective — lacking in any emotional content — or whether the crucial point was to express in an architectural medium a mood of objectivity, matter-of-factness. In practice, architects took the latter course. Consider the houses that Mart Stam designed for the Weissenhof exhibition in Stuttgart in 1927 — their lack of shadow and projection; the openness of those oblong windows that seem like bright unblinking eyes; the paleness and smoothness of the building's skin (fig. 91). What is being expressed is the mood of the kind of youthful person who can look at the world with a steady gaze, without the texture of age on their skin or the frown of sorrow or fear on their brow. The person is 'unexpressive' in the sense of undemonstrative, unflinching, but nevertheless in the grip of that feeling of clear-sighted objectivity.

These expressive effects come from careful attention to detail: we might say that creating such undemonstrative expressions involves the most cunning artifice of all. Most certainly it does not involve matter-of-fact building. Stam had originally intended the building to have a steel frame, which would have had expressive potential but little matter-of-factness in terms of building economics. In the end, most of the planned steel frame was cut in order to save money but one column remained and is exposed in the living room – an elegant young limb frankly revealed, but actually the only remaining part of a larger intention (fig. 92).

Other buildings might be truly unexpressive in this sense. Ordinariness or matter-of-factness, and emptiness of emotional content, can be an aesthetic programme and it moves the centre of gravity back in the direction of realistic seeing. The architecture of ordinariness, whether in the Arts and Crafts tradition, or the work of Alison and Peter Smithson, or the current work of architects such as Tony Fretton, derives pleasures from materials, construction, qualities of light. We do not need to invent a special kind of expressiveness to account for such cases: it is quite satisfactory to say that they are lacking in expressiveness and have other attractions (figs 93 and 94).

7   Expression that harks back to human demeanour can be important, but it need not be; some human feelings and virtues can be expressed, but not all; and there is no obvious rule to determine which can and which cannot be expressed. The best I can make of these ragged conclusions is to suggest that this form of expression is a resource that architects can use. Its scope is wide but it also has limits,

and it is not clear why they should be in one place rather than another. Let us return to considering individual cases, and follow through some of the difficulties involved in making the argument work. The first point to note is that a heavy rhythm such as that encircling the Mausoleum at Castle Howard could be that of a marching army as well as that of a grief-stricken individual; openness, on the other hand, could be that of innocence or frankness as much as that of joy. Howard Robertson remarks that 'The shaping of a window into tall and narrow proportions, crowned with an arch of slightly stilted centreing may suggest gravity, dignity and aspiration.'[28] His suggestions might lead an architect to use such a window on a government ministry building. But the window may also suggest elegance and a haughty manner and was used in the 1920s to impart glitzy smartness to the commercial buildings around Piccadilly Circus (fig. 95). The general point is that the smaller-scale elements of a design do not necessarily have a single expressive significance: a stilted arch or a heavy rhythm or a sense of openness can each have various kinds of expressive significance.

The problem has roots in our actual human expressions. For example, I might be creased up with laughter and my expression, frozen in time, would be just the same as if I were in a rage. In both cases the expressive process that I described above can be operating, but it may be operating to produce demeanours that are similar, at least momentarily. Understanding the context can help to resolve these difficulties. Human expressions are not a series of semaphore flags waved in front of the face, but gain meaning from the unfolding of the life of the face itself.

The fact that buildings can have numerous expressive features is helpful here. There is an openness about the configuration of the Chambers Casino which could be part of other kinds of expression such as frankness or simplicity. There is also a playful complexity in the movement of recessions and projections, and there is delicacy in the decoration. As features multiply they form the context for the interpretation of other features. So in my interpretation I am gradually drawn away from frankness towards joyfulness. Indeed, the density of

93   Interior detail at Bath University, England, designed by Alison and Peter Smithson (1984–88).

94   Interior of the Lisson Gallery, London, designed by Tony Fretton (1991).

95   Piccadilly Circus, London: Regent Street and Piccadilly corners, designed by Sir Reginald Blomfield and Ernest Newton (1910–24).

features in the expressive configuration of a building helps to compensate for the fact that it is frozen in time. In interpreting a person's feelings, the context is the flux of their actions. Buildings are static and have frozen features, but can have a much wider repertoire of expressive configurations than any individual face, simply because the architect can choose from a vast range of building materials, types of details, forms of decoration and so on. Consequently, a building can express a feeling in a manner unique to itself. We cannot make our faces quite so unique: individuality comes from the lives we lead.

Now we have to square two sets of ideas. One is that a building which has an expressive configuration is made out of parts which together form the context for each other's interpretation: this is the only way that distinctive emotional expressions can be realised. The joyfulness of Chambers's Casino, for example, can be analysed into openness plus playfulness plus a springing rhythm. On the other hand, our perceptual experience of expression hangs on the sense that it resides in the whole configuration. We see a building as modest or pompous or haughty, not as a collection of parts which lead us to deduce that particular expression; and the joyfulness of the Casino is a property of the whole building. The mask analogy now sits rather uneasily. Expression has the unity of a mask but not its sense of a rigid shell-like object. Our feeling is rather that the expressive building is an articulated whole and we want some explanation for this.

I can suggest some ways of thinking through this problem, but they fall far short of a solution. It is helpful to take as a model a trial and error process of design, rather as Le Corbusier described in his essay 'If I had to teach you architecture':

> Another point, just as important: Where do you make the window-openings? You realise that according to where the light comes from you get a particular feeling, so draw all the possible ways of arranging window-openings and then tell me which are the best.
>
>   As a matter of fact, why have you made your room that shape? Think out other workable shapes, and put in openings for doors and

windows. You had better buy a big notebook for this job – you'll need pages and pages.[29]

This shifts the emphasis away from the question of why particular small-scale forms have expressive significance, and towards the practical business of recognising expressive whole designs, of knowing them when we see them. The process of testing alternatives is not as systematic as the quotation from Le Corbusier suggests, but neither is it random. It moves towards the sense of rightness by a series of steps, each building on the previous one. These steps occur to the architect intuitively: they occur rather than are chosen. This intuitive process does important work in throwing up certain possibilities for testing and amending. It is true that the problem of explaining why certain mental states are linked to certain architectural elements is now transferred into this unconscious process. But it is possible that the unconscious mind does indeed entertain a great variety of connections between inner states and physical objects; that some of these occur intuitively to the architect; and that the conscious process of assessment revises and tests them.

The notion of a trial and error process allows for the possibility that an expressive intention may not be formulated in advance. The architect may have in mind a definite expressive mood for a building and may achieve it by testing out a number of possibilities, rather as Le Corbusier suggests. Recall that in Collingwood's terms this would be essentially a craft activity. Other cases might correspond more closely to Collingwood's description of 'art proper', namely those where the process of trial and error helps to define what the mood or virtue of the building should actually be. In yet other instances, a process of trial and error might modify the design in such a way that the architect recognises it as satisfactorily expressive but, rather along the lines that Bouwsma suggests, he or she may be unable to define what that expression is.

The idea of achieving an expressive effect by trial and error connects with an idea that I sketched out in the previous chapter in relation to visual meaning. This was the notion that the architect moulds, adapts or modifies an object, in order to make it responsive to a certain kind of non-realistic seeing. There has to be a physical object as the basis of these manipulations. The architect can make it expressive but the physical object will always remain accessible to realistic seeing. Expression, as a form of non-realistic seeing, brings realistic seeing with it, just as architectural meaning brings realistic seeing with it. The links are essential since it is the manipulation of physical objects in certain ways that makes non-realistic construals possible. That is simple enough but it is more difficult to connect it with the architect's working practices and I will say a little more on the subject in Chapter Eight.

Finally, consider a further part of the argument set out in the previous chapter. I suggested that architectural meaning exists in a movement between realistic and unrealistic ways of seeing buildings. There is something un-architectural about representations that are sharply realistic – the restaurant designed as a duckling or the dragon on the roof. In wanting buildings to be humanised we do not want them to cease to be buildings and become statues, but to be animated and melt into significance in their own way. Perhaps the same point applies to expression in architecture. We do not want buildings to laugh and sing or cry: we want them to be emotionally animated in a manner that is appropriate to them as buildings, a manner that respects their other lives as practical objects. If a building is to be joyful or sad it must be so in a way that is appropriate to a building. Once again, this leaves a great deal for the unconscious mind to do, carrying out the basic assembly work by which the outer world is invested with human feelings and virtues. The process of design, with its intuitive trial and error procedures, brings those parts together into a satisfactory articulated whole, but we may remain ignorant of the unconscious's basic craft of projecting human states onto the world.

Chapter 7

Purpose, Function, Use

1   I began the book by discussing the proposition that architecture is aesthetically distinctive because it is an art of design. This was a useful idea but it turned out to be limited in scope. In the intervening chapters I have followed a number of arguments that tried to remedy that limitation. This led eventually to the attempt in Chapters Five and Six to show how architecture could be meaningful and expressive in its own distinctive ways. The matter was two-sided: that architecture contributes to larger projects of meaning and expression, and that it does so in its own way. In this final part of the book I make another proposition about architecture's aesthetic distinctiveness, and I shall follow the arguments that result. The proposition is that architecture's individuality comes from the fact that it is a useful art, and that the aesthetics of architecture should be based on recognising its usefulness. The similarities with the opening chapter of the book should be evident. There the suggestion was that architecture takes a distinctive place among the arts because it is an art of design; here the suggestion is that it has a distinctive place by virtue of being useful.

It is possible that a distinctive kind of architectural experience is involved in using buildings, one that is not involved in contemplating them. In earlier chapters, I discussed the question of architectural experience but in doing so I avoided making any distinction between the way that users on one hand and enthusiasts and tourists on the other might experience buildings. If it turns out that the use of buildings does involve a special kind of experience, it might then provide the basis for understanding the relationship between usefulness and aesthetics.

Using buildings does indeed involve a different mode of experience from that involved in contemplating them. However, I suggest that the difference lies in the modes of attention that are employed in each case. Using buildings leads us to engage kinds of attention – for example, 'distracted' and repetitive kinds – that are part of our common repertoire in daily life and in our other cultural pursuits. The experience of contemplating and using architecture do have different characteristics but the latter are not unique to architecture, or distinctive of it. This means that the connection between usefulness and the experience of architecture is a loose one, and it is not likely to provide the basis for a clear conceptual link between usefulness and aesthetics.

In the next section of the chapter I turn away from experience towards the idea that usefulness can be given symbolic or representational significance in the design of buildings. Perhaps this will provide a firmer link between usefulness and aesthetics: that this kind of meaningfulness is constitutive of architecture as a distinctive kind of art. This type of approach can be found in Kant's discussion of the place of architecture among the fine arts. His arguments are of great interest in themselves, but also by virtue of their close links with the larger precepts of aesthetic theory developed in *The Critique of Judgement*. The problem of Kant's approach, and of others of a similar type, arises from the fact that usefulness is treated as an attribute of the building which can be put in the form of a concise statement, or a concept, to use Kant's term. The relationship between usefulness and aesthetics then comprises something really quite external to the use of the building in a practical sense. At root, the approach involves a process of naming or labelling: this is an X kind of building from the point of view of usefulness, and the salient aesthetic issue is that X-ness is given appropriate symbolic or representational form.

This imparts a feeling that the relationship between usefulness and aesthetics does not go much below the surface: it does not have connections deep into the nature of usefulness, but only connects with a procedure for categorising it. As we have seen, the argument for a connection between the experience of using buildings and their aesthetics lacked depth and specificity, and here too it seems that the connection is plausible but lacks depth.

Note that the assumption has been made that usefulness does have a nature, that there is something complex in it which invites a rich aesthetic response. This assumption needs some discussion and I set this in motion with a fairly gruelling trek through definitions and clarifications of the terms 'use', 'purpose' and 'function'. I believe this unpromising dissection of terms has an important outcome. It points to the impossibility of the notion that use or function or purpose can be defined separately from a design, with the expectation that a design can then be made to fit that use, function or purpose. In fact, usefulness and design are not related in a problem–solution manner: the real relationship is one where design and usefulness constitute each other. A deep connection between usefulness and aesthetics is then problematic, because the two sides of the proposition cannot be conceptually separated, prior to being brought back together again. There can be no depth where there is no sense of independence of the two sides, or of the possibility of pulling them apart.

This is a highly abstract way of putting things, and I hope that this chapter will put some life into it. It may be that we should consider designing with usefulness in mind as a process of finding rather than making. The shift would recognise the fact that we shall always see usefulness and design cohabiting, and that we cannot invent one partner simply as a solution to the other. It also moves the focus of architectural aesthetics away from the modification of traditional forms towards the way that buildings are designed – away from prescriptions about products towards the design process. The aspiration to forge compelling links between usefulness and design via the medium of the design process is, very broadly conceived, the grand theme of modern architecture, considered in a historical perspective that extends from the early part of the nineteenth century to almost the present day. We lack a word for what is involved here: I call it the sustaining outlook of modernism in architecture and I attempt to outline its characteristics.

Even the phrase 'the design process' may be misleading, if it gives the impression of a series of procedures that can be codified. I want to point to a set of attitudes and views which together underpin or support the practices of design that have developed since the early nineteenth century, but which are half submerged in architectural writing and commentary. For clarity's sake, I shall piece together a composite version of the outlook as it can be excavated from the writings of modernists such as Walter Gropius and Louis Kahn, and I shall trace their antecedents. But I admit that I provide only a sketch of a very complex phenomenon.

Romanticism is the source for the idea that truth can be found by looking inwards, by following a personal sense of authenticity. The inner life of the architect connects with the life of the object that is being designed. The exercise can take numerous forms, ranging from Romanticism's imbuing of objects with human feeling, through numerous types of pervading spirits or transcendental life, to the explicit mysticism that can be found in Louis Kahn's writing. These are powerful ideas which make it possible for the sustaining outlook to achieve that depth of connectedness between a new use, function, purpose and a new design. A revived awareness of biological coherence leads to the idea that finding an appropriate design will reveal an object that has a natural-seeming integration of form and function. Significant also is a stress on finding designs which are appropriate to a moment, and not just conceived timelessly.

This sketch of the sustaining outlook of modernism is at odds with the common view that modernism embodies a reductive and schematic approach to the relationship between usefulness and design. I can make little sense of this view, except to speculate that what it observes is actually the creation of the sustaining outlook itself – its bad other, its straw man, a mechanistic view of the nature of design that it took delight in puncturing. A second type of criticism has become current among architectural theorists in recent years, to the effect that the sustaining outlook is based on mistaken reasoning and that the idea of a deep connection between usefulness and design is implausible.

In the final part of Chapter Eight I shall discuss the influential contributions that Peter Eisenman has made to this stream of discussion about architecture and usefulness. There are two aspects to his critique of the sustaining outlook of modernism. The first is the suggestion that because usefulness is always a matter of values that are socially and culturally changeable, there is no firm basis of thematic material on which the art of architecture can work. This overlaps with a second argument in which the artist is given a duty to criticise and subvert the assumptions of the society in which they find themselves. Thus whatever thematic material might present itself in the usefulness of buildings should be the object of criticism, not artistic elaboration.

Eisenman develops an extreme scepticism about the nature of architecture. Accordingly, he suggests that in the absence of compelling connections between architectural content and design, architecture as an art can play as it wishes with any thematic material. However, this scepticism does not appear to extend to the possibility that architecture might not be an art at all. That seems always to be a background assumption, so the scepticism leads to the possibility that architecture is an art in general, but not an art in particular. The point is an important one, since if we want to avoid the emptiness of an art-in-general we will have to accept that it is made particular by human choice. We are then on the edge of a much more complex relationship between usefulness and aesthetics than the earlier discussions have allowed, one in which usefulness is itself transformed by artistic activity and in which aesthetic and ethical matters overlap.

2   The first proposition that I wish to examine in detail is that use – actual use – involves a distinctive kind of architectural experience, a kind that is different from the experience of simply being a spectator of buildings. The aesthetic experience of architecture, properly considered, is therefore only open to users of buildings. This obviously implies

that the pleasures of looking at buildings, as a tourist or as an enthusiast of architecture, are now deemed strictly un-aesthetic. We could
accommodate the fan or the tourist by saying that their pleasure in
architecture derives from seeing its forms, spaces, textures and so on,
as if it were a complex large-scale kind of sculpture; but we would
have to tell them that they are not experiencing architecture in its aesthetic distinctiveness. We could soothe the fan's pique at being excluded
from architecture proper by suggesting that they can participate imaginatively in the experience of users, incidentally suggesting that this
would be the appropriate way in which to 'experience' historic
buildings.

If we were considering the great workroom at the Johnson Wax
headquarters, designed by Frank Lloyd Wright, we would assert that
an aesthetic experience of the building could only truly be had by a
person working there (fig. 96). The tourist or the architecture fan visiting the building could aim to imagine what it would be like to work
there, and might thereby get some access to the aesthetic experience
of architecture. But it would always be limited by the distance between
experience and imagined experience.

The architecture fan might reply by objecting that the argument is
overblown. All the Johnson Wax Company needs to do is set aside one
desk and chair at which visitors can sit if they wish. They will then
have precisely the architectural experience that the office workers have.
They will see the mushroom columns, the even glow of the light, the
soft red of the brickwork, the lift gliding up and down in its glinting
metal cage. The visitor will not be processing invoices, it is true, but
how can that be constitutive of architectural experience?

The architecture fan and the user may indeed experience just the
same things, seeing, hearing and touching the building in very similar
ways. However, the argument could still be made that the user's experience is quite different in texture from that of the architecture fan. We
could point to two features, the first of which depends on the idea of
'divided attention'. The office worker differs from the tourist by paying
attention to the invoices, the phone calls from anxious creditors and
the manager's enquiries, while at the same time having a greater or

lesser awareness of the building and its space, colours, forms, textures. There is a stream of consciousness[1] in which the building varies in significance moment by moment, rising to conscious attention and then falling away. The second feature is that the office worker does this every day so that an essential aspect of the aesthetics of use is its sheer repetition. Obviously, the architecture fan cannot experience this, though he or she can try to imagine it. In essence these are aspects of a phenomenology which is open to the users of buildings, but not to tourists and visitors.

This could be the starting point of an account of what is specific to the aesthetics of architecture, by virtue of its usefulness. However, if by specific we meant unique, implying that divided attention and repetition are unique to architectural experience, then we would be heading for problems. A remark of Walter Benjamin's alerts us to the difficulty. In 'The Work of Art in the Age of Mechanical Reproduction' he discusses changes in modes of perception in the modern world and in particular the ways in which modern culture has created new modes of aesthetic attention.[2] He suggests that one of the characteristics of watching movies (by the masses at any rate) is that it involves a 'distracted' attention, in contrast to the conventional idea of concentrated aesthetic attention. The significance of 'distracted' attention goes beyond the experience of movies and of art generally: it provides a cover under which the masses will take on new attitudes and learn new skills. Benjamin views the process with considerable anxiety and argues instead for cultural forms where politics is made explicit, rather than communicated during the audience's state of distraction.

Benjamin's model for 'distracted' attention is none other than architectural experience. He takes a view broadly similar to the one that I am testing here: that we properly experience architecture by a process of repetition and habitual use. The experience of 'the attentive concentration of the tourist before a famous building'[3] should not be taken as the paradigm of architectural experience. We should take distracted experience as the paradigm. Benjamin's view fits the daily experience of the accounts clerk: distraction, not attentive contemplation, characterises his or her daily practical relation to architecture. But the interesting point is not that architecture is unique in all this, that we could take this particular phenomenology as constitutive of it as an art, but precisely that it is a generalised feature of cultural experience. Benjamin makes the case for the cinema but once the matter is raised we can see distraction everywhere. The obvious example is music, where dual attention and repetition may be even more characteristic of the experience than in the movies.

Now consider a further issue, pointing in the opposite direction. Distracted experience is important but it is unikely that, in itself, it exhausts the aesthetic experience of architecture by users of buildings. Indeed, it can create its opposite and suddenly deliver moments of concentrated aesthetic attention of a quite conventional kind. So the accounts clerk, taking a break from the invoices, sees undistractedly for a moment that the light in the great workroom is just such a light, that the space is just such a space, that the columns are just such columns and the sense of finality – the Kantian finality that we shall shortly discuss – reigns.

Again, the point may be of general application. Aesthetic attention to music is difficult on a first hearing. Repetition and familiarity are the means by which we become able to confront a piece in a mood of concentrated attention. Indeed, repetition is generally inscribed in the musical structure itself, as if recognising the fact that concentration can only be built on familiarity.

A user experiences buildings differently from the way that a fan or a tourist does but not because they experience different things, or because the nature of their experience as a user is unique to being a user. Rather, their use of the building inserts them into a different pattern of responses, but responses which nevertheless exist generally in the culture. So the user of the building has a different range of kinds of experience, a different collection of types of attention, from the visiting spectator. Users are caught in a distinctive web of experiences, but that web is spun out of patterns of attention that are common in other areas of culture and daily life. Experience does not provide us with a distinctive route by which usefulness in itself can become constitutive of architecture as an art.

3   Let us now turn to an alternative view of the way that usefulness and aesthetics can be related. This centres on the idea that the designs of buildings can incorporate symbolic or representational reference to usefulness. The emphasis moves away from a general type of experience towards the detailed visual configuration of buildings. Kant's account of the place of architecture among the fine arts provides a good example of how such an argument can be structured.

We can take up Kant's argument at the point where he develops an overall classification of the fine arts.[4] Architecture belongs to the sub-group of 'formative arts'. This comprises the visual arts – painting, sculpture and architecture – as we would nowadays understand them, although it differs in including landscape gardening, on the grounds that it is a kind of painting. The distinctiveness of the formative arts is that they communicate 'aesthetic ideas' via 'figures in space'. In the case of architecture and sculpture 'figures in space' can be thought of as the detailed forms that the objects take; and in the case of paintings the relevant 'figures' are depictions of objects. By contrast, rhetoric and poetry – 'the arts of speech' – give access to aesthetic ideas via the interplay of the understanding and the imagination; in the third group of arts, which comprises music together with Kant's proposal for an art of colour, aesthetic ideas have their basis in the play of the sensations of hearing and sight in themselves. 'Figures in space' are aspects of physical buildings, but we should note that for the spectator their significance lies not in their physicality but in the fact that they represent forms which are of aesthetic interest.

Kant's argument depends on the interplay between these 'aesthetic ideas' and the 'concept' of a building. He means by the latter term the kind of use or purpose to which the building is put. His examples are 'temples, splendid buildings for public concourse, or even dwelling-houses, triumphal arches, columns, mausoleums etc., erected as monuments', and in fact he extends the range to include household furniture. Architectural concepts refer to artefacts made for human use and can be distinguished from sculptural concepts which refer to works of nature – 'men, gods, animals etc.'[5] The architectural concepts that Kant cites are of the kind that would enable us to identify certain kinds of objects in the world: that is a dwelling-house, that a triumphal arch, that a mausoleum. The criterion for differentiating one object from another is its use – as dwelling-house, triumphal arch and so on. We have to assume that Kant has in mind that each of these types of buildings will be recognisable from their general appearance.

The phrase 'aesthetic ideas' is best understood by considering the role that such ideas perform within works of art. An aesthetic idea is a 'representation which induces much thought, yet without the possibility of any definite thought whatever, i.e. *concept*, being adequate to it, and which language, consequently, can never quite get on level terms with or render completely intelligible'.[6] Kant is pointing us towards visual images or objects, or passages in literature, which are food for numerous thoughts. Alongside this richness we experience a difficulty in pinning down exactly what an aesthetic idea is referring to. Concepts are clear but limited; aesthetic ideas range widely but they have no sharp focus. Aesthetic ideas, it seems, would be marvellous things to have but only if they were coupled with concepts in a way that provided them with some greater exactness of reference.

Kant suggests three ways in which we can imagine aesthetic ideas being profitably coupled with concepts. They could help us towards a more complete and grounded understanding of notions which are outside our actual experience. So, for example, they could help us to grasp notions of 'invisible beings, the kingdom of the blessed, hell, eternity, creation, etc.', the objects of which are strictly inaccessible to us. The second use for aesthetic ideas is in bringing completeness to our grasp of aspects of experience such as 'death, envy, and all vices, as also love, fame and the like'. In such cases they can bring multiplicities of thoughts to bear which extend our grasp of these concepts beyond immediate experience. Thirdly, and this is the area which is most relevant to architecture, aesthetic ideas can extend the scope of concepts that we are able to understand, 'giving aesthetically an unbounded expansion to the concept itself'. Aesthetic ideas bring concepts to life, make abstract ideas concrete, make our partial experiences fuller, and surround the core of a concept with a wealth of associations and meanings. That is the general case across all the arts.

The uses of buildings are also concepts, and so in this sense temples and dwelling-houses stand in elevated company, alongside death, envy, love and fame, hell, eternity and so on. They share a density of meaning and significance that cannot be exhausted in words and to which only the multiplicities of imaginative form can do justice. In architecture 'aesthetic ideas' flesh out and give a wealth of meaning to the concept of a building's use. Kant does not provide an example to illustrate his point, but we can surmise what he had in mind from other examples. He talks of visible attributes which are used to flesh out concepts in visual art: 'In this way Jupiter's eagle, with the lightning in its claws, is an attribute of the mighty king of heaven, and the peacock of its stately queen.'[7]

The spirit of the proposal would encompass the varieties of sculptural and pictorial meaning that we discussed in Chapter Five. The variety of means by which Labrouste referred to the function of the Bibliothèque Ste-Geneviève would fall into the category of aesthetic ideas which fleshed out that larger concept. Or this more recent example of the notion that aesthetic ideas give depth of meaning to a building's function: 'The design by Santiago Calatrava [for the Bilbao airport] is an elegantly conceived metaphor for the dynamics of flight. Like his renowned TGV station and airport at Lyons-Satolas, Calatrava's design uses a bird-like image with open wings to express its function as an air terminal (fig. 97).'[8]

The aesthetic ideas which surround the concept of a building's use give that concept a fullness and richness of meaning and make our grasp of it more secure. But Kant makes a further important point when he says that the art of architecture also consists of the presentation of these concepts 'with aesthetic finality'. This brings to bear an idea which is central to his discussion of aesthetics. For Kant, 'aesthetic finality' carries the sense of rightness or inevitability, and although this is not in itself an obscure notion, his explanation of its origins is dauntingly complex. It rests on his view that our ordinary perceptual hold on the world arises from the interaction of a number of levels of mental activity. We construe the world out of our sense-experience, but we have to structure these initial impressions in some way. This involves

96　The 'great workroom' at the Johnson Wax Headquarters, Racine, Wisconsin, designed by Frank Lloyd Wright (1936–39).

97　Railway station at Lyons-Satolas Airport, designed by Santiago Calatrava (1989–94).

the interaction of two levels, or faculties of the mind, namely imagination and understanding. In imagination we construe the world and we do so in a manner that is congruent with the categories of the understanding. This meshing of the two faculties is an entirely practical and everyday matter, but Kant also suggests that it can be felt, as a sense of 'rightness', beyond its practical origins. Thus when a work of art has a distinctive sense of finality or rightness, it is activating, out of its original context, a feature of the mind's basic operation.

The striking feature of Kant's argument about architecture now becomes its degree of abstraction from actual experience. The distinguishing aesthetic feature of architecture is not an actual encounter with a physical object: buildings are not important from a tactile or visual point of view, but because they instantiate certain forms. Those forms are not important in themselves, but only as 'aesthetic ideas'. It is not the actual use of buildings that is important, but the concept of their use. And ultimately concepts and aesthetic ideas are only important as grist to the mill of aesthetic finality. At each stage of the discussion we are looking upwards to the next level of abstraction.

Why did Kant wish to insulate his theory of aesthetic experience so carefully from our ordinary pleasure in objects? The explanation lies in his desire to explain how aesthetic judgements can arise from subjective experience and yet have objective validity. He wished to account for the fact that the pleasures of art can involve something more than an assertion of a personal taste. This led him to the thought that if aesthetic judgements are to have objective validity they must be universally held by humans. Therefore they cannot be dependent on the immediate feelings of pleasure we have when confronted with objects. These by definition are individual, of 'private validity' only. Then he makes the suggestion that aesthetic satisfaction is based on a universal feature of the mind, one that we all possess by virtue of the fact that we are able to understand the world at all. The feature of the mind that attracted Kant's attention was that sense of rightness that has its origins in normal perception.

Now, Kant does refer to another kind of rightness which is much more practical and straightforward than the 'aesthetic finality' that he

claims is central to aesthetic experience. This is our sense that a building may feel just right for its purpose, in a practical sense, leading us
to consider it beautiful by virtue of its fittingness. So, as he points out,
we might find a 'church, palace, arsenal, or summer-house'[9] beautiful
because it is so well suited to its ends. This, however, he describes as
'appendant beauty' and is not to be confused with the 'free beauty'
which characterises those objects that have aesthetic finality. The reason
why this sense of practical fittingness is not truly aesthetic is that it is
based on the individual appropriation of an object, and on an individual experience of pleasure in doing so. This individuality means that
it does not meet Kant's requirement that true aesthetic experience
should derive from a mental power that all humans have in common.

Kant wants to find a place for architecture in an aesthetic system.
An essential principle of this system is to exclude individual pleasure
in the useful appropriation of objects, so that aesthetic experience can
lay claim to a universal application. However, he also wishes to recognise architecture's usefulness and the way that he squares these two
impulses is to make usefulness itself into an abstraction. Indeed, the
notion of aesthetic finality, which has its origins in ordinary practical
perception, returns to architecture having been highly abstracted. In
Kant's theory, usefulness is not located in our pleasure in the practical
adaptedness of buildings, but in concepts of use and the aesthetic ideas
that bring them to life.

We should not overlook a positive feature of Kant's suggestion. By
making the aesthetics of use into a symbolic aspect of buildings it can
now be common property for spectators as well as for users. We do
not need actually to use a building in order to respond aesthetically to
it: it will be enough that we see those aesthetic ideas that are incorporated into its design. This is relevant to urban settings where a building may have many more passers-by than users. But a negative feeling
might overcome that train of thought. It centres on the idea that, in
order to squeeze architecture into his theoretical structure, Kant has
taken away from it exactly that intimate relationship to experience that
we value in it. In response, we might be tempted to turn Kant's argument on its head and devise a theory of the aesthetics of architecture

based on the experience of use, not on symbolic representations of it. This would return us to the issues discussed in the first section of the chapter and we might then swing unhappily between the deficiencies of an experience-based view of the relation between usefulness and aesthetics, and those of an abstracted representation-based view.

The high level of generality of the theory means that it can be applied in the context of numerous styles and architectural outlooks. In fact, Kant's view is strikingly different from the Neo-classical argument that gave architecture its entry ticket to the status of a fine art in the *Encyclopédie*. He does not define architecture as an art of imitation, and the great importance given in the late eighteenth century to convention and decorum as the connectors between building use and form are not mentioned. There is nothing in Kant's argument that contradicts the Neo-classical approach, and nothing that would exclude other ways of linking concepts of use and 'aesthetic ideas'. This is because his interest is not in setting criteria for appropriate designs but establishing a basis for judging whether a given design, however it is derived, might be productive of the feeling of beauty.

When Kant discusses 'concepts of use' he refers to what we would call 'building types'. He assumes that a type has a one-to-one relationship to a use: a certain kind of use or function of a building is embodied in a type-concept. He alludes to building types with a very broad brush, noting temples, 'splendid buildings for public concourse', dwelling-houses and so on. This breadth makes it easier for his examples to stand comparison with the other kinds of verities around which aesthetic ideas are gathered – death, envy, love and fame.

In Kant's account, building types arise out of practicality: they begin as buildings. Then the architect lavishes aesthetic ideas on them, giving depth of meaning to essentially practical objects and making them into works of art. That originating building is at once mundane, full of profundity and also highly abstract. This is an attractive view, but it does contain the difficulty that concepts at this level of abstraction are unlikely to generate common type-designs for buildings. The design that is appropriate to the concept of a dwelling-house will vary across the world and over time. We would have to set up a much wider range of concepts of use, and this gain in historical and geographical realism would be offset by a sense that aesthetic ideas are no longer clustering around concepts of profound human generality.

4   From another viewpoint, Kant's suggestions involve a superficiality in the relationship between usefulness and design, one that co-exists with his assertion of the human profundity of building types. The essential thing in his account is the identifying phrase or word – dwelling-house, temple and others – and its link with a certain kind of object. The phrase is a label or an 'identifier' that is attached to those regularly occurring objects. Kant's discussion does not delve below that label: the nature of the usefulness of a dwelling-house is taken for granted. The role of aesthetic argument is to show how that label is given artistic expression and contributes to aesthetic fulfilment. Kant provides us with an argument that links usefulness and aesthetics, but in an important sense it remains on the surface, since it takes the existence of various kinds of usefulness as given and merely attaches labels to them. The idea to which I alluded in the first part of the chapter, that usefulness imparts something distinctive to architectural experience, held out the possibility of a much greater intimacy between the nature of usefulness and aesthetic experience. In the event, the idea turned out to be less profitable than we had hoped, but it seems that now we are faced with a more plausible, but shallower, argument. There is a lack of gravity, of rootedness in Kant's argument which goes against our desire that the aesthetics of architecture should make a link between the practical complexity of ordinary life and the special complexity of works of art.

   This difficulty underlies the discussions from here until the end of the book. I wish to probe other possibilities for a deep connection between usefulness and aesthetics, and I also wish to discuss the opposite view that the search for depth is quite misguided and will be fruitless. However, in order to move towards these discussions it is necessary to sketch out what usefulness, considered in depth, could possibly mean and entail. The remainder of this chapter is taken up with this sketch.

It begins by discussing (in an admittedly dry manner) a number of definitions – of purpose, function and use. From there it will be possible to make some general suggestions about the nature of usefulness in architecture. These in turn will help us to probe that key question about the possible depth of the relationship between usefulness and aesthetics.

My starting point is to allocate more precise meanings to the terms 'use', 'purpose' and 'function', which have been employed more or less interchangeably so far. At first this will seem narrowly prescriptive, because in ordinary life no great harm comes from overlapping the meanings of such terms. But I believe that in order to understand the complexity of usefulness we need to pull apart its various conceptual aspects, and one way of doing so is to give more particular meanings to terms which are in current use. In everyday life we may say that the use of a particular room is as a lecture theatre, its purpose is to be a lecture theatre, its function is to be a lecture theatre, and mean the same thing in each case. The ambiguity is helpful and quite benign in practice, but underneath it distinct ideas can be identified. My suggestion for distinguishing them is as follows. Purpose denotes a human intention in relation to an object, and function denotes the object's execution of that purpose. For example, my purpose in putting up an umbrella is to prevent myself getting wet; the function of the umbrella is to keep the rain off. To take the more common example of a knife, my stipulation is that we use the term 'purpose' for the intention or goal that I entertain of cutting something, and that we reserve the term 'function' for the knife, the function of which is to cut.[10] The core of the third term in the group, 'use' considered as a noun, refers to what goes on in buildings. As we shall see, 'use' is a highly elusive concept and for the moment I simply wish to stress that a notion of human activity is central to it.

Some initial observations on these definitions can be made. First, it is a practical matter to devise an artefact in such a way that it successfully discharges its function. This is where our interest in design enters. A knife can be designed in such a way that it succeeds in its function of cutting. Obviously, there is no necessary connection between a human purpose and the function of an artefact: the latter may fail to carry out the function expected of it, or carry it out partially or badly. The knife might not cut, my umbrella might turn inside out in the slightest wind and rats might get in and eat the grain in the silo that had the function of storing grain. For the present purposes I shall say that the success of a silo in storing grain is a tribute to its design and its failure is an indication of a design fault. If a building does successfully discharge its function it has thereby fulfilled the purpose that was intended. Purpose and function are related, but only in such successful cases.

Then, three aspects of 'use' should be noted. First, human subjects must be involved: the concept of use has no relevance to the stones on the beach. Many interesting things could be said about where they came from and what they are made of, but to try to account for or describe them in terms of use would be futile. However, people do not need to be present in a building in order to be involved in its use. Many kinds of storage and industrial buildings such as silos and electricity sub-stations may have no continuous human presence yet still serve a human use.

Secondly, use must involve the physical world. True, I can imagine uses, but I will always be imagining a physical world. Use has no conceptual structure beyond its instances in the world and it has no inner logic. Thirdly, in making distinctions between purpose, function and use, I am not suggesting that use merely comprises a series of bodily movements, changes of location and so on, and that these are set in motion by 'functions'. It is tempting to identify use merely as a series of traces: recall the tracks of cars in the snow that delighted photographers in the 1930s, the tracks of housewives as they moved around their kitchens, or the imagined traces of activity that came out of Bernard Tschumi's murder mystery in *The Manhattan Transcripts*.[11] In contrast, my notion of use incorporates the intention that goes along with the actions, as well as the actions themselves.

5   We can test how these terms 'purpose', 'function' and 'use', each wearing their crisp new meanings, actually relate together in a building or a building type. Take the example of a school and imagine someone saying, 'The function of this building is to be a school.' This is a straightforward descriptive remark, bearing none of the weight of the purpose–function relationship that I have just outlined. It is simply the case that this building is a certain kind of thing, namely a school. This is the way that I used the term in the discussion of natural meaning in Chapter Five, and it is essentially the way in which Kant appears to employ 'concepts of use', as labels or 'identifiers'.

If we wish to explore the purpose–function relationship we shall need to specify a purpose that can be identified separately from the function. So imagine someone expressing the purpose that 'children should be educated' and then saying that 'the function of a school is to educate children'. A school may fail to perform that function, so the statement is not necessarily circular. Suppress for the moment any scepticism about the truth or profundity of this view of a school's purpose: we are only interested in the general character of the argument.

It is unlikely that what is meant is that the school, considered as a building and hence as a physical object, does the educating. A knife can perform the function of cutting, perhaps a silo can perform the function of storing, but a building cannot perform the function of 'educating'. Evidently, the person has some other notion in mind of what a school is. They might say that it is teachers that educate children and therefore it is teachers that make a school. We might then pursue the point that books, paper, pens, blackboards, computers, science equipment, musical instruments and so on are also needed if children are to be educated. We would then conceive of a school as a distinctive kind of system that has many aspects. There is a purpose, namely that children should be educated, and the function of a school is to fulfil that purpose. However, what is meant here by 'school' is not a building but that complex system – let us call it a 'pedagogic system' – of human activity and practical resources.

All this might be interesting but unfortunately it has the effect of pushing the building out of the discussion altogether. We have stated a purpose and discovered that the building is irrelevant to its fulfilment. One way of getting the building – the building as physical object – back into the argument is to suggest that phrases like 'the function of this building is to be a school' are contracted versions of a phrase such as 'the function of this building is to accommodate a pedagogic system'. The purpose that corresponds to this function would then be along the lines that 'the pedagogic system be accommodated in an artificial climate, protected from the weather and intruders'. The underlying point is that whereas a building, considered as a physical object of a certain design, cannot educate a child, it can modify the local climate and it can be a barrier against intruders.

The building, as a physical object, might then be considered as neutral in relation to the process that takes place within it. This is plausible in some circumstances. Consider the pumping station designed by John Outram in East London (fig. 98). The purpose of the building was to accommodate and protect from the weather and intruders a series of pumps that regulate the surface water level in a low-lying part of the city. Describing its function as 'a pumping station' does appear to be a contraction of a phrase such as 'the accommodation, etc. of an array of pumps and other equipment'.

This kind of approach is not adequate for school buildings, however. They are not neutral in relation to the process that takes place in them. School buildings do not just throw a roof over a group of teachers and their equipment. They are divided into rooms of different shapes and sizes, with defined relationships one to another. Separate rooms may be provided for different age groups and for teaching certain subjects, and there may be a room which is large enough for the whole school to assemble and identify itself as a single community. These arrangements are essential aspects of certain kinds of educational practice. The design of schools is part of the 'pedagogic system' and changes in educational practice typically involve some change in the design of school buildings. A notable example occurred in the 1950s, when open-plan design combined with 'home bases' replaced an array of separate classrooms. This new architectural arrangement was constitutive of a new approach to education (fig. 99).[12]

98   Pumping station at the Isle of Dogs, London, designed by John Outram (1988).

99   Woodside Junior School, Amersham, designed by Buckinghamshire County Architects Department (1956–57).

It remains true that important aspects of school buildings are climate modifying and security devices. However, these roofs and walls are not just thrown over a group of teachers, children and furniture, but over an internal organisation that brings together a way of teaching, a mode of administration and an architectural setting. I propose that we call such an internal organisation a 'programmatic whole'. The key point is that the programmatic whole of a school is conceptually separate from its component parts. Only the system as a whole has the function in question. The component parts make possible on a practical, empirical level the execution of that function, but they are not part of the function itself. This logical point enables us to make sense of the fact that buildings cannot, as mute physical objects, do something like educating but that they can, as a practical, empirical matter, contribute to that process. In other words, buildings do not have functions by virtue of their being physical objects but by virtue of what goes on in them; and the building is instrumental in what goes on in them. Strictly speaking, then, school buildings do not have functions. Their significance lies in the way that they contribute to a systemic arrangement which also comprises human activities, practical resources, furniture and so on, and which, when properly mobilised, does fulfil a function.

By contrast, those parts of buildings that are engaged in controlling internal climate and providing security can be in a direct purpose–function relationship, along the lines of our umbrella example. Buildings, considered as physical objects, are the kinds of objects that can logically be involved in changing climate, creating barriers; but objects of that kind cannot educate children. It is the latter case that interests us for the moment, not because climate control and security are unimportant but because the aim is to understand the relationship between use and design.[13]

6   At this point I suggest that we return to the original hypothetical purpose and function – 'that children should be educated' and 'that the function of a school is to educate children' – and regard them with some of the scepticism that we have so far held in check. Statements of this kind are of limited value and interest. Perhaps the purpose in question is that children should be socialised, or trained, or civilised, or prepared for work: there are numerous possibilities. The interesting point is that it is hardly necessary for there to be any clear answer to questions of purpose and function in order for schools to continue to exist and develop as pedagogic systems.

This is not just a matter of the difficulty of pinning down the functions of social institutions like schools. It is an example of the common situation that building types generally do not have plausible statements of purpose or function associated with them. The term 'function' simply operates as the identifier of a building type and the functions that such building types discharge can only be expressed by reference to the kind of buildings that they are. Thus the function of an office block is to enable the carrying-out of those activities appropriate to an office block; the function of a hospital is to provide the kinds of services that a hospital provides; the function of a prison is to effect the kind of incarceration that takes place in a prison; the function of a court-house is to administer those elements of the system of justice that take place in a court-house; the function of a house is to provide the kind of setting and amenities that a house provides; the function of a church is to carry out those liturgical and other activities which are appropriate to a church, and so on.[14]

In none of these cases can I see any virtue in trying to formulate a statement of purpose to which the building would be a functional response. Nor, of course, are such institutions founded, adapted and developed by reference to such functional statements, but rather by a constant process of revision of the relationship between the configuration of the building and its inner system. These processes of revision might take place in unexpected ways. For example, Adrian Forty has suggested that the development of the hospital as a building type in the nineteenth century owed as much to the growing professionalisation of medicine, and the needs of medical training, as to the improvement of the hospital as a 'machine for healing'. So blanket purpose–function statements might be quite unhelpful in understanding the historical development of building types.[15] These building types comprise 'programmatic wholes' in the same sense that I have outlined in relation to a school, but it is neither necessary nor possible to make overall purpose–function statements for them.

The counter-argument to this train of thought is to say that of course buildings are responses to purposes, since their design and construction is not a matter of accident: it is simply that we are looking in the wrong place for the purposes. An office building can be a response to the purpose of making money, a school can be a response to the purpose of providing school places in a new neighbourhood, and so on. Buildings can fulfil innumerable institutional and commercial purposes. The purposes are fulfilled by the operation of these 'programmatic wholes', the inner functions of which are so obscure. However, if we ransack that outer purpose for an explanation of the inner systemic nature of a building type, we will not find it. Outer purposes simply assume that such and such a systemic character will be present, and will be profitable or institutionally appropriate. Compare the situation with that of farmers. They can put crops and animals to profitable use: those are their purposes and the land and the animals obligingly become functions. But in another sense the farmers' purposes shed no light on the function of a cow or a blade of wheat: indeed, it is doubtful whether cows or wheat, considered as species, have functions at all.

I want to explore the consequences of this scepticism about the explanatory value of ideas of function in trying to understand the relationship between the designs of buildings and their usefulness. But let us hold onto the idea that building types are systemic, programmatic wholes, and bearing that in mind, consider in more detail what is entailed in 'use'.

7   The central difficulty is that in many cases it is hard to define what 'use' really means. We could start with a straightforward example. Imagine a sports hall designed to accommodate a basketball pitch. Basketball is an activity, and there is little difficulty in calling it a use

so far as the building is concerned. The building has a similar relationship to the use as did John Outram's pumping station. In the one
case the building provides accommodation for a set of pumps and in
the other for a basketball pitch. Both uses could take place without a
building were it not for requirements of climate control and security.
The building in both cases is neutral in the way that the use is carried
out. In both cases there would be a convincing formula that linked
purpose and function: the purpose is that the internal use be protected
from weather and intruders and the function of the buildings is to
accomplish this.

Now consider the case of the auditorium in a theatre, or rather the
combination of the visible stage and the auditorium where the audience sits. This combination I will clumsily call a 'use' for the moment.
Elsewhere in the theatre are other 'uses': the bars, dressing rooms, back-
stage area, foyer and so on. Theatres as 'programmatic wholes' contain
such a constellation of 'uses'. The architecture of the auditorium differs
from that of the sports hall in the obvious but important respect that
it is not neutral in the way that the 'use' is carried out. The design of
an auditorium and the visible stage is constitutive of the kind of theatrical use which takes place.

In fact, the 'use' now becomes quite elusive. Is it what happens on
the stage, or is it the audience's experience? If it is some composite of
the two then we would certainly have to accept that the design of the
auditorium, from practical matters of sight lines and acoustics, to more
intangible ones such as atmosphere, immediacy of impact, was constitutive of the kind of use that takes place. Furthermore, of the two cases
– the sports hall and the theatre – it is the latter that we consider to
be the paradigm for architecture, the one that brings the greater
difficulty to the architect but also the larger gratification to both architect and user.

A number of issues begin to emerge. Although activity, as I have
said, is central to use, it would be inadequate to say that the use simply
is a certain activity. The use of a theatre auditorium is not just the
activity of the actors, no matter how energetically they stride around
the stage. Secondly, given that the perimeter of 'use' now seems to be

obscure, it would be misleading to suggest that the architecture is simply a response to it. Since we cannot clearly say where the conceptual separation is between the originating activity and the architectural response, it seems truer to suggest that use is what happens in a dialogue with the building.

In response to the difficulty of pinning down elusive 'uses', I shall coin another piece of terminology – 'ensembles of use'. The term will not solve the difficulty but it will draw attention to the point that, in cases which we find architecturally interesting and challenging, uses are partly constituted by the configuration and detail of the building and by the furniture and equipment within it. These do not simply serve or respond to a pre-existing 'use'.

I suggest that an ensemble has three components – a certain pattern of human activity, a certain configuration and detail of architectural form, and a certain arrangement of furniture or equipment. The first two aspects are indispensable: there cannot be an ensemble of use without a specific part of a building and a particular human activity being involved. Some distinctive furniture or equipment is nearly always involved. An empty office block does not yet contain its intended ensemble of use because the associated human activities are absent. The Hill House, designed by Charles Rennie Mackintosh for the Blackie family, no longer contains the ensembles of use that it once did, because the family left long ago, although in many of its rooms the beautiful combinations of space, architectural detail and furniture designed by Mackintosh have been kept (figs 100–102).

An ensemble of use need not necessarily have its own walls. A workstation in an open office, consisting of a definable space, a desk, a chair, a computer and so on, combines with a set of human activities to make an ensemble of use. A priest celebrating mass at an altar, surrounded by the altar plate and furniture that the liturgy demands, all set in a larger space, participates in an ensemble of use. The nature of the surrounding space and of adjacent ensembles also constitute the nature of the use-ensemble, just as do the enclosing walls of a theatre auditorium.

The point to stress is that an ensemble of use is not an arrangement of furniture and architecture in which a piece of use takes place, for

100 The empty interior of an office block, London Docklands 1998.

101 Bedroom at The Hill House, Helensburgh, Scotland, designed by Charles Rennie Mackintosh (1902–04).

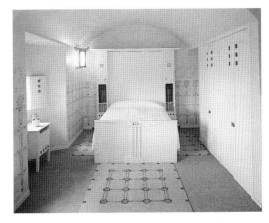

102 Patient and doctor at Glenavy Surgery, Co. Antrim, Northern Ireland, designed by Tim Ronalds (1993).

the reason that the pattern of activity cannot be specified separately from the architecture or furniture. The activity of working at a desk both requires and is constituted by a desk and chair; the activity of celebrating communion both requires the altar, the chalice and other requisites, the surrounding space and is constituted by them. Someone might say that a certain design of desk and chair determines the way in which 'the office activity' operates. This could be just a label for what goes on, but it would have no explanatory power. 'The office activity' is precisely what the desk and chair ensemble constitutes, in all its historical development. It is not the determinant of a use-ensemble, but an abstract description of it.

There are similarities with my suggestions about the nature of the 'programmatic whole'. We can state a function for an ensemble of use, but it will really be no more than an identifier – the dining room, the parlour of the working-class English house, an operating theatre. These are not function responses to external purposes. A dining room, for example, is constituted by its nature as a certain kind of room, not as a response to the purpose of dining.[16] The general point is illustrated by a story about Gerrit Rietveld. When he started work on the design for Mrs Schröder's house, he is said to have asked her 'How do you want to live?', to which she replied 'upstairs'.[17] Rietveld was asking an unanswerable question: tell me your style of life in abstract so that I can make a building for it. Mrs Schröder refused to talk in abstractions: she wanted to live the way that happens when the living rooms are upstairs.

The issue is also revealed more clearly when it is turned on its head, as in Christopher Alexander's 'pattern language'. The 'patterns' are recommendations for small-scale elements of design, mostly for houses. They bring together activity, furniture and architectural arrangement into a defined setting. Alexander's recommendations create an extraordinarily vivid image of a way of life, his answer to the question 'how do you want to live?' The way of life is partly constituted by the bringing together of a number of architectural traditions: the Arts and Crafts interior, the houses of better-off European peasants, the flexibility of American timber-frame construction, the nookiness of the Edwardian suburban house and so on. However, Alexander is keen to present the patterns as solutions to problems. For example, 'in rooms lit from one side, the glare which surrounds people's faces prevents people from understanding one another',[18] a problem which is solved by the proposal that there should be light on two sides of every room. This seems like inventing a problem in order to justify a 'pattern' that has quite enough charm and justification in its own right.

Buildings considered as programmatic wholes gather up and embrace a number of ensembles of use. Conversely, ensembles of use are at the end point of analysis in trying to understand the relationship between design and usefulness. There is nothing to be gained by analysing separately the activity, the furniture, the architectural configuration. Usefulness inheres in them as ensembles, not in their constituent elements, and no amount of shaking them will make the use fall out on its own.

8   There is a difficulty with the argument. My case is that there is a certain combination of architecture, furniture and so on, and that it not only responds to a certain use but also helps to make it possible, since the use could not be conceived in isolation from some kind of physical setting. How then do we deal with the case of someone who uses a building in a way that doesn't conform to that ensemble? It would be foolish to suggest that certain arrangements of architecture, furniture, equipment necessarily force people to act in a certain way. A school hall or a dining room can be used for purposes other than those central ones intended by the architect and building owner. There may be innumerable possible ensembles of use which can take advantage of a given physical arrangement of architecture and furniture.

It is true that there is a question of precedence. The unorthodox use of a building is only possible because an owner and architect have developed an intention to provide for a certain ensemble of use in the first place. They decide not only the physical arrangement but they are also the source of authority for the use-ensemble which will take place. We could then call that the central case, recognising that it is not the only possibility and that other kinds of uses, unexpected and unwanted, can cluster around it. For example, a school hall might temporarily be used as a polling station. This poses no problems for the building owner, and we could say that it is merely parasitic on the original intended ensemble. On the other hand, a student who walks straight into the headteacher's room has devised their own ensemble of use, transgressing the central case in which children are only invited into staff areas. But these uses are, on the face of it, straightforward instances of putting a building to a certain kind of use. They therefore involve exactly the conceptual separation of use and physical setting that I have argued against at such length.

The underlying issue has been pursued by Bernard Tschumi in several essays.[19] He suggests that uses other than the central case should be taken as the paradigm for the relation between usefulness and design in architecture. On his account, my treatment of the central case is both cosy and oppressive. It is not simply that he re-casts the hierarchy which links the uses that owners intend and those that are unapproved. He suggests that there are three sorts of uses: possible ones intended by the owner, possible ones not intended by the owner, and impossible ones. The latter two kinds exist as a challenge and a reproach to the owner's intended uses. Tschumi's point is part of a broader project of re-defining the relationships between authority, order and pleasure in architecture – another aspect of which I noted in the discussion of order and architectural meaning.

But what can be meant by impossible uses? The idea rests on Tschumi's overall view of how uses arise in buildings. He suggests that sequences of events and sequences of spaces can be considered as operating on separate but overlaid levels. Each level has its own pattern and rhythm. Uses are defined by selecting any point where a moment of activity overlays a particular spatial arrangement. Uses are fundamentally the result of a combinatory process: some will be impossible but interesting, some will be possible and out of these some will gain approval as central cases sanctioned by the building owner. Uses in total are outside the scope of human intention and purpose: they are the sum of all the possible points of overlay between the two levels.

The argument assumes a world of structured events, which continue along their way unchanged by the spaces with which they intersect;

and a world of ordered spaces which are unchanged by the events that take place in them. This is the basis of Tschumi's exploration of the nature of use in architecture. However, as I have tried to show, it is difficult to envisage this kind of abstract separation. It is hard to conceive of what a space-less world of events would mean, and what an event-less world of space would mean. Space and events are founded in each other, and uses arise when space, activity and equipment mutually constitute one another, not when they merely intersect.

Perhaps we should consider the transgressive user as an owner architect *par excellence*. In practice, an ensemble of use comes out of a design process in which a physical setting is imagined. This imagined setting makes a certain pattern of use posssible. It focuses an unfocused aspiration or an unfocused desire to change or improve an existing ensemble. Architects have to imagine all this and, with the approval of the building owner, get their imagined physical setting built. The transgressive user has the good fortune to be faced with an actual building, but they in turn imagine how that physical setting can be constitutive of their own use. For them too the building will focus an aspiration or a desire and turn it into a use. The owner, in the final analysis, cannot have a use in mind in abstraction from a physical setting that will make it real; and nor can the transgressive user entertain the idea of a use except when faced with the opportunities that a real building offers.[20]

9 The point I want to stress is the difficulty of pinning down the exact relationship of the building, considered as a physical object, to questions of use and function. In some instances it is reasonable to say that the physical building does have a function, for example in modifying the local environment and keeping out intruders. But buildings which we find interesting and complex on account of their human and social content will have an additional relationship to function. This is the sense in which a school building is implicated in the function of a school. Here my suggestion is that buildings, considered as physical objects, cannot have functions, since physical objects in themselves cannot have the kinds of effects – such as educating children – that are likely to be at issue. Instead, I suggest that they contribute to the 'programmatic whole' of the building, considered as a socially operating entity. The design of the building has an interactive relationship with that whole and makes a contribution to its operation.

I also doubt whether programmatic wholes can invariably be considered as having functions. Indeed, for interesting and complex building types it is difficult to make plausible statements of purpose and function at all. Of that most complex of all building types, the dwelling, it is virtually impossible to make statements that will not be merely circular: a dwelling is the kind of thing that a dwelling is. In these cases we may have to be content with a programmatic account. A dwelling is what a dwelling does, or is what it makes possible.[21] Then statements of a building's function, such as 'this is an office block' or 'this is a school', become descriptive rather than teleological in character. They tell us the kind of thing that the building is, not what its function is.

Since buildings, as physical objects, do not respond to functions, it is unreasonable to ask what its function is and expect that the answer will point in the direction of a physical configuration. It may point towards a programmatic whole or there may be no answer at all. Now we can draw a conclusion, which is that functional-seeming statements are unlikely to help us in devising a design which is appropriate to a certain kind of usefulness. So, if someone wished to re-cast Kant's theory by suggesting that aesthetic finality can be found in the relation of function to design, this would be a doomed endeavour. If they persisted with the project they would probably be forced back to the kind of position that Kant took up, in which the concept of use is simply a descriptive, identifying phrase for a familiar object.

10   My argument has implications for how we think about the success of buildings in providing for usefulness. If a use can be defined separately from the design of a building, we can talk about success or satisfaction in terms of question and answer or problem and solution. But, as we have seen, it is difficult to put the matter into that format. It would involve a formula along the lines that 'aspects of y building are a good solution to x problem'. In practice, however, y and x are likely

to be the same terms: a given auditorium building may be a good solution to the auditorium problem. So nothing is gained by putting the question in this problem–solution format: it simply amounts to saying that a building has a good auditorium.

It appears that the issue is not whether an aspect of the design is a good solution to a particular use problem, but simply whether this is a good design, from the point of view of usefulness. More elaborate ways of talking, in terms of problem and solution or question and answer, are likely to resolve into that simpler question. This more economical way of putting it also has the benefit of emphasising the qualitative aspects of a design. For example, it could give a sharper focus to critiques of functionalism. These are often expressed in an abstract manner, countering the suggestion that 'form follows function' with the argument that numerous forms can follow a given function, and that a given form can follow various functions. In this spirit, Aldo Rossi argued that there have been enough forms in architectural history already, and that a limited stock of inherited simple forms can continue to accommodate varieties of present-day uses.[22]

This is true if we take a sufficiently abstract view both of functions – strictly speaking, 'identifiers' of building types rather than functions – and of forms, considered perhaps as outline containers. But at a smaller scale these generalisations about function and form will evaporate and we will be left with questions like 'is this a good housing scheme?', or 'is this a good theatre?' We can take the thought in another direction: rather than accepting the general truth of Rossi's observation that the large, simple formal structures of the Palace of Diocletian at Split, for example, can be recycled to make a series of present-day urban spaces, we could ask what specific changes and adaptations had to be made in order to make the structures good for present-day use. Or we could consider the vast architectural and constructional effort that is involved in converting Bankside Power Station – a simple and flexible volume – into the Tate Gallery of Modern Art (fig. 103).

Suggesting that discussions of use should be re-cast from form–function, problem–solution or question–answer into the form 'is this a good x?' does not mean that systematic discussions are impossible.

There are innumerable ways of discussing whether an ensemble is good or not, from the point of view of usefulness, and these can involve public discussion as well as individual intuitive judgements. They can also involve measurement and comparison, not so as to quantify goodness itself but to sharpen analysis of the characteristics of the ensembles that are liked and disliked.[23] The point is quite uncontroversial, and indeed the overall shape of my argument is close to the consensus position that has been reached in recent years in studies of 'design methods'.

According to this view, what the architect does is produce designs which can then be the subject of evaluation and improvement, either in an imaginative 'dialogue' with the drawings, or else in discussions with clients, users, colleagues and others. It entails a shift away from the idea that there is a straightforward logic connecting problems and solutions, and instead embraces a good deal of discussion about the perplexing character of the logic that is involved. It recognises the plurality of ways in which designs can be produced, prior to evaluation and testing. There is a move away from the abstract logic of design, towards an ethnographic approach which recognises the importance of the social and professional context in which architects work. This in turn connects with an interest in design as a practical skill rather than a systematic procedure.[24]

An architect designing with usefulness in mind designs an object which has features relevant to certain kinds of usefulness. He or she may imagine such an object in detail, but it is not at all clear to us how an appropriate object is arrived at. In most cases, architects adjust and modify their first attempt at a design in order to improve its usefulness. At one extreme, an architect might produce a sculptural object and gradually adjust it to make it more useful. For example, Ledoux designed a collective house for the coopers who would work in the ideal city of Chaux, made it resemble the hoops and circles of a barrel, and then squeezed into it an arrangement of useful spaces – living quarters, bedrooms and workshops (fig. 104). At the other extreme, the initial design may need only the merest tinkering to make it appropriately useful.

103 Early stages of construction (1998) at Bankside Power Station, London, for its conversion into the Tate Gallery of Modern Art, to the designs of Herzog and de Meuron.

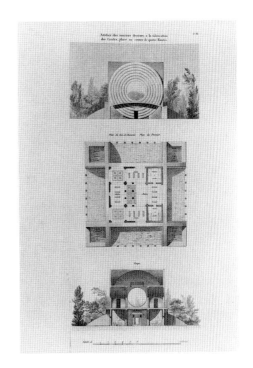

104 Design for a house for coopers at the ideal city of Chaux, designed by C.-N. Ledoux, from *L'Architecture considérée sous le rapport de l'art, des moeurs et de la législation* (1804).

By contrast, the arguments of this chapter rule out the possibility of a design process in which the architect states certain kinds of purposes and then works according to some logical procedure in order to make an appropriate design. The point is striking because we are accustomed to the idea that it is just that logical progression from use to design that is characteristic of modern architecture. It seems to expose a contradiction very near to the surface of modernism: that it claims to operate with a logical progression from purpose to design but, if the arguments of this chapter are on the right lines, such a claim would be a delusion, would involve a quite mistaken understanding of the real relations of design and usefulness.

I do not believe that modernism, as a general rule, did operate on the assumption that there can be a simple logical progression from stating purposes or uses to deriving a design. In the next chapter I shall begin by sketching out the ideas on which modern architects did base their view of the relationship between usefulness and designs. These developed over a long period, forming a 'sustaining outlook' which enabled architects to avoid that stark, logical difficulty. In its place they were able to make an underlying perplexity manageable and fruitful. But the perplexity still remained at the core of modernism's 'sustaining outlook'. Put in the broadest terms, I shall ask how it is possible to arrive at projects which have that interdependence of usefulness and design, if not by a logical process. The examples that I shall cite add nothing to the standard accounts of the development of modernism. However, my interest is in employing them to further our understanding of the possible ways in which usefulness can become thematic to architecture, thematic to the art of architecture perhaps, and so I intend to move through a historical sketch towards an ahistorical outline of that conceptual issue.

Chapter 8

Usefulness, Life and Art

I   I now wish to discuss a quite different way of thinking about the relationship between usefulness and design from the schematic analysis that dominated the previous chapter. It is, in the main, the outlook that lies behind the main stream of thinking in modern architecture. We can usefully take the writings of modernists such as Walter Gropius and Louis Kahn to indicate the overall shape of the ideas in question, but I believe it is also important to show how they developed out of attitudes that were current at the begining of the nineteenth century. We lack a term for this developing complex of ideas and in the absence of any other I have simply described it as the 'sustaining outlook' of modern architecture. The historical bearings are important but I shall also turn to the question of whether the sustaining outlook can still stand scrutiny today: considered ahistorically, can it contribute to our understanding of the relationship between usefulness and aesthetics in architecture?

By comparison with Kant's notion of the relationship between usefulness and aesthetics, the sustaining outlook is immeasurably more ambitious. Kant focused on the relation between categories of building types and the detailed aesthetic ideas that fleshed them out, and that relation was essentially between a concise statement and its representation in visual form. The sustaining outlook, by contrast, wishes to find aesthetic significance in the relationship between the design of the building and the actual human demands, needs and wants out of which it arose.

It rejects on two grounds the idea that architects should elaborate and develop designs which had been handed down by tradition. The first is that in those cases where such forms did exist, the tradition was considered to be exhausted and incapable of further development. The second is that new kinds of practical tasks had arisen for which there was, as yet, no tradition-sanctioned generic form. Both of these kinds of arguments lead to the notion that new types of forms have to be devised, ones which would adequately express, in some deep and non-trivial way, the usefulness that is entailed in them.

There is an obvious challenge here to the argument that I sketched in the previous chapter. The sustaining outlook suggests that usefulness and design have to be separated in order that they can subsequently be reconciled, but it was just this possibility that I was at pains to reject, for the reason that usefulness and design are interdependent. What makes the challenge important is that it engages a quite different style of argument from the one that I employed, arising from a parallel world of debate about the relationship between usefulness and design. The latter kind of argument can begin by accepting that usefulness and design are interdependent. Then the task is not to make something that fits a given kind of usefulness that is understood and defined from outside, but to find just the design which has the required sort of inter-dependency. That shift of emphasis from making to finding is of great importance. What might it entail? One possibility is to assume that usefulness does operate in some sense as a force, as a mode of influence on designs, but that this force cannot be discerned from the outside. It could be argued that biological systems work like that: viewed from the outside they have an integration of form and function that cannot be prised apart.

The next thought is that if it were possible in some manner to get inside the life of the organism its constituent forces might become discernible. In fact, this is one of the most notable features of the sus-

taining outlook of modernism. It raises the question of how an architect can immerse himself or herself in the inner life of a design, to
which the answer comes – and here the outlook begins to seem daring
and bizarre by turns – that they should do so by looking into themselves. Put a little more circumspectly, analysis and study from outside
will be a part of the process of design, but unless at some stage the
architect looks inwards that connection with the lives of designs will
not be made. The daring in the argument, the move that makes it possible, is the notion that the inner imaginative life of the designer is
moulded by the same forces that mould the forms of objects. The connection between the designer and the object that is being designed
goes beyond a cognitive relationship: it is not just a question of
knowing what a design is to be but in some sense being joined with
it, with the architect's introspection making this bridge between subjectivity and the nature of the object.

One of the typical moves within the sustaining outlook is to answer
questions of the kind 'what should a railway station, or a school, or an
office block, be like?' by throwing them back rhetorically. Thus, a
railway station should be like a railway station, a school like a school,
an office block like an office block. This is a reminder that the outlook
does not provide recipes for design or a design method in the sense
of practical step-by-step procedures that could make the link between
problem and solution. It is an approach, a mentality, a way of thinking, that is at issue. Now, it would be possible to place these sorts of
formulations – famously expressed by Pugin when he said that a
railway station should look like a railway station – within the style of
argument that I developed in the previous chapter. We would say that
Pugin is playing on two meanings of the term railway station. One of
these refers to the physical configuration of the building, the other
refers to the programmatic whole, summed up in that descriptive term
(as we have seen, only loosely a 'function') 'railway station'. So, if successfully designed, a railway station as physical building will look just
as a railway station as programmatic whole should. But whereas the
schematic kind of logic of the previous chapter gives us no help in
understanding the inner logic that connects those two parts of the

proposition, it is the purpose of modernism's sustaining outlook to give just that assistance.

Let us turn to the writings of Walter Gropius in order to illustrate some of these points. He states that the spirit of the epoch can be discerned, but that the forms appropriate to it have yet to be clearly defined. Modern architecture is growing up from the roots but (he makes the point in 1954 as well as in the 1920s) it has not developed into a style. So Gropius advises patience, just as many nineteenth-century commentators advised patience. We need to let modern architecture grow, and the style will develop as it grows. In the first instance the spirit of an epoch manifests itself in ideas. Architects have a crucial role in giving these abstractions visible expression. Gropius's view is that learning the history of architecture is irrelevant to this task, since it can only result in old forms of expression being repeated. Instead, architects need to learn competence in 'the language of vision' – those means of visual communication which are of general trans-historical value and which may therefore be used for the expression of new realities.[1]

At the centre of Gropius's outlook is the aspiration to overcome the split between the self and the material world. Art can resolve the conflict between the two sides by creating a new form of unity. This does not involve a compromise, or a reconciliation between the two: on the contrary, an achieved unity will signify the success of the spirit's struggle against the material world. This idea is linked with a conception of the relationship between the organic and artificial worlds. A modern building should be true to itself, an affirmation of the contemporary world, an instance of an organic architecture 'whose inner logic will be clear and naked.' It is necessary to search for the appropriate design-type, but Gropius states that its form may be surprising and unexpected when we find it.

Architects and designers can in turn endow artefacts with souls. Gropius's point here is that the creative force of the designer is fused with the object, so that it lives on, embodied in the artefact's outward form. The content of that creative force is the architect's crystallisation of the client's needs. The architect makes those needs explicit, turns them into a coherent expression, and they in turn become the life of the building. A design for an artefact or a building may be merely an exercise in ingenuity: to create a work of art requires individual talent. Gropius repeatedly talks of the need for the 'creative spark' to endow objects with life. The spark comes from the individual, complementing the collaborative work which is necessary in the technical sphere. The process by which organic form arises in nature is the model for human creativity.

Gropius's interests changed and developed over a long career, but this sketch of his views would hold good for the period before the First World War when he was involved in debates in the Deutscher Werkbund, for the inter-war period and for his career in the United States in the 1940s and 1950s. In the case of Louis Kahn, we can piece together a coherent and very engaging viewpoint from his lectures and interviews from the 1960s up to his death in 1974, remembering that a long period of professional and political activity had already preceded this burst of public activity.[2] In his later career Kahn repeatedly grappled with the question of how the animate and the inanimate worlds can be connected. Lying in the background is the idea that the essence of life, considered at the most abstract level, is continuous and unchanging. Hence the repeated formula 'What was has always been. What is has always been. What will be has always been.' His conceptions of art and of architecture are similar in structure, so that typically there is a difference between the essence and the human realisation. Living is the exercise of life; a work of art is an offering to art; and works of architecture are offerings to the spirit of architecture.

All living things have consciousness to varying degrees. Goethe is referred to in this connection. However, humans not only participate in life but can also make it: making a work of art is making a life, and making a building is making a life. To achieve this the architect must, as Kahn puts it, 'instill consciousness into the wall of the building.' This connects to the anthropomorphism which is so delightful and so easy to parody. The architect must find out what the wall wants to be, must see what the concrete wants to be, can listen to the brickwork asking to be an arch, can listen to the stainless steel – 'a thin, little man with a high voice'.

These animated materials are what Kahn calls 'the orders of construction'. They have their own natures and the architect must respect
them. The idea is more highly developed in his account of how architects should design for usefulness. He rejects the idea that the nature
of a building can be derived from the programme that the client provides. In most cases, he advises, the programme will have to be
changed. The architect's approach to the task is necessarily introspective and involves a search for the essential character of the building
type, of its species. It is, as he puts it, a search for the nature of 'School',
not 'a school'. Both thought and feeling are necessary in this introspective process. The feeling side implies something more than the distinction between thought and emotion, since Kahn links it to 'the
essence religion', with the sense that some form of spirituality is vital.
It is the merging of thought and feeling that can bring the architect
into contact with what a thing wants to be: what Kahn calls 'Psyche'.
The style of introspection that he suggests thus makes a bridge between
the individual and the essence that lies behind objects. This is the
beginning of Form, but only at a highly abstract level of the sense of
order, the distinctiveness of one thing vis-a-vis others, 'the inseparable
parts of something'. Form is not shape, or design. Those are the particular realisations that architects make of the abstract Form.

Kahn's treatment of the relation between finding the general truth
about a building and devising its particular design is of great interest.
He stresses that the realisation of Form does not belong to any one
individual. Just as oxygen does not belong to the discoverer of oxygen,
as he puts it, so nobody possesses the order of brickwork, nor the
nature of 'school' nor of 'the apartment' and so on. These things are
discovered. However, the specific way that something is designed is
essentially individual, an individual expression. Groups or committees
cannot design buildings. A design reveals the individual and the individual self is the starting point for the task of designing. That self, that
individuality, may itself have been discovered in the earlier search for
the general truth of the building.

Kahn has a useful formula here, which is to point out that he does
not talk about 'my architecture' – since no one can own such a thing

– but about 'my expression'. Expression, we should then note, is not a subsidiary kind of activity to that earlier introspective search. Kahn states repeatedly that to live is to express, the reason for living is to express, to express is the soul of the soul and so on. The distinctive way that humans participate in life is through expression. Hence also art is the language of humans, their distinctive way of communicating. Expression is still inextricably tied to that search for what is essential. This is because the essential Form has to have specific shape, design: in itself it is abstract, impersonal, though we can only get access to it by personal search. Thus it is the desire to individuate the essence that is the distinctively human expressive activity. In fulfilling this desire architects endow buildings with life.

One curious coincidence is worth noting. When Kant wished to illustrate the point that aesthetic ideas can body out a concept he noted the following example: 'Perhaps there has never been a more sublime utterance, or a thought more sublimely expressed, than the well-known inscription upon the Temple of *Isis* (Mother *Nature*): "I am all that is, and that was, and that shall be, and no mortal hath raised the veil from before my face".'[3] The example recalls Kahn's 'What was has always been . . .' and reminds us of the continuities that run from the opening of the Romantic period to the architectural world of the 1960s.

In Gropius's writings the client's needs are seen as the content of the architect's creative force, and this in turn endows the building with life. A client's needs do not in themselves offer answers to questions of design but rather provide the material for a process which is brought into life by a 'creative spark'. These metaphors help to negotiate the ambiguous character of the design process as both making and searching. Kahn, however, takes the notion of the building's inner life in a more radical sense. A building partakes in life, it is given its own individual life by the architect. The Form is found by introspection, via the essence religion, and it is only at a less abstract level of realisation that it is given shape by the architect.

Gropius and Kahn provide alternative versions of the sustaining outlook of modernism, but they do not differ at a strategic level. A number of ideas and attitudes flow together to create the outlook. In the following section I aim to show how each of these ideas, considered independently, has been discussed in detail in histories of modern architecture. My suggestion is that we should also consider how they join together into a whole and how, in particular, they inform background ideas about usefulness and aesthetics.

2   Be yourself, never imitate, be of your time. Search for the right design. Designs belong to their own world, as well to the human world, and have their own laws of development. Style too inheres in the world of designs: it cannot be made but only discovered. To trust oneself, one's individuality, will lead not to a merely private expression but towards the character of the moment itself, since the self is a product of that moment. So to be yourself is also to realise the external moment. Find the moment, and the design will be partly found.

Some of these attitudes are prefigured in Goethe's *On German Architecture* of 1772.[4] The essay praises the Gothic of Strasbourg Cathedral, the product of the soul of the German people at a moment in its history. But the building itself is not an anonymous product. One of Goethe's objectives is to re-assert the identity of the architect, Erwin of Steinbach, and to show that his individual genius was precisely to exemplify the collective spirit at a moment in history. The outlook began to gather force in the 1830s. Hugh Honour points out that in the 1830s the phrase *il faut etre de son temps* (one must be of one's time) was current in French artistic circles. He reports one writer who urged that the slogan *Soyons Français, soyons de notre epoque* be inscribed on the facade of the Académie.[5]

David Van Zanten has described the ideas and outlooks that influenced young architects in Paris in the 1830s, among them the notion that architectural forms develop out of the forces that drive a society. He quotes the writer Jean Reynaud in making the link with biological forms: 'One may, in a profound sense, compare human monuments to those shells formed by animals who give them the shape of their bodies and live in them: the method of the naturalist makes no distinction between the description of the shell and that of the mollusc.'[6] His contemporary, Hippolyte Fortoul, concluded that because the proper style of the period develops out of circumstance, it cannot be predicted, only discovered. Accordingly, the generation of 1830 explored the nature of the moment, not the essence of Classicism, as was expected of them. The young Labrouste irritated the establishment of the Ecole des Beaux-Arts by drawing reconstructions of ancient buildings full of the objects and graffiti of daily life; Félix Duban did so by designing an austere Protestant church at a moment when it was said that 'Romanticism is Protestantism in the arts'; Léon Vaudoyer, trying to educate his crusty architect father, pointed out that 'Lord Byron, and not Biron, was never an admiral, but a very distinguished poet and defender of the liberty of the Greeks'.[7] The liberal and Romantic students of the 1830s duly became key figures in architectural teaching. By 1847 a design brief at the Ecole des Beaux-Arts could specify that submissions should 'leave no doubt as to the epoch in which the new structure was built'.

Romantic individualism and an interest in the biological character of architectural forms were also conjoined in the United States. In the 1840s the American sculptor Horatio Greenough elaborated the analogy between nature and architecture. The forms of animals, and their beauty, derive from their adaptation to function: 'The law of adaptation is the fundamental law of nature in all structure.' A Lamarckian view of evolution is suggested, one which allows adaptations to circumstance to be transmitted, and which thus embraces human artefacts as well as natural forms. Thus, 'the struggling and cumbersome machine becomes the compact, effective and beautiful engine.'[8] Architects must do as nature does and devise a structure for the building based on its essential functional requirements. The building's 'dress' will remain to be designed, but an organic understanding will take the architect far into the details of the design.

Leopold Eidlitz, who arrived in the United States in the 1840s from Prague (and helped to found the American Institute of Architects in 1857), remarked that 'a work of art, like a work of nature, is a realized idea, and the ideal is the essence of architecture. It is the godlike attempt to create a new organism, which, because it is new, cannot be an imitation of any work of nature, and, because it is an organism, must be developed according to the methods of nature.'[9]

One distinctive view of the connection between architecture and biology can be traced back to Goethe's theory of the *urpflanze*, the type-plant from which all others derived.[10] Harry Francis Mallgrave suggests that Goethe's views influenced Semper's formulations of the relation between architecture and nature, via the intermediary of the physician and writer Carl Gustav Carus.[11] Quatremère de Quincy opposed the idea that architecture had a single type-origin in 'the primitive hut', and stressed that different architectural forms grew out of distinctive material and geographical cultures. As Sylvia Lavin has noted, he employed biological metaphors: each mature style of architecture developed out of 'foetal' structures or seeds of elementary building forms.[12] This brings to mind an aspect of teaching in the Ecole des Beaux-Arts under Quatremère's direction. Candidates for the Prix de Rome had to produce a sketch scheme in a gruelling 24-hour preliminary session. Those considered suitable would then be chosen to work up the scheme in more detail over a period of four months. The Ecole kept the original sketches, only allowing the students to make an outline copy. The point was to prevent the students from deviating from the principal elements of the sketch and finally to judge their skill in elaborating that original idea: in eliciting what was already contained within that design seed.[13]

In Chapter Four I pointed out the importance that Quatremère attached to the elementary features that were repeated in an architectural style, so that if one fragment were discovered it would indicate the whole style to which it belonged. The notion has strong affinities with the view of animal structures that was developed by Georges Cuvier. David Van Zanten suggests that Cuvier's ideas would have been influential in the circles of the radical young architects of the 1830s, and Philip Steadman discusses the effect of the doctrine on Viollet-le-Duc's writing on Gothic architecture in the 1850s, and then notes the wider spread of the idea, for example to Leopold Eidlitz and Montgomery Schuyler in the United States. Here, for example, is his quotation from Schuyler, writing in 1894:

This character of the organisms of nature is shared by at least one of the organisms of art. A person sufficiently skilled in the laws of organic structure can reconstruct, from the cross-section of the pier of a Gothic cathedral, the whole structural system of which it is the nucleus and prefigurement. The design of such a building seems to me to be worthy, if any work of man is worthy, to be called a work of creative art. It is imitation not of the forms of nature but of the processes of nature.[14]

The idea that works of architecture are, or should be, distinctive products of their time, was congruent with the re-thinking of the age of the natural world that gathered force early in the nineteenth century. The tradition of evolutionary theory initiated by J. B. de Lamarck created a supportive background for ideas about the evolution of type-forms in architecture and design. Lamarck held that creatures adapted to changes in their environment by the more frequent or sustained use of particular organs; this in turn led to the enlargement and development of those organs and the change was duly transmitted to later generations.[15] The idea of the progressive development of type-forms of artefacts, in a Lamarckian fashion, is central to Le Corbusier's polemics in the 1920s and a possible intermediate stage of influence, Philip Steadman has suggested, came in the writings of Samuel Butler, who pressed the case for a Lamarckian view of evolution of artefacts.[16]

The term 'biology' – the science of life – which was coined by Lamarck around 1800, signals the shift away from an outlook in which the key distinction between humans and the rest of the world was that they possessed souls. Edward de Zurko has pointed out that the former view created an interchangeability of attitudes to animals and machines. In the outlook that derived from Descartes, a clock could be described as an organism, and an animal as a machine.[17] Neither possessed souls but both had organic complexity and unity. The science of biology, on the other hand, makes the crucial distinction between living and non-living things. Humans, animals and plants now stand on one side of a divide, human artefacts on the other. On the face of it, this should have consigned architecture to the world of artefacts, and severed the organic analogy.

Then another gap opened within biology, between 'vitalism' and 'mechanism', dividing the idea that there is a sustaining spirit and purpose behind the natural world from the view that it can be understood using the non-teleological methods of physics and chemistry. It is important to note that this controversy continued actively in scientific circles until the 1920s.[18] Its significance for our purposes lies in the fact that the anti-mechanist viewpoint straddled both biology and the arts.[19] Architecture could be brought across the divide and into the living world, but it required a powerful notion of the spirit within nature, one that could see that spirit extending across nature into human action.

Hence also the attraction of Schopenhauer's philosophy, for example for Louis Sullivan. His interest was less in Schopenhauer's theory of aesthetics and its implications for architecture and more in the continuity that was suggested between the operation of the will in the world as a whole and its operation through the functional forces in the design of buildings.[20] Sullivan attended the Ecole des Beaux-Arts briefly in 1874–75 and was taught in the tradition established by the Romantic generation of 1830. The French influence contributed to his conviction of the biological character of architecture. Building types are responses to types of functions. Just as in nature the form of an animal or plant expresses its inner life, so in architecture designs grow out of functions. The architect needs to understand the inner functional forces in a building type, because this will unlock the possibilities of expression that lie within it. The idea sustaining the argument is that 'problems contain their own solutions'. So, having posed the problem of the functional determinants of the building, the architect can then understand, at higher and higher levels of detail, the form of expression that is implied. The architect must begin by searching within the problem, but this in turn will free his or her individuality. The self, and its unique expressiveness, will be liberated rather than confined by submission to the laws which organically determine form.

In a later period, Theosophy entered the background of ideas about the continuity of life across its usual boundaries.[21] Wassily Kandinsky and Theo van Doesburg, both influential teachers who taught at, or were associated with the Bauhaus, were sympathetic to the move-ment.[22] These interests did not necessarily entail commitment to an esoteric or 'expressionist' style. For example, J. A. Brinkman and L. C. Van der Vlugt – exemplary modernists in the clear and elegant style of the 1920s – were participants in the Dutch Theosophical movement.[23]

In the nineteenth century the idea that architectural forms should bear an organic relationship to the functions of buildings, and to the moment in which they are designed, was commonplace. It also led to the expectation that such forms should be part of a coherent stylistic expression, but it was precisely a coherent style that was felt to be lacking. This created ingenious solutions and heartfelt anxiety in equal measure.[24] As interesting as the proposed styles, and their intricate justifications, were the voices that pointed out the sheer difficulty of trying to bring a style into existence, and the foolishness of trying to do so against its will. Robert Kerr, in the *Newleafe Discourses* of 1846,[25] portrayed both the Gothic and the Greek styles as being no longer viable options for the present day, and urged their replacement by a new style; but he could not as yet specify what such a style would be like.

These kinds of anxieties have been discussed many times and are central to accounts of the development of modernism in architecture. Peter Collins takes the example of J. P. Seddon, who in 1850 urged architects to pay no attention to style, but leave all classifications to posterity.[26] Nikolaus Pevsner pointed out the interesting transitional case of Beresford Hope who advocated a style – Gothic 'Middle Pointed' – as the appropriate one for the time in 1865, but who never-theless thought that it would gradually develop into something new and more deeply organic to its time. Similarly William Burges, also an enthusiast for the Gothic style, could detect no distinctive architecture of his time, and doubted whether it would arise before the twentieth century.[27] This line of thought put a particular responsibility on the young architect. Peter Collins refers to an article in *The Builder* in 1848, expressing the hope that the younger generation of architects would produce the germs of a new style. It was left to Robert Kerr to defend the youthful professionals against the expectation that they could solve all their elders' problems: he pointed out that it may be his children's generation who would eventually find the proper style for the age.[28]

The idea becomes a truism, especially after its elaboration in the Arts and Crafts movement. Then we can find it expressed by Herman Muthesius, in a lecture of 1907 that paved the way for the founding of the Deutscher Werkbund:

> Styles do not grow up overnight and cannot be invented to order. They can only be the fruit of periods of serious striving, when inner forces are made explicit. If the new trends are genuine, then an original lasting style will emerge, and if they are superficial and vain they will ultimately lead to something resembling the fickle imitations of the last fifty years. . . . Nor can style be anticipated; it can only grow up as the all-embracing expression of the spirit of the age. It is up to the next generation to sort out what exactly our style was, that is to say to detect the common ground in the most meaningful achievements of our best architects and craftsmen.[29]

W. R. Lethaby, writing in 1920, put it thus: 'To design in "a style" is to design a seeming which stands in the place of style proper.'[30] However, it was Adolf Loos who carried the argument to its conclusion, away from the architect and designer altogether, presenting them as imposters in the world of true makers. Style, he claimed, is what is produced unconsciously from a culture of production; it develops bit by bit in a process of feedback between user, maker and the techniques of production. In a gruesome metaphor Loos warns architects off trying to define what the style of the time should be like: 'No one has yet thrust his podgy hand into the spinning wheel of time without having it torn off by the spokes.'[31]

The idea then became familiar in modernism in the inter-war period. Hannes Meyer's address to the students of the Bauhaus in 1928 pointed to the dilemma faced by those who wished to be 'of their time' in a period of rapid change, where a period might not be measured in decades but in years or months. The Weimar years of the Bauhaus had been the post-war period of revolution and Expressionism and those who participated in these movements, feeling like the 'children of their time' were right to do so. But the conflict they experienced was that they 'have not been aware that a new age has begun. They should, for once, open their eyes and look around in their environment; then they would notice that conditions have changed radically. Today, as yesterday, the only correct thing is to be "children of [one's own] time".'[32]

A typical statement of the matter, around which nineteenth-century attitudes continued to reverberate, is that of J. J. P. Oud, writing in 1918: 'One thing is certain; the aesthetics of modern buildings will not be based on the buildings of the past: they will be shaped by the essential characteristics of modern society and technology, and will therefore be completely different from those of any previous period.'[33]

In place of trust in the adaptation and further development of traditional models grew the sense that the forms appropriate for the present day might not be immediately apparent, and that another kind of trust and patience was necessary to allow them to become evident. The idea that a style might develop from a process of patient search spread into the way that individual projects were conducted, as well as colouring the architect's view of the way that the whole culture was heading. By searching within their own selves architects might get closer to the spirit that animated the period; and more specifically, looking inwards would bring them closer to the inner forces that joined usefulness and designs.

3   Counter-examples can be suggested. The obvious question, given his commanding position in modern architecture, is where Le Corbusier would stand in relation to this sustaining outlook. His fierce egotism affirmed the Romantic commitment to the individual. As a young man he took to heart Renan's *Vie de Jésus* and, like countless others of his generation, took Nietzsche as a guide to his personal artistic search.[34] There is also no doubt of the pervasiveness of organic and biological references in Le Corbusier's writings and practice. This extends from the discussions of type-objects and their evolution, as I have noted, through the idea of the biological connectedness of parts

within buildings and of functions within cities, and reaches an astonishing conclusion in his unbuilt scheme for the Olivetti factory, in
which the anticipated movement of workers through the building is
exactly represented as the movement of corpuscles through the circu-
lation system of the body (figs 105 and 106). No other modern architect came near Le Corbusier in the range, audacity and literalness with
which the biological analogy was employed. His phrase 'creation is a
patient search' brought together the notion of individual creativity with
the sense that designs are already there to be explored in the world.

But how would we place Le Corbusier on another co-ordinate that
I have suggested, the integration of material and spiritual, animate and
inanimate? Here we would pause, because it is exactly the sense of
confrontation between subject and object, of artefacts standing against
nature, that is so pervasive in his work. Buildings have effects and they
may move us, but they do not aspire to become truly animate and we,
as spectators, do not aspire to become merged with them. In this
respect at least, we feel that Le Corbusier stood at a distance from the
sustaining outlook that dominated modern architecture for so long.

We can observe different combinations of attributes in other
instances. Hannes Meyer stressed that biology forms a model for the
design of artefacts and, as we have seen, he was committed to the principle that architects should respond to the nature of the moment, to
the practical tasks it sets and its larger spirit. It is also true that he
opposed the stress on the personal search, and emphasised, to the contrary, the collective nature of architectural work. Nevertheless, it would
be wrong to exaggerate the extent of Meyer's difference from the sustaining outlook of modern architecture. I am not persuaded by the
argument that figures such as Meyer form part of a coherent 'posthumanist' strain within modern architecture, with fundamentally different values from those of the sustaining outlook.[35]

This might provoke the suspicion that my 'sustaining outlook' just
yokes together three separate sorts of issues – the links between architecture and biology, the consequences of the architect's enhanced individuality, and the question of the search for the solution appropriate
for the moment. All three may be present together, but it depends on

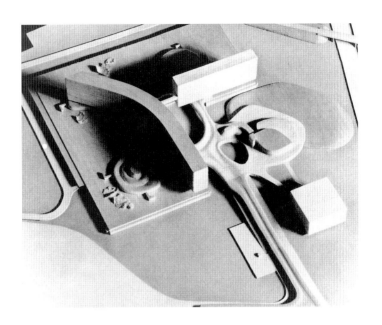

105 Model of the proposed Olivetti Research Centre, near Milan, by Le Corbusier (1962).

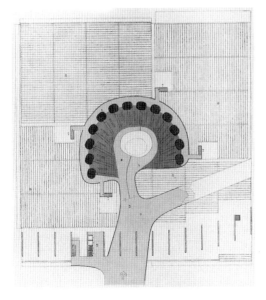

106 Olivetti Research Centre: plan of upper floor, showing the transition to the 'clean' production area below. The arrangement is modelled on the structure of the lung, where oxygen passes into the bloodstream.

the case. However, I am still impressed by the continuity and strength of the urge among architects in the nineteenth and twentieth centuries to bring these elements together into a coherent outlook. It is said that some of Kahn's old friends, who knew him as a fairly hard-headed and practical man, were surprised when he began to lecture in his distinctively philosophical way. Perhaps this was just garrulousness, a kind of sublime waffle, that came with the nervousness of speaking to large groups. I prefer to think that he was elaborating and making alive to a new generation a project that already had a long history.

4 I have tried to emphasise the contrast between the sustaining outlook that actually lay behind modern architecture and the widely held view that the modernist frame of mind was resolutely utilitarian, that architects manipulated usefulness merely on the surface of life.[36] The latter view shades into the opinion that this utilitarian attitude was responsible for the failure of modernism, on the grounds that it refused to engage with deeper human feelings and the sense of the continuity of life between humans and other objects. I hope it is clear that I can make little sense of this argument. It rests on the idea that it is the absence of art and philosophy that explains modernism's failures and it entails the comforting illusion that an immersion in matters of the spirit would necessarily bring beauty in its train. The reality is that a concern with matters of the spirit is no guarantee of aesthetic success: the failures of modernism confirm this point rather than the idea that they arose from a narrowly utilitarian outlook.

My argument exposes a complex question about the definition of functionalism. Gropius was insistent that he was not a functionalist, and by this he meant to distance himself from the ideas that went under the heading of 'objectivity'. These were associated with the pre-war Werkbund and enjoyed a revival in the 1920s, and they rested on the principle that fitness for purpose inevitably brings beauty. Gropius, as we have seen, explored instead the idea that beauty needed to be discovered in the inner life of the object. To be faithful to Gropius we should not call him a functionalist, but the difficulty is that the term has, with time, acquired a much looser meaning and in practice it provides a convenient label for that un-named but dominant stream of thinking in modern architecture which I have inelegantly termed the 'sustaining outlook' – and for which Gropius is such an eloquent spokesperson.

5   At this stage I wish to move the discussion away from its historical bearings and ask whether the sustaining outlook of modernism offers an alternative to the sceptical view of the relationship of usefulness and design with which I concluded the previous chapter. I do not believe that there is continuity between biological life and the inner lives of buildings. There is a divide between living and inanimate objects, and human artefacts are in a strict sense inanimate objects. It is true that a compelling metaphor is in play which turns an abstract point about the interdependence of usefulness and design into a living force. The attractiveness of the metaphor is that it can fill a gap in our ability to explain the design process: architects do actually produce designs which have that sense of interdependence, but we do not understand the combination of anlaytical and creative processes which makes that making or finding possible.

In fact, the metaphorical connections can gain credibility from real comparisons between designs and organisms, although the comparisons I have in mind are not quite those that are made in the sustaining outlook of modernism. I suggested in Chapter Seven that the designs of buildings need not be explained by reference to an outer purpose, but that they may be understood to have an inner programmatic unity. Similarly, we do not need to assume that biological organisms have a function by which they effect an outer purpose, in order to make sense of them as programmatic wholes. The connection between an organism and its environment can be seen as part of another larger system, an ecological niche perhaps, and the idea of biological systems can be extended in scale – systems within larger systems – so that the idea of response to purposes becomes unnecessary.

On this kind of argument, buildings and living organisms have the important similarity of being wholes by virtue of their inner relationships rather than by virtue of their response to an outer purpose. Biological systems are complex in a systematic manner, and so are buildings considered as useful objects. Biological organisms are not made in response to outer purposes but they do have inner coherence, structured relationships with other organisms and specific ecological settings. Buildings certainly have those latter features and I have also suggested that it is often difficult to state their outer purpose without merely repeating a summary of their internal organisation. In practice, we can rest the analogy there, seeing buildings as programmatic wholes within a larger social and cultural ecology. This would fit with the discussion of usefulness and design that was outlined in Chapter Seven.

It is possible to assert a distinction between the biological and the artefactual – between living and non-living objects – and yet still make use of the biological analogy. Both the sustaining outlook of modern architecture and the more schematic approach outlined in Chapter Seven may use biological analogies to illuminate the relationship between the worlds of artefacts and living objects. But there is still a very wide gap between them. The sustaining outlook of modernism uses the analogy in order to make sense of its assumption that the subjectivity of the architect, and the nature of the outer object that is being designed, are connected. The kind of argument that I employed in Chapter Seven makes no allowance for such a connection and so the issue is absent from the analogies it makes.

I doubt that more detailed discussions of the relationship between buildings and biological systems would close the gap. The biological analogy is pressed into the service of two quite distinct positions, one of which asserts the continuity of life from the artefactual to the natural and thence the human, the other asserting that life belongs to the natural world only. The first of these positions is of great importance to the sustaining outlook of modern architecture because it helps to make sense of the perplexities of the design process. It makes intuitive sense, allowing a busy professional life to continue, rather than making logical or scientific sense.

This is perplexing in itself, since it seems that a large part of the working practices of modern architecture rely on a kind of reasoning that is at a tangent to the systematic procedures of engineering and production. And yet it is precisely the pressure to produce designs, to prepare drawings for the world of production, that sustains this recourse to a Romantic conception of the flow of life between nature and artefacts. It seems that dealing with those practical problems brings with it a quite impractical, un-commonsense view of the world.

Having identified that there is such an issue lying behind the cluster of ideas in the sustaining outlook, it is useful to construe it in a different context. We could put to further use the ideas about expression that were discussed in Chapter Six. In the sustaining outlook it could be said that two processes of expression are going on side by side. The architect is expressing himself or herself in that creative process of making and discovery: as we have seen, the sustaining outlook emphasises that this is essential not just for the architect's private satisfaction but because it also assists in finding the design. In a second parallel process, however, the design is expressing itself. This is the idea that Louis Kahn returns to again and again – a building wants to be a certain way, the appropriate design is a consequence of it expressing its inner character and so on – but, as we have seen, its roots can be traced back to the early nineteenth century.

Note also the idea, common in modern architecture, that when the design of a building emerges it may be unexpected and strange. There is a similarity here with the treatment of expression in Collingwood's theory. It is characteristic of artistic activity that the artist does not know what the work of art will be until it is made: he or she begins with an unfocused impulse and makes that coherent. The work of art is both the consequence of an expressive process and the means by which its underlying impulse is made explicit. The point helps us to locate a negative aspect of the sustaining outlook, namely its tendency towards a certain grandiosity and over-simplicity. This comes with the desire to find an idea in which the whole inner nature of a building will be compressed so that, as in Louis Kahn's case, a school is the expression of School, or an assembly building is the expression of

Assembly. Roger Scruton has written persuasively on this question, arguing that expressive effect comes from the accumulation of parts and their answering one to another, and is unlikely to come from putting a single idea into physical form.[37]

We can relate these applications of the theory of expression to Chapter Seven's schematic view of the relationship between usefulness and design. They offer another way of thinking about the intimacy of the connection between the building as a physical object and as a pro-grammatic whole. The architect has a descriptive term for the build-ing that he or she is to design, a functional-sounding term but really just a label, as I explained. In the design process this is analogous to the artist's unfocused impulse. Then the architect has to engage skill, intuition and expressive energy in order to design an object that will correspond with the label. Note, in passing, the sense that searching is involved here as much as making, which captures the feeling of sub-mergence in an intuitive process, followed by a recognition that the basis of a design has been found. The product defines and makes con-crete the unfocused impulse, and the architect gains this prize from the obscurity of the design process.

6   Ideas about expression may help us to flesh out the detailed impli-cations of the sustaining outlook of modernism. However, I now want to explore an opposing viewpoint, one that has grown in importance since the 1960s. It focuses on the proposition that because usefulness is not logically compelled to be thematic, it cannot be truly thematic to architecture as an art. This is a very cursory way of putting the argu-ment and it will take some time to unpack its implications. In what follows I will use Peter Eisenman's work as a guide, rather as I used Gropius and Kahn to illustrate the sustaining outlook of modernism.

Underlying this outlook is the issue that I have already sketched out, namely that there can be no logical, step-by-step connection between the statement of the purpose of a building and its design. Implicit in the sustaining outlook of modernism is a recognition that, since every-day logic cannot do the job then another kind of deep connection will need to be achieved between thematic material and architectural expression. Usefulness, which can be construed in the most elevated sense, as in Kahn's writings, can be what architecture is about, and therefore it becomes a central aesthetic issue. The opposing viewpoint asserts that, since there can be no logical step-by-step connection, there can be no basis for usefulness being aesthetically thematic. The absence of a logical connection is a reason to remove usefulness from that central position in the aesthetics of architecture. The absence of a connection was the cause of an anxiety which the sustaining outlook of modernism in turn sought to assuage. But now the anxiety of that search for depth in the relation between usefulness and design can be allowed to melt away, leaving a sense of freedom and lightness in design, an opening up of possibilities.

On the face of it, the idea of an un-profound, lighter and less anxious connection between usefulness and design – an idea that is central to post-modern thinking – seems at odds with the importance that I gave in Chapter Seven to their interdependence. The point about that interdependence is that functions of buildings cannot be specified separately from the way that they are configured as objects. A useful building has a certain configuration and it is the one that is appropriate to a certain function. It will offer itself up in a particular way, making itself useful to a greater or lesser degree in its own distinctive way. Architects design such objects, with varying skill in predicting what the outcome of their use will be. Beyond that point, I have suggested, theorising comes to an end.

Focusing on the idea that usefulness is offered by the object helps us to grasp the full force of that interdependence, and enables us to correct the mistaken view that the object is a servant of a pre-determined use. Then the contemporary theorist may reasonably say that a building could be designed from numerous starting points, with symbolic, representational or iconographic matters uppermost; then it could be assessed for usefulness; then it could be modified and tuned as necessary. That process of adaptation could be considered of limited aesthetic significance, and the final conclusion could be that usefulness need not be thematic or central to the design process. All this would

be congruent with the argument I made in Chapter Seven, a quite
valid way of developing it.

The perplexity that underlies the sustaining outlook of modernism
– which proceeds from the direction of usefulness and asks how it is
that designs can have a profound relationship to it – now seems to
arise from a position freely taken. If we choose we can work the issue
the other way: going from an object in the direction of its usefulness.

Let us examine how Peter Eisenman developed these kinds of ideas.
A good way to begin is to note his comments on a celebrated paper
by Sir John Summerson, given in 1957, entitled 'The Case for a Theory
of "Modern" Architecture'. The paper became a boundary marker for
the view of modernism that I have already described, so it is under-
standable that Eisenman should have taken it as a starting point for his
own critical discussion of the topic in the early 1970s. The passage in
Summerson's article that Eisenman responds to is as follows:

> The source of unity in modern architecture is in the social sphere,
> in other words in the architect's programme. . . . Whether you
> accept this statement as a basic principle and a specifically modern
> principle depends on a number of things. Mainly, there is the ques-
> tion, what a 'programme' is. A programme is a description of the
> spatial dimensions, spatial relationships and other physical conditions
> required for the convenient performance of specific functions . . .[38]

This is the key passage in Eisenman's response:

> There is often an attempt made to rationalize architecture in terms
> of its program. In a paper given at the RIBA in 1957, Sir John
> Summerson represented this position quite explicitly when he
> attempted to make a case for a theory of architecture with such a
> programmatic basis. In essence, Summerson said the source of unity
> in modern architecture is in the social sphere, in other words in the
> architect's program. But it would seem that the situation is more
> complicated than Summerson allowed. For if the program is to
> sustain such an emphasis it should be able to specify and distinguish
> what the facts of a particular situation are, and except for certain

physical laws, facts in a programmatic sense are really a series of value judgements. Much of the oeuvre of modern architectural theory is involved in a basic dilemma precisely because it has refused to distinguish between problems of fact and problems of value. And, more specifically, because it has refused to recognize problems of form as predicated by anything except ideas of social and technological change or as a matter for stylistic and aesthetic speculation.[39]

Eisenman is seeking some solid foundation on which the strategy for a building's design can be erected. He wants facts against which the values incorporated in a design can be juxtaposed and argues that Summerson's suggestion offers no such certainty. Someone might quibble with this and say that the client's value judgements become facts so far as the architect is concerned, in the sense that the demanding client will brook no discussion of or change to those requirements. However, I believe that Eisenman's meaning is clear: the content of a programme is comprised not of facts but of value judgements. In isolation the point is a correct and useful one, but in its context it is curious for two reasons. The first is that Summerson may well have agreed that the content of a programme comprises value judgements rather than facts. It is clear that the 'dimensions', 'spatial relationships', 'physical conditions' that he refers to are ways of specifying the wants and desires of a client. Those wants themselves are social *par excellence*, and for Eisenman to point out that they are not like facts of nature is to elaborate Summerson's point, not to criticise it.

Secondly, and more importantly, our curiosity is alerted by the suggestion that something can only be thematic to architecture if it is factual. Eisenman stresses that usefulness has no solid, factual claim to be thematic to architecture. Looking back, it is a strange argument, implying that architectural expression has a thirst for natural laws as its content, rather than the contingencies of human life. In fact, the idea was linked with Eisenman's engagement with structuralism and the search for 'deep structures' of architectural organisation which would have law-like validity. Individual works of architecture were to be thought of as expressing those laws rather than the practicalities of human life.

According to Eisenman, making usefulness thematic – and this is what Summerson's view of the 'programme' amounted to – pushes the architect into a dilemma. If there is no solid starting point there can be no logical progression towards an architectural expression. To achieve the sense that usefulness is truly thematic architects have to pretend that it is more factual than it really is. The next step in the argument is the idea that, since usefulness is not thematic for some solidly grounded logical reason, it is therefore wrong to make it thematic at all.

Eisenman has described how his views gradually changed in the process of carrying out the sequence of formal investigations provoked by a structuralist view of architectural form. His interests became more critical and dialectical, focusing on the artistic responsibilities of the architect rather than the search for formal structures. A key idea was that the artist's central role is to 'dislocate' the assumptions (the 'metaphysic') on which the current cultural consensus is based. He gave a number of historical examples such as Palladio, who 'dislocated the existing metaphysic by applying a classical idea to a vernacular building, literally creating the villa type.'[40] Perhaps the argument is heavy-handed here: a new kind of design becomes a metaphysical challenge. Its weightiness was more appropriate when he came to discuss modernism in architecture.

Another kind of dilemma faced architects in the nineteenth and twentieth centuries: during this period, Eisenman held, architecture's existing 'metaphysic' was that it should serve the needs of industrial society and the improvement of the conditions of everyday life. However, if they were to follow the logic of their role as artists, architects should have aimed to dislocate exactly this kind of consensus. Their failure to do so meant that they were not truly modernists, in an artistic sense, at all. Eisenman's provocative suggestion was that modernism as it occurred in architecture was, and is, quite false. Its apparent stylistic radicalism masks a deep compliance with the ruling cultural ethos. The model for modernism proper would be James Joyce, on the grounds that he challenged the inner 'metaphysic' of literature, rather than say William Morris or Hannes Meyer (the examples are mine), who wished to distribute the fruits of architecture differently, but who accepted the presumption that the basis of architecture as an art lay in its usefulness.

The argument then takes a further step. The architect's responsibility is to challenge the ruling metaphysic of architecture wherever it occurs. In Eisenman's case this involved projects designed to be positively difficult to use, which would force users to behave in unexpected ways. Even so, he warned against supposing that this would lead eventually to understanding the true origins and basis of architecture. In the end architecture has no origins, no compelling logic. He pointed to Vitruvius as the most powerful originary figure in architecture. Vitruvius's claims to setting a basis for architecture have to be challenged, but once that is done nothing can be put in its place. At this juncture the post-structuralist view of language comes into the picture, with its assertion that terms in language refer to other terms, then to other terms, and so on, with little hope that there is an end-point of meaning where language refers to something entirely outside itself.

In a number of design projects of great brilliance, Eisenman explored the implications of challenging the basic ideas of architectural procedure, namely scale, place and time, and the consequences of treating them not as fixed referents but as meanings that are open to ranges of further interpretation.[41] Jeffrey Kipnis, in introducing some of this work, alludes to its playfulness: 'What is being proposed is an expansion beyond the limitations presented by the classical world to the realisation of architecture as an independent discourse free from external values; that is, the intersection of the meaningful, the arbitrary and the timeless in the artificial.'[42] It is serious play, of course, just as the assertion of the architect's artistic role in defiance of social demands is one of high seriousness.

I believe that this corrosive scepticism about architecture's thematic basis – usefulness included – actually rests on a very firmly held view of architecture's status among the fine arts. To be truly an artist, Eisenman tells us, the architect must question everything. But that questioning does not extend to the critical role to which architecture lays claim: that is the rock on which the artist stands. A thread runs through all the brilliance and complexity of the writings and projects: that there is an origin after all, and it is the assumption that architecture belongs to the system of the fine arts.

This assumption leads us towards a broader debate about the position of architecture among the arts. I have suggested that the notion of a system of the fine arts, in its eighteenth-century form, was double-sided. There was an overall assumption about what the arts had in common, but each individual art had to have its own distinctive reason for admission. The *Encyclopédie* held that architecture was the particular art of imitation that imitated the way in which nature itself hangs together; for Kant, the distinctiveness lay in architecture's usefulness. Eisenman's argument poses a different proposition, which is that architecture is an art but there is no distinguishing feature, no special origin, that makes it this art, the art that it is. Architecture is not an art of anything: it is, so to speak, an art in general but not an art in particular.

The argument raises the stakes for the significance of aesthetics in architecture. Eisenman has rejected the idea that architects should subordinate their work and their ideas to social values; the architect has nowhere else to stand but on that eminence of fine art. The claim brings a sense of vertigo. Our anxiety is that architecture, lacking particularity, might slide into critical debate and then, gathering speed, disappear altogether into philosophy. We might begin to suspect that what keeps an art back from the brink is the sense that it does have a particular kind of thematic material, or mode of expression, or physical material. It is only by being a particular art that it can claim to be art at all, and can avoid that slide into philosophy.

7   The question I raised at the beginning of Chapter Seven was whether architecture's distinctiveness as an art comes from the fact that it is involved in the making of useful objects. There is some similarity with the opening chapter of the book. There the suggestion was that architecture took a distinctive place among the arts because it is an art of design; here the suggestion is that it has a distinctive place by virtue of being useful. So far, the conclusions of these enquiries are not encouraging. There is no doubt that usefulness is essential to architecture; the difficult question is whether it is central to it as an art and earns it a distinctive place among the other arts.

The term 'central' is helpfully vague, but it indicates that we should at least be looking for connections between usefulness and aesthetics. One way of making a connection is to say that usefulness is what architecture is about, with the assumption in the background that this kind of relationship is important. Saying what something is about asserts something fundamental about it. An application of this idea can be found in Kant's treatment of architecture in his discussion of the division of the fine arts. It turned out to be unsatisfactory, mainly because it seemed to take a rather summary view of usefulness, treating it as a categorising or pigeonholing exercise. It did not seem to approach usefulness itself, but surveyed it from a distance. This led us to enquire quite what usefulness might mean and we were faced with the situation that something eminently practical, part of everyday life, was surprisingly difficult to pin down conceptually. Indeed, this led me to employ another helpfully vague term – 'usefulness' – as a means of pointing to those complex issues.

I discussed the question of the interdependence of designs and usefulness at some length. I argued that it is implausible to construe usefulness as something separate from designs, and misleading to suggest that designs are solutions to problems that usefulness sets up. As Sullivan noted, problem and solution are intertwined. So in one sense it is impossible for architecture to be 'about' usefulness, if aboutness were thought to mean that one thing, usefulness, fits into another, which is the design. This would be a simple relation of content and form, with the form holding or enclosing the content. The difficulty raised by the interdependency of designs and usefulness is that the 'form' already contains the 'content', in fact is constituted by it.

Then I asked what happens if we accept this interconnectedness, this joining, of usefulness and design. How could aesthetic significance be discerned in this relationship? I suggested that it was just this problem that underlay the sustaining outlook of modernism in architecture. We can easily forget its vaulting ambition: it held that usefulness can become aesthetic when an architect has an introspective connection with the inner forces that join usefulness and design. Then the architect can become one with that inseparable whole, and make it aesthetically significant. I suggested that it is possible to see the usefulness of the outlook as a means of structuring difficult design tasks, and that its marshalling of biological arguments was particularly helpful. But in truth, the products of the outlook were often over-simple in their effect, as if the problem of Kant's approach had re-surfaced and we were again dealing with representations of quite abstract ideas.

So I came to Peter Eisenman, as a representative of theorising that has taken place after the decline of the modernist outlook. He has put a quite different construction on the interdependence of designs, stressing the social, historical, cultural and political contingency of those relations. At one stage, this led him to make the criticism that an art based on these contingent, changeable connections will lack compelling force. Later, the criticism was made in a stronger form, namely that architects actually have a responsibility to subvert and criticise just those sort of connections. The argument led him to the conclusion that there could be no thematic material that would have the required strength: all kinds of thematic material could be contested and argued against. And so we reached the dizzying cliff edge that architecture is an art in general but not in particular.

In fact, Eisenman's argument forces us to confront an important issue. If architecture is to have usefulness at its centre, and if it is to be definitive of it as an art, then it will be because we make it so, not because it is necessarily so. We shall have to take a position on those contingent issues of social purpose within which usefulness is placed. We shall have to commit ourselves to judgements, based in a time, a place, a society, of what is useful, and we shall have to make commitments to practical values such as ease and comfort where vague usefulness comes down to earth. There can only ever be usefulness in particular: usefulness in general helps us to organise our ideas but not spaces, walls, furniture, corridors, stairs. If we then make a connection between usefulness and aesthetics, it will be significant because we want it to be so, because we have chosen it to be so.

There must be a human project underlying this type of interest in and commitment to the practical details of buildings. Towards the end of his discussion of functionalism Theodor Adorno pointed to one such possibility. He suggested that functionalism can engage with the project of humanising a world that bourgeois society has separated off and exploits for its own purposes. Admittedly, this is intertwined with pessimism, but there can be a hope that 'The useful object would be the highest achievement, an anthropomorphised "thing", the reconciliation with objects which are no longer closed off from humanity and which no longer suffer humiliation at the hands of men.'[43]

This is a stirring idea, that underlying a commitment to usefulness is a project to deliver human beings from oppression by objects alien to them, and conversely, as Adorno says, to allow '"things" to come into their own'. Physical objects do offer usefulness to us, as I have tried to explain, and so this project of reconciliation could be central to the aesthetics of architecture. Yet in another sense usefulness does not reside in objects themselves but in those ensembles where human activity, buildings and furniture are joined. The project that is entailed is therefore of much greater conceptual subtlety than Adorno's suggestion of the relationship between humans and outer objects allows. And I confess that I cannot add anything more that would help to illuminate that subtlety.

That is the place for breaking off. Building specifications often use the phrase 'making good', meaning that something rough is smoothed off, cracks are filled, jagged edges covered. It would be satisfying if this ragged ending could be made good. Return for a moment to that problematic idea that the relationship of an art and its thematic material is one of content and form, and the associated tendency to think that form contains, holds or wraps a certain content. Consider another possibility, that what we expect of the arts is that they transform their content and do not merely package it. Paintings and dramas present us with objects and events which have been touched and transformed by the artist so that we are made aware of them with a new intensity.

If we decide that usefulness is to be thematic to architecture as an art we may embark on such a transformative project. It would be wise to work on a more modest scale than modernism's attempts at 'expressive totalities', which have their roots in the Beaux-Arts notion that a building in its totality should be contained within an original seed or *parti*. But how would the analogy with the other arts work and how would art transform usefulness? The previous discussions do not help us here, since they have been centred on that containing relationship between form and content, rather than on the sense of a transformative activity. Architecture would be part of a larger project that includes the other arts, but what it would transform in particular would be usefulness. To put it very abstractly, we would expect some intensification of the ensemble of use, so that it became more redolent of use itself. I do not know how the point can be elaborated conceptually: it becomes real in the practice of architecture.

What is certain is that in transforming usefulness, architects transform practical life, and thus aesthetics and everyday life come into contact. This is a cause for great anxiety: at its worst, imposing an aestheticised life on others can be a kind of oppression. The temptation is to avoid this danger by placing the question of architecture's relationship to usefulness into the framework of ethics rather than aesthetics. I doubt if re-naming the problem would make it go away, since detailed issues of design would merely shift from one category to another. Indeed, it seems strange to suggest that aesthetics should give way to ethics simply because everyday life is involved – as if the other arts were not also intent on showing us how life might be transformed. An overlap seems inevitable: the architect who takes usefulness as thematic to architecture takes on ethical responsibilities, as I have noted, but the detailed way these are discharged is likely to be elaborated within the context of an aesthetic outlook.

I do not believe that usefulness in architecture stands at a boundary where aesthetics ends and ethics takes over. In fact, it is the binding together of usefulness and aesthetics that prevents architecture from sliding into philosophy, by giving it a foothold in daily life. The interest and usefulness of aesthetic discussion continue past this boundary. Many senses of the term 'making good', with its commingling of what is right and what is good to look at, remain to be explored.

Notes

Chapter One

1 Patricia Lee Rubin, *Giorgio Vasari: Art and History*, New Haven and London (Yale University Press), 1995, pp. 241–42 and 212–14.

2 See Richard A. Goldthwaite, *The Building of Renaissance Florence: An Economic and Social History*, Baltimore and London (John Hopkins University Press), 1980, ch. 7, pp. 351–96.

3 *Ibid.*

4 Leon Battista Alberti, *On the Art of Building in Ten Books* (*c.*1450), trans. Joseph Rykwert, Neil Leach and Robert Tavernor, Cambridge, Mass. (MIT Press), 1988, p. 3.

5 Catherine Wilkinson, 'The New Professonalism in the Renaissance', in *The Architect: Chapters in the History of the Profession*, ed. Spiro Kostof, Oxford (Oxford University Press), 1977, p. 130.

6 Howard Burns in collaboration with Lynda Fairbairn and Bruce Boucher, *Andrea Palladio 1508–1580: The Portico and the Farmyard* (exh. cat.), London (Arts Council of Great Britain), 1975, p. 259.

7 Wilkinson, 'The New Professionalism in the Renaissance', pp. 132–33.

8 Leopold D. Ettlinger, 'The Emergence of the Italian Architect during the Fifteenth Century', in *The Architect*, ed. Kostof, p. 104.

9 James S. Ackerman, 'Architectural Practice in the Italian Renaissance', in *Renaissance Art*, ed. Creighton Gilbert, New York (Harper and Row), 1970, pp. 170–71.

10 Ettlinger, 'The Emergence of the Italian Architect during the Fifteenth Century', in *The Architect*, ed. Kostof, p. 111.

11 *Ibid.*, pp. 113–17.

12 *Ibid.*, pp. 114–15.

13 See Frances A. Yates, *Theatre of the World*, London (Routledge and Kegan Paul), 1969, and Eileen Harris, *British Architectural Books and Writers 1556–1785* (Cambridge University Press), 1990.

14 On the changing relationship between 'polite' and vernacular architecture see R. W. Brunskill, *Illustrated Handbook of Vernacular Architecture*, London (Faber and Faber), 1970, and Colin Platt, *The Great Rebuildings of Tudor and Stuart England*, London (University College London Press), 1994.

15 See Alison Kelly, *Mrs. Coade's Stone*, Upton-upon-Severn, Worcestershire (Self-Publishing Association), 1990.

16 See Adrian Forty, *Objects of Desire: Design and Society 1750–1980*, London (Thames and Hudson), 1986, ch. 2.

17 W. L. Goodman, *British Plane Makers from 1700*, London (G. Bell and Sons), 1968.

18 On the Adams's innovations in decoration see Geoffrey Beard, *Craftsmen and Interior Decoration in England 1660–1820*, Edinburgh (Bartholomew), 1981, and *Decorative Plasterwork in Britain*, London (Phaidon), 1975; Eileen Harris, *The Furniture of Robert Adam*, London (Alec Tiranti), 1963; Damie Stillman, *The Decorative Work of Robert Adam*, London (Alec Tiranti), 1966.

19 On the drawings of Robert Adam and the drawing practices of the Adam office see A. A. Tait, *Robert Adam: Drawings and Imagination* (Cambridge University Press), 1993, and *Robert Adam: The Creative Mind: From the Sketch to the Finished Drawing*, London (The Soane Gallery), 1996; Alistair Rowan, *Robert Adam: Catalogue of Architectural Drawings in the Victoria and Albert Museum*, London (Victoria and Albert Museum), 1988, and 'The Adam Brothers and Contemporary Office Practice,' in Giles Worsley, ed., *Adam in Context: Papers Given at the Georgian Group Symposium*, London (The Georgian Group), 1992.

20 George Richardson, Architect, *A Book of Ceilings, composed in the style of the Antique Grotesque*, London, 1776.

21 Richard Wollheim, *Art and its Objects*, 2nd edition (Cambridge University Press), 1980, p. 78.

22 See Paul Oskar Kristeller, 'The Modern System of the Arts', in *Renaissance Thought II: Papers on Humanism and the Arts*, New York (Harper Torchbook), 1965, p. 202; Jean Le Rond d'Alembert, *Discours Préliminaire de l'Encyclopedie*, Paris (Editions Gonthier), 1965.

23 In present-day speech we can talk about the art of motorcycle maintenance,

and in doing so we would be nodding towards an older and more inclusive use of the word art, but we cannot say, without being eccentric, that motorcycle maintenance is one of the arts. We negotiate these two kinds of uses in daily life without any difficulty.

24 The view can be found in Peter Collins, *Changing Ideals in Modern Architecture 1750–1950*, London (Faber and Faber), 1965; Henry-Russell Hitchcock, *Architecture: Nineteenth and Twentieth Centuries*, 3rd edition, Harmondsworth (Penguin), 1969; Kenneth Frampton, *Modern Architecture: A Critical History*, 3rd edition, London and New York (Thames and Hudson), 1992.

25 Kevin Harrington, *Changing Ideas on Architecture in the Encylopedie, 1750–1776*, Ann Arbor, Michigan (UMI Research Press), 1985, ch. 1, 'Launching the *Encylopedie*', pp. 1–40.

26 Kristeller, 'The Modern System of the Arts', p. 202.

27 D'Alembert, *Discours Préliminaire*, pp. 49–50.

28 David Watkin, *Sir John Soane: Enlightenment Thought and the Royal Academy Lectures* (Cambridge University Press), 1996, p. 118.

29 A. W. N. Pugin, *Contrasts* (1836), with an introduction by H. R. Hitchcock, Leicester (Leicester University Press), 1969, frontispiece.

30 Pugin, *An Apology for the Revival of Christian Architecture in England* (1843), reprinted Oxford (St Barnabas Press), 1969, pp. 14–15, n. 10.

Chapter Two

1 For an outline of the issues involved see William J. Mitchell and Malcom McCullough, *Digital Design Media*, 2nd edition, New York (Van Nostrand Reinhold), 1995, ch. 9, 'Lines in Space'. See also Robin Evans, 'Architectural Projection', in Eve Blau and Edward Kaufman (eds), *Architecture and its Image: Four Centuries of Architectural Representation*, Montreal (Canadian Centre for Architecture), 1989, pp. 19–35.

2 For the historical importance of sectional elevations see Wolfgang Lotz, *Studies in Italian Renaissance Architecture*, Cambridge, Mass. (MIT Press), 1977, ch. 1, pp. 1–65. 'The Rendering of the Interior in Architectural Drawings of the Renaissance'.

3 In Chapter Five I discuss the question of pictorial seeing in more detail.

4 On the question of the interaction between drawing and imagining in the process of design see Edward Robbins, *Why Architects Draw*, Cambridge, Mass. (MIT Press), 1994; 'Alvin Boyarsky interviews Zaha Hadid', in Zaha Hadid, *Planetary Architecture Two*, London (Architectural Association), 1983, p. 2.

5 I use the term 'builder' in what follows as shorthand for the enterprise that

carries out building work. It is unlikely to be a single person and the tasks that I describe as the builder's are usually carried out by various individuals within a large enterprise.

6   Nelson Goodman, *Languages of Art: An Approach to the Theory of Symbols*, 2nd edition, Indianapolis (Hackett Publishing), 1976, pp. 218–21, gives more emphasis than I to the dimensional information that drawings contain. This is an omission in my account but the priority that Goodman gives to it leads him to the conclusion – incorrect in my view – that an architectural plan 'counts as a digital diagram and as a score', rather than a picture-type representation.

7   Peter Blundell-Jones, *Hans Scharoun*, London (Phaidon), 1995, p. 187.

8   For a further discussion of the issues involved see Richard Wollheim, 'Are the Criteria of Identity for Works of Art Aesthetically Relevant?' in his *Art and Its Objects*, 2nd edition (Cambridge University Press), 1980, pp. 167–76.

9   *Ibid.*, pp. 74–91.

10 Antonio Gramsci, *Selections from Cultural Writings*, ed. David Forgacs and Geoffrey Nowell-Smith, London (Lawrence and Wishart), 1985, p. 131.

11 See Brenda Vale, *Prefabs: A History of the UK Temporary Housing Programme*, London (Spon), 1995.

12 See Raglan Squire, *Portrait of an Architect*, Gerrards Cross (Colin Smythe), 1984, p. 100.

13 See Andrew Saint, *Towards a Social Architecture*, New Haven and London (Yale University Press), 1987.

14 Walter Segal (1907–1985), the son of the painter Arthur Segal, was brought up in artistic communities in Switzerland and Berlin. He studied architecture in Berlin and moved to London in 1937. His approach to one-man practice crystallised in the 1950s and his involvement in self-build housing developed in the late 1960s. See John McKean, *Learning from Segal: Walter Segal's Life, Work and Influence*, Basel (Birkhauser Verlag), 1989.

15 *Ibid.*, p. 96.

16 On the performance analogy see Jonathan Miller, *Subsequent Performances*, London (Faber and Faber), 1986.

17 David E. Brownlee and David G. DeLong, *Louis I. Kahn: In the Realm of Architecture*, New York (Rizzoli International Publications), 1991, p. 418.

18 See Anthony Blunt, *Philibert de L'Orme*, London (Zwemmer), 1958, pp. 134–35.

19 See Janne Ahlin, *Sigurd Lewerentz, Architect*, Cambridge, Mass. (MIT Press), 1987, pp. 165–74. For further material on Lewerentz, see also Claes Dymling (ed.), *Architect Sigurd Lewerentz*, Stockholm (Byggforlaget), 1997; *Mega X:*

Sigurd Lewerentz, 1885–1975, The Dilemma of Classicism, London (Architectural Association), 1989.

20 Colin St John Wilson, *Architectural Reflections: Studies in Philosophy and Practice of Architecture*, London (Butterworth Architecture), 1992, p. 126. For the suggestion that Carlo Scarpa's work also has analogies with painting, see Rafael Moneo, 'Representation and the Eye', in Francesco Dal Co and Giuseppe Mazzariol, *Carlo Scarpa: The Complete Works*, London (The Architectural Press), 1986, p. 236.

Chapter Three

1 Reprinted in George Berkeley, 'An Essay towards a New Theory of Vision', in *Philosophical Works*, introduction and notes by M. R. Ayers, London (Everyman), 1992, pp. 3–59.

2 For discussion of the context and later consequences of Berkeley's theory see Michael J. Morgan, *Molyneux's Question: Vision, Touch and the Philosophy of Perception* (Cambridge University Press), 1977.

3 Quoted in Nicholas Pastore, *Selective History of Visual Perception: 1650–1950*, New York (Oxford University Press), 1971, p. 71.

4 Lisa Heschong, *Thermal Delight in Architecture*, Cambridge, Mass. (MIT Press), 1979, p. 24.

5 Steen Eiler Rasmussen, *Experiencing Architecture*, Cambridge, Mass. (MIT Press), 1959, pp. 17–18. A further development of Rasmussen's type of argument can be found in Iain Borden, 'Body Architecture: Skateboarding and the Creation of Super-Architectural Space', in Jonathan Hill (ed.), *Occupying Architecture: Between the Architect and the User*, London (Routledge), 1998, pp. 195–216.

6 August Schmarsow, 'The Essence of Architectural Creation', in Harry Francis Mallgrave and Eleftherios Ikonomou (eds), *Empathy, Form and Space: Problems in German Aesthetics 1873–1893*, Santa Monica (Getty Center for the History of Art and the Humanities), 1994, p. 286. Another source of the idea, especially for readers of English, was the work of Bernard Berenson: see *The Italian Painters of the Renaissance*, rev. edition, Oxford (Clarendon Press), 1930, p. 62, for his statement of the space–kinaesthesia argument, as the basis for 'tactile values' in painting. For the context of Berenson's outlook see Ernest Samuels, *Bernard Berenson: The Making of a Connoisseur*, Cambridge, Mass. (Belknap Press), 1979; Meryle Secrest, *Being Bernard Berenson: A Biography*, London (Wiedenfeld and Nicolson), 1980. Berenson's influence overlaps with that of Geoffrey Scott and Vernon Lee: see ch. 4 below.

7 Heinrich Wölfflin, *Principles of Art History: The Problem of the Development of Style in Later Art* (1915), trans. M. D. Hottinger, New York (Dover Publications), 1950, p. 21.

8 Robert Vischer, 'On the Optical Sense of Form: A Contribution to Aesthetics,' reprinted in Mallgrave and Ikonomou, *Empathy, Form and Space*, p. 94.

9 *Ibid.*, 'Introduction', p. 36.

10 See Michael Podro, *The Critical Historians of Art*, New Haven and London (Yale University Press), 1982; Wilhelm Worringer, *Abstraction and Empathy: A Contribution to the Psychology of Style*, trans. Michael Bullock (1908), London (Routledge and Kegan Paul), 1953.

11 Sigfried Giedion, *Space, Time and Architecture: The Growth of a New Tradition* (1941), London (Oxford University Press), 1949; *The Eternal Present: The Beginnings of Architecture*, London (Oxford University Press), 1964; *Architecture and the Phenomena of Transition: The Three Space Conceptions in Architecture*, Cambridge, Mass. (Harvard University Press), 1971. See also Sokratis Georgiadis, *Sigfried Giedion: An Intellectual Biography* (Edinburgh University Press), 1993.

12 Giedion, *Space, Time and Architecture*, p. 440.

13 See Peter Collins, *Changing Ideals in Modern Architecture*, London (Faber and Faber), 1965, ch. 24, 'New Concepts of Space', pp. 285–93; Roger Scruton, *The Aesthetics of Architecture*, London (Methuen), 1979, pp. 51–52; Spiro Kostof, 'Architecture, You and Him – The Mark of Sigfried Giedion', *Daedalus* (no. 105), 1, 1976, pp. 189–204; Linda Dalrymple Henderson, *The Fourth Dimension and Non-Euclidean Geometry in Modern Art* (Princeton University Press), 1983, p. 337.

14 *Space, Time and Architecture*, Giedion, p. 425.

15 Le Corbusier used the phrase 'promenade architecturale' in relation to this aspect of the Villa Savoie. See Le Corbusier and Pierre Jeanneret, *The Complete Architectural Works, Vol. II, 1929–34*, ed. W. Boesiger, London (Thames and Hudson), 1964, p. 24.

16 Bruno Zevi, *Architecture as Space*, New York (Horizon Press), 1957, p. 158. Georgiadis, *Sigfried Giedion*, p. 85, quotes an article written by Schmarsow in 1914 in which he counterposed the principle of permanence in religious architecture with 'the living principle of *movement* in housing'. Housing, he points out, must be given both practical and theoretical priority over religious and monumental buildings. Here we can observe social, ethical and aesthetic principles converging on the idea that movement is paramount in architecture.

17 For an introduction to the neurophysiology see Semir Zeki, *A Vision of the Brain*, Oxford (Blackwell Scientific), 1993; for a general account of the psy-

chology of vision see Margaret W. Matlin and Hugh J. Foley, *Sensation and Perception*, 3rd edition, Boston (Allyn and Bacon), 1992, pp. 47–243.

18 See Annette Karmiloff-Smith, *Beyond Modularity: A Developmental Perspective on Cognitive Science*, Cambridge, Mass. (MIT Press), 1992, esp. ch. 3, 'The Child as a Physicist', pp. 65–89.

19 See Colin McGinn, *The Character of Mind* (Oxford University Press) (1982), 2nd edition, 1996, ch. 1, 'Mental Phenomena', pp. 1–16, and ch. 3, 'Acquaintance with Things', pp. 49–72.

20 See Matlin and Foley, *Sensation and Perception*, ch. 11, 'Motion', pp. 339–65.

21 Peter Blundell-Jones, *Hans Scharoun*, London (Phaidon), 1995, p. 183.

22 See Matlin and Foley, *Sensation and Perception*, pp. 172–73. For a discussion of parallax in architecture, see Peter Collins, *Changing Ideals in Modern Architecture 1750–1950*, London (Faber and Faber), 1965, pp. 26–28 and ch. 24, 'New Concepts of Space', pp. 285–93. Collins attributes to parallax the characteristics of architectural seeing that Giedion refers to in his discussion of 'space-time'.

23 See Matlin and Foley, *ibid.*

24 Note however that computer simulations of the interiors of buildings that are based on connecting a set of two-dimensional images, such as Quick Time VR, will not show parallax effects. Simulations derived from CAD systems will do so, but are likely to provide realistic renderings only for a chosen route. I am grateful to Kim Foo-Jones for help on this topic.

25 See McGinn, *Character of Mind*, p. 41 for a discussion of the part–whole relation in perception.

26 On the significance of rapid-eye movements see Matlin and Foley, pp. 116–19.

27 See Anthony Kenny, *The Metaphysics of Mind* (Oxford University Press), 1992, ch. 7, 'Sensation and Observation', pp. 97–112.

28 See Matlin and Foley, p. 370.

29 Newgate Prison was demolished, but in the Museum of London there is a reconstruction of part of the rusticated facade. The effect is rather odd, because although looking like stone it is actually fibreglass and has a certain tacky smoothness rather than stony roughness. The hand is deceived a second time.

30 *Ibid.* pp. 395–97.

31 Quoted from Goethe's *Baukunst* in Rudolf Arnheim, *The Dynamics of Architectural Form*, Berkeley and Los Angeles (University of California Press), 1977, p. 152. Reference to Goethe's text can also be found in Heinrich Wölfflin, 'Prolegomena to a Psychology of Architecture', reprinted in Mallgrave and Ikonomou, *Empathy, Form and Space*, p. 155.

32 For discussion of the general concept of the 'haptic system' see J. J. Gibson,

The Senses Considered as Perceptual Systems, London (George Allen and Unwin), 1968, ch. 6, 'The Haptic System and its Components', pp. 97–115. Gibson's use of the term 'haptic' covers both touch and kinaesthetic perception and argues strongly for their systematic connection. For the application of his approach to architecture see Kent C. Bloomer and Charles W. Moore, with a contribution by Robert J. Yudell, *Body, Memory, and Architecture*, New Haven and London (Yale University Press), 1977.

33 See David Summers, *The Judgment of Sense: Renaissance Naturalism and the Rise of Aesthetics* (Cambridge University Press), 1987, esp. pp. 311–35.

34 Kenneth Frampton, *Studies in Tectonic Culture: The Poetics of Construction in Nineteenth and Twentieth Century Architecture*, ed. John Cava, Cambridge, Mass. (MIT Press), 1995, p. 12.

35 For a philosophical and practical discussion of the loss of sight see Bryan Magee and Martin Milligan, *On Blindness* (Oxford University Press), 1995.

Chapter Four

1 Edmund Burke, *A Philosophical Enquiry into the Origin of our Ideas of the Sublime and Beautiful* (1757), ed. James T. Boulton, Oxford (Basil Blackwell), 1958.

2 I confess that I have borrowed the term 'feelingful' from S. J. Petock 'Expression in Art: The Feelingful Side of Aesthetic Experience', *Journal of Aesthetics and Art Criticism* vol. 30, no. 3 (Spring 1972), pp. 297–309. Petock's article is relevant to the discussion of expression in Ch. 6 below.

3 Heinrich Wölfflin, 'Prolegomena to a Psychology of Architecture' (1886), in Harry Francis Mallgrave and Eleftherios Ikonomou (eds), *Empathy, Form and Space: Problems in German Aesthetics 1873–1893*, Santa Monica (Getty Center for the History of Art and the Humanities), 1994, p. 169.

4 Geoffrey Scott, *The Architecture of Humanism* (1924), rev. edition, Foreword by David Watkin, London (Architectural Press), 1980, p. 213. Scott provides an alternative route into the connected issues of 'space' and 'empathy' to that charted in Mallgrave and Ikonomou's anthology. Scott was influenced by Bernard Berenson's notion of 'tactile values' in painting (see ch. 3, n. 6) and by the writings of Vernon Lee, for which see Vernon Lee and C. Anstruther-Thomson, *Beauty and Ugliness and Other Studies in Psychological Aesthetics*, London and New York (John Lane), 1912; Vernon Lee, *The Beautiful: An Introduction to Psychological Aesthetics*, Cambridge (Cambridge Manuals of Science and Literature), 1913; Peter Gunn, *Vernon Lee: Violet Paget 1856–1935*, London (Oxford University Press), 1964.

5 See Mallgrave and Ikonomou, *Empathy, Form and Space*, pp. 39–56.

6   See Henri F. Ellenburger, *The Discovery of the Unconscious: The History and Evolution of Dynamic Psychiatry*, London (Allen Lane, Penguin), 1970.

7   See Robert Vischer, 'On the Optical Sense of Form: A Contribution to Aesthetics', in Mallgrave and Ikonomou, *ibid.*, and their Introduction, pp. 17–29; see Ellenburger, *ibid.*, p. 493 for the relationship of Freud, Volkelt and Scherner.

8   Vischer, *ibid.*, p. 100.

9   Sigmund Freud, *Introductory Lectures on Psycho-Analysis* trans. Joan Riviere, 2nd edition (1929), London (George Allen and Unwin), p. 16.

10 *Ibid.*, p. 17.

11 I do not know whether Scott had read Freud. But Theodor Lipps, who was Vernon Lee's point of reference among empathy theorists, was involved in early discussions of psychoanalysis. See Sigmund Freud, *The Interpretation of Dreams* (1900), trans. James Strachey, Harmondsworth (Penguin Books), 1976, pp. 771–73 and 775.

12 Adrian Stokes makes the link between psychoanalysis and architecture on many occasions but see, for example, *Smooth and Rough*, London (Faber and Faber), 1951; 'The Impact of Architecture', *British Journal of Aesthetics*, vol. 1, 1960–61, pp. 240–53; *The Invitation in Art*, London (Tavistock Publications), 1965. Peter Fuller discusses the idea of 'aesthetic emotions' in the context of other psychoanalytic approaches, in 'Abstraction and "The Potential Space"', in *Art and Psychoanalysis*, London (Writers and Readers Publishing Cooperative), 1980, pp. 177–238. Freud's interest in the specific feeling of 'the uncanny' is discussed in relation to architecture in Anthony Vidler, *The Architectural Uncanny: Essays in the Modern Unhomely*, Cambridge, Mass. (MIT Press), 1992.

13 Richard Wollheim (ed.), *The Image in Form: Selected Writings of Adrian Stokes*, Harmondsworth (Penguin), 1972, p. 11, 'if Stokes's early work can be read much as though it belonged to the tradition of nineteenth century aestheticism, it is to be observed that, throughout, there is a place reserved for psychoanalytic theory, at which it can be introduced when the moment is right.'

14 See David Watkin, *Sir John Soane: Enlightenment Thought and the Royal Academy Lectures* (Cambridge University Press), 1996, p. 59. Watkin also points out, p. 214, Soane's interest in Le Camus de Mézières's remarks on lighting effects.

15 Scott, *Architecture of Humanism*, pp. 237–38.

16 Colin St John Wilson, *Architectural Reflections: Studies in the Philosophy and Practice of Architecture*, London (Butterworth Architecture), 1992, ch. 1, 'The Natural Imagination', pp. 2–19.

17 Adrian Stokes, *Venice: An Aspect of Art*, London (Faber and Faber), 1945.

18 Roger Scruton, *The Aesthetics of Architecture*, London (Methuen), 1979, p. 89. The argument is to be found in ch. 4, 'Experiencing Architecture', pp. 71–103.

19 Robert Venturi, *Complexity and Contradiction in Architecture*, New York (Museum of Modern Art), 1966.

20 Nicolas Le Camus de Mézières, *The Genius of Architecture; Or, The Analogy of that Art with our Sensations* (1780), introduction by Robin Middleton, Santa Monica (Getty Center for the History of Arts and the Humanities), 1992, p. 96.

21 For a recent discussion of the topic, see David Chipperfield, *Theoretical Practice*, London (Artemis), 1994.

22 For more extended thinking of this kind see Adrian Stokes, *Stones of Rimini*, London (Faber and Faber), 1934, ch. 2, 'The Pleasures of Limestone', pp. 27–58. A more recent example can be found in Peter Zumthor, 'Thermal Baths Vals', in *Three Concepts* (exh. cat.), Berlin (Birkhauser), 1997.

23 Adrian Stokes, *Smooth and Rough*, London (Faber and Faber), 1951, p. 56.

24 See David Summers, *The Judgment of Sense: Renaissance Naturalism and the Rise of Aesthetics* (Cambridge University Press), 1990, which puts the idea of the supremacy of touch underlying perception into a historical perspective.

25 Anthony Kenny, *The Metaphysics of Mind* (Oxford University Press), 1992, pp. 111–12.

Chapter Five

1 The distinction between natural and unnatural meaning is drawn in H. P. Grice, 'Meaning', *The Philosophical Review*, vol. 66, 1957, pp. 377–88.

2 Natural meaning in architecture is referred to by Roger Scruton, *The Aesthetics of Architeture*, London (Methuen), 1979, p. 160. He considers, mistakenly in my view, that 'to treat buildings in terms of their "natural meaning" is a trivial exercise'. The underlying issue is discussed in the context of semiology and with different terminology by Roland Barthes, *Elements of Semiology*, trans. Annette Lavers and Colin Smith, London (Jonathan Cape), 1967, pp. 41–42: 'This semantization is inevitable: *as soon as there is a society, every usage is turned into a sign of itself*; the use of a raincoat is to give protection from the rain, but this use cannot be dissociated from the very signs of an atmospheric situation' (Barthes' emphasis). For a discussion of Barthes's and others' formulations see Umberto Eco, 'Function and Sign: The Semiotics of Architecture', in G. Broadbent, R. Bunt and C. Jencks, *Signs, Symbols and Architecture*, Chichester (Wiley), 1980, pp. 11–58.

3 A version of Sullivan's article can be found in Tim and Charlotte Benton

(eds), with Dennis Sharp, *Form and Function: A Source Book for the History of Architecture and Design 1890–1939*, London (Crosby Lockwood Staples), 1975, pp. 11–14.

4 To be precise, it is 'natural languages' which are at issue. But they still deal in 'unnatural meaning' in the sense discussed above.

5 John Summerson, *The Classical Language of Architecture*, London (Thames and Hudson), 1980, p. 40.

6 *Ibid.*, p. 64.

7 William J. Mitchell, *The Logic of Architecture: Design, compututation and cognition*, Cambridge, Mass. (MIT Press), 1990, ch. 8, 'Languages of Architectural Form', pp. 131–81.

8 On the relation of grammar to architectural meaning see also Scruton, *Aesthetics of Architecture*, pp. 164–5.

9 Mitchell, *Logic of Architecture*, p. 135.

10 Frank Lloyd Wright, *The Natural House*, New York (Horizon Press), 1954, p. 181.

11 Sylvia Lavin, *Quatremère de Quincy and the Invention of a Modern Language of Architecture*, Cambridge, Mass. (MIT Press), 1992, p. 88, quoting from Quatremère's *De l'architecture égyptienne* (1803).

12 Philip Steadman, *The Evolution of Designs: Biological Analogy in Architecture and the Applied Arts* (Cambridge University Press), 1979, p. 40. For a modern view of 'nested hierarchies' in classical architecture see Alexander Tzonis and Liane Lefaivre, *Classical Architecture: The Poetics of Order*, Cambridge, Mass. (MIT Press), 1986, pp. 98–101.

13 I am grateful to Andrew Floyd for making this observation.

14 John Onians, *Bearers of Meaning: The Classical Orders in Antiquity, the Middle Ages and the Renaissance* (Princeton University Press), 1988, chs 16 and 17, pp. 216–46.

15 Summerson, *Classical Language of Architecture*, p. 27.

16 Tzonis and Lefaivre, *Classical Architecture*, chs 4 and 5, pp. 171–255.

17 Onians, *Bearers of Meaning*, p. 8.

18 Bernard Tschumi, *Architecture and Disjunction*, Cambridge, Mass. (MIT Press), 1994, p. 88.

19 George Hersey, *The Lost Meaning of Classical Architecture*, Cambridge, Mass. (MIT Press), 1988, p. 36.

20 John Ruskin, *The Seven Lamps of Architecture*, 2nd edition, London (Smith Elder), 1855, p. 8.

21 Victor Hugo, *Notre-Dame of Paris* (1831), trans. John Sturrock, Harmondsworth (Penguin), 1978, pp. 189–93.

22 *Ibid.*, p. 196.

23   Ruskin, 'Interpretations of "The Bible of Amiens"' (1881), *The Works of John Ruskin*, vol. 33, ed. E. T. Cook and Alexander Wedderburn, London (George Allen), 1908, pp. 5–187.

24   Neil Levine, 'The Book and the Building: Hugo's Theory of Architecture and Labrouste's Bibliothèque Ste-Geneviève, in Robin Middleton (ed.), *The Beaux-Arts and Nineteenth Century French Architecture*, London (Thames and Hudson), 1982, pp. 138–73.

25   Neil Levine describes Labrouste's interest in the notion that classical buildings were the setting for ephemeral displays of notices and other information in 'The Romantic Idea of Architectural Legibility: Henri Labrouste and the Neo-Grec', in Arthur Drexler (ed.), *The Architecture of the Ecole des Beaux-Arts*, New York (Museum of Modern Art), 1977, pp. 325–416. On the general question of flexibility of meaning see also Eco's concluding remark in 'Function and Sign', p. 58.

26   Kenneth Frampton, *Studies in Tectonic Culture: The Poetics of Construction in Nineteenth and Twentieth Century Architecture*, Cambridge, Mass. (MIT Press), 1995, p. 275.

27   See Robin Evans, *Translations from Drawing to Building and Other Essays*, 'Mies van der Rohe's Paradoxical Symmetries', London (Architectural Association), 1997, pp. 233–72.

28   The argument can be found in Richard Wollheim, *Art and its Objects*, 'Seeing-as, Seeing-in, and Pictorial Representation', Supplementary Essay v, 2nd edition (Cambridge University Press), 1980, pp. 205–26; and Richard Wollheim, *Painting as an Art*, 'What the Spectator Sees', ch. 2, London (Thames and Hudson), 1987, pp. 43–100.

29   Wollheim, *Art and its Objects*, p. 223.

30   *Ibid.*, p. 222.

31   See Alice T. Friedman, *Women and the Making of the Modern House: A Social and Architectural History*, 'Family Matters: The Schröder House, by Gerrit Rietveld and Truus Schröder', ch. 2, New York (Harry N, Abrams Inc.), 1998, pp. 64–91.

Chapter Six

1   See Guy Sircello, 'Expressive Properties of Art', in Joseph Margolis (ed.), *Philosophy Looks at the Arts*, rev. edition, Philadelphia (Temple University Press), 1978, p. 325, 'Romantic ideas about mind and its relation to art did not receive their clearest expression until the twentieth century. Then philosophers like Croce, Collingwood, Cassirer, Dewey and Langer tried to spell out exactly how it is that art can be expressive.'

2   R. G. Collingwood, *The Principles of Art* (1938), Oxford (Clarendon Press), 1958, p. 128. I assume that Collingwood does not mean craft in the 'arts and crafts' sense: studio pottery, for example, is closer to his definition of an art. I take it that motorcycle maintenance or computer programming would be crafts in his sense.

3   *Ibid.*, p. 32.

4   *Ibid.*, p. 236.

5   *Ibid.*, pp. 234–41.

6   *Ibid.*, p. 147.

7   *Ibid.*, ch. 14, pp. 300–24. Collingwood was writing in 1938 and the contemporary interest in collective artistic activity shines through. Compare also his treatment of the question with that of Walter Benjamin in 'The Work of Art in the Age of Mechanical Reproduction', in *Illuminations*, ed. Hannah Arendt, London (Fontana/Collins), 1977, pp. 219–53.

8   Frank Rutter, *The Poetry of Architecture*, London (Hodder and Stoughton), 1923. For a view of architecture which derives from a similar viewpoint to Collingwood's see also Suzanne K. Langer, *Feeling and Form*, London (Routledge and Kegan Paul), 1953, pp. 92–102. And for the influence of Langer in turn see Niels Lunning Prak, *The Language of Architecture: A Contribution to Architectural Theory*, The Hague (Mouton), p. 17, 1968: 'A work of art, just as a word, symbolises the concept of an emotion, and through that concept the emotion itself'; see also Sven Hesselgren, *The Language of Architecture*, 2 vols, Lund (Student litteratur), 1972.

9   Bruce Allsopp, *Art and the Nature of Architecture*, London (Sir Isaac Pitman and Sons Ltd.), 1952, p. 79.

10 *Ibid.*, p. 24, 'Shelter, refuge, security, home, hearth, family, neighbours, work, the land, animals, crops, weather, divinity, religion, devotion, dedication, aspiration, play, comfort, luxury, strength, stability, soundness, construction, fitness, shape, texture, colour, stress, strain, pattern, economy of effort, perfection of means to end, rhythm, balance, unity, space enclosed.'

11 *Ibid.*, p. 25.

12 H. S. Goodhart-Rendel, *Vitruvian Nights*, 1932, pp. 10–11.

13 Langer, *Feeling and Form*, p. 389.

14 Collingwood, *Principles of Art*, p. 52.

15 O. K. Bouwsma, 'The Expression Theory of Art', in W. Elton (ed.), *Aesthetics and Language*, Oxford (Basil Blackwell), 1954, p. 98.

16 See Robert Wilkinson, 'Art, Emotion and Expression', in Oswald Hanfling (ed.), *Philosophical Aesthetics: An Introduction*, Oxford (Blackwell), 1992, p. 229.

17 This discussion draws on Virgil Aldrich, '"Expresses" and "Expressive"', *Journal of Aesthetics and Art Criticism*, vol. 37, no. 2 (Winter 1978), pp. 203–17.

18   Roger A. Shiner, 'The Mental Life of a Work of Art', *Journal of Aesthetics and Art Criticism*, vol. 40, no. 3 (Spring 1982), pp. 253–68, discusses the surface–depth aspect of expression in relation to Wittgenstein's idea of 'language-games'. Stephen Mulhall, 'Expression', in *A Companion to Aesthetics*, ed. David E. Cooper, Oxford (Blackwell), 1995, pp. 144–49 also draws on Wittgenstein's idea of 'secondary' uses of language.

19   Bouwsma, 'Expression Theory of Art', p. 99.

20   *Ibid.*, p. 74.

21   See Malcolm Budd, *Music and the Emotions: The Philosophical Theories*, London (Routledge and Kegan Paul), 1985, p. 4.

22   Talbot Hamlin, *Architecture: An Art for All Men*, New York (Columbia University Press), 1947, p. 15.

23   Stanley Abercrombie, *Architecture as Art: An Esthetic Analysis*, New York (Van Nostrand Reinhold), 1984, p. 135.

24   Howard Robertson, *Architecture Explained*, London (Ernest Benn), 1926, p. 120.

25   Eugene Raskin, *Architecturally Speaking*, New York (Reinhold Publishing Corporation), 1954, pp. 128–30.

26   John Ruskin, *The Seven Lamps of Architecture*, 2nd edition, London (Smith Elder), 1855, p. 77.

27   William R. Lethaby, *Architecture, Mysticism and Myth* (1891), Bath (Solos), 1994, p. 16.

28   Robertson, *Architecture Explained*, p. 122.

29   Le Corbusier, 'If I had to teach you architecture', in *Focus*, no. 1 (Summer 1938), London (Percy Lund Humphries), pp. 3–12.

Chapter Seven

1   The phrase comes from William James, 'The Stream of Consciousness', ch. 11 of *Psychology: Briefer Course* (1892), reprinted in William Lyons (ed.) *Modern Philosophy of Mind*, London (Dent), 1995, pp. 3–23.

2   Walter Benjamin, *Illuminations*, ed. Hannah Arendt, London (Fontana/Collins), 1977, pp. 219–53.

3   *Ibid.*, p. 242.

4   The discussion of architecture can be found in Section 51 of Kant's *The Critique of Judgement* (1790), trans. James Creed Meredith, Oxford (Clarendon Press), 1928. On the general question of how Kant's division of the fine arts relates to his larger aesthetic theory see Michael Podro, *The Manifold in Perception: Theories of Art from Kant to Hildebrand*, Oxford (Clarendon Press), 1972, pp. 7–35.

5   Kant, *Critique of Judgement*, p. 186.

6   *Ibid.*, pp. 175–76.

7   *Ibid.*, p. 177.

8   Dennis Sharp (ed.), *Bilbao 2000: Architecture and Urban Regeneration*, London (Book Art), 1995. p. 48.

9   Kant, *Critique of Judgement*, p. 73.

10   This usage is as proposed in Andrew Woodfield, *Teleology* (Cambridge University Press), 1976, p. 27.

11   Bernard Tschumi, *The Manhattan Transcripts*, 2nd edition, London (Academy Editions), 1994.

12   For a discussion of the relationship between changes in educational ideas and school design see Andrew Saint, *Towards a Social Architecture: The Role of Schoolbuilding in Post-war England*, London (Yale University Press), 1987.

13   When William J. Mitchell, *The Logic of Architecture* Cambridge, Mass. (MIT Press), 1990, chs 9 and 10, pp. 183–239, embarks on the formal functional analysis of building designs it is significant that his examples deal with climate control, specifically the pitches of roofs that are desirable in order to shed water. However the attempt at systematic functional analysis is effectively abandoned when issues about the internal use of buildings are discussed.

14   For an example of the kind of discussion that is entailed see Nigel Yates, *Buildings, Faith and Worship: The Liturgical Arrangement of Anglican Churches 1600–1900*, Oxford (Clarendon Press), 1991.

15   Adrian Forty, 'The Modern Hospital in England and France: The Social and Medical Uses of Architecture', in Anthony D. King (ed.), *Buildings and Society: Essays on the Social Development of the Built Environment*, London (Routledge and Kegan Paul), 1980, pp. 61–93. For discussion of these topics in other contexts see Thomas A. Markus, *Buildings and Power: Freedom and Control in the Origin of Modern Building Types*, London (Routledge), 1993.

16   For the development of the design and use of the interiors of British houses see Alison Ravetz with Richard Turkington, *The Place of Home: English Domestic Environments 1914–2000*, London (Spon), 1995.

17   Lenneke Büller and Frank den Oudsten, 'Interview with Truus Schröder', in Paul Overy et al., *The Rietveld Schröder House*, London (Butterworth Architecture), 1988, p. 56.

18   Christopher Alexander *et al.*, *A Pattern Language: Towns, Buildings, Construction*, New York (Oxford University Press), 1977, p. 159. Part of the interest of this book lies in its differences and continuities with Alexander's earlier work, *Notes on the Synthesis of Form*, Cambridge, Mass. (Harvard University Press), 1964, in which the idea of the separation of problems and forms was given more abstract treatment. The consensus, with which I agree, is that *Notes on*

the Synthesis of Form failed to demonstrate that architectural forms, in any recognisable sense, can be derived from systematically stating problems. However, I believe that the problem carries through into the later work. See also Stephen Grabow, *Christopher Alexander: The Search for a New Paradigm in Architecture*, Stocksfield (Oriel Press), 1983.

19 Bernard Tschumi, *Architecture and Disjunction*, Cambridge, Mass. (MIT Press), 1994 and *Manhattan Transcripts*. For discussion of projects in which these ideas are elaborated see Tschumi, *Event-Cities: (Praxis)*, Cambridge, Mass. (MIT Press), 1994.

20 For an intriguing example of transgressive uses of buildings see Eamon Duffy's description of 'squints' made through the inner screens of churches, which allowed the devout to observe the critical moment of the communion, in *The Stripping of the Altars: Traditional Religion in England c. 1400–1580*, New Haven and London (Yale University Press), 1992, pp. 96–98.

21 I use the term dwelling as a convenient term to embrace houses, flats, etc. To avoid confusion, I should stress that I do not have in mind the usage that appears in English translations of Heidegger.

22 Aldo Rossi, *The Architecture of the City* (*L'Architettura della città*, 1966) trans. Cambridge, Mass. (MIT Press), 1982; and *A Scientific Autobiography*, Cambridge, Mass. (MIT Press), 1981.

23 For an early account of systematic methods for the appraisal of designs see Dennis Chapman, *The Home and Social Status*, London (Routledge and Kegan Paul), 1955. Note his adoption of the terms 'manifest' and 'latent' functions to account for some of the perplexities that I have described. A typical account of appraisal techniques can be found in John Zeisel, *Inquiry by Design: Tools for Environment–Behaviour Research* (Cambridge University Press), 1984.

24 The development of this consensus can be traced in the following: B. Hillier, J. Musgrove and P. O'Sullivan, 'Knowledge and Design', in H. M. Proshansky, W. H. Ittelson and L. G. Rivlin (eds), *Environmental Psychology: Man and His Physical Setting*, 2nd edition, pp. 69–83.

Bill Hillier and Adrian Leaman, 'How is Design Possible?', *Journal of Architectural Research*, vol. 3, no. 1, 1974, pp. 4–11. The interactivity between problem and solution is discussed in terms of a 'manifold', p. 7: 'Even to name an architectural problem – say, "design a school" – implies a whole range of solutions which will be more or less immediately activated in some sense through the designer's manifold.'

James A. Powell, I. Cooper and S. Lera (eds), *Designing for Building Utilisation*, London (Spon), 1984.

Barrie Evans, James A. Powell and Reg Talbot (eds), *Changing Design*, Chichester (John Wiley and Sons), 1982.

Bryan Lawson, *How Designers Think: The Design Process Demystified*, 2nd edition, London (Butterworth Architecture), 1990. Lawson develops his argument through a series of case studies of architects' design methods in *Design in Mind*, Oxford (Butterworth Architecture), 1994.

The logical character of the design process is discussed in Lionel March, 'The Logic of Design and the Question of Value', in March (ed.), *The Architecture of Form* (Cambridge University Press), 1976, pp. and by William Fawcett, 'A Note on the Logic of Design', *Design Studies*, vol. 8, no. 2 (April 1987), pp. 82–87.

Many of the themes are brought together in an important series of papers by Jane Darke: 'Architects and User Requirements in Public-sector Housing: 1. Architects' Assumptions about Users', *Environment and Planning B: Planning and Design*, vol. 11, 1984, pp. 389–404; 'Architects and User Requirements in Public-sector Housing: 2. The Sources for Architects' Assumptions', *ibid.*, pp. 405–16; "Architects and User Requirements in Public-sector Housing: 3. Towards an Adequate Understanding of User Requirements in Housing', *ibid.*, pp. 417–33.

Chapter Eight

1   I have used the following as sources of Gropius's views: Tim and Charlotte Benton (eds), with Dennis Sharp, *Form and Function: A Source Book for the History of Architecture and Design 1890–1939*, London (Crosby Lockwood Staples), 1975, sections 26, 59, 73 and 74; Walter Gropius, *The New Architecture and the Bauhaus*, London (Faber and Faber), 1935; Gropius, *Scope of Total Architecture*, New York (Collier Books), 1962; Peter Gay, *Art and Act: On Causes in History – Manet, Gropius, Mondrian*, New York and London (Harper and Row), 1976. For a disapproving view of Gropius's later career see Klaus Herdeg, *The Decorated Diagram*, Cambridge, Mass. (MIT Press), 1983.

2   For Kahn's views in the later period of his career see Richard Saul Wurman, *What Will Be Has Always Been: The Words of Louis I. Kahn*, New York (Access Press and Rizzoli), 1986. There is a good deal of repetition in the lectures and interviews and I have assumed that the repeated passages indicate key issues for Kahn.

3   Immanuel Kant, p. 179, n. 1.

4   Goethe, *On German Architecture* (1772): see the translation by Geoffrey Grigson, with marginal commentary by Nikolaus Pevsner, 'Act 2: Romantic Gothic; Scene 1: Goethe and Strassburg', *Architectural Review*, 98, 1945, pp. 155–59, or the translation in Elizabeth Gilmore Holt (ed.), *A Documentary*

History of Art, vol. 2, Garden City, New York (Anchor Books), 1958, pp. 360–69.

5   Hugh Honour, *Romanticism*, London (Penguin), 1981, p. 364, n. 1.

6   David Van Zanten, *Designing Paris: The Architecture of Duban, Labrouste, Duc, and Vaudoyer*, Cambridge, Mass. (MIT Press), 1987; The references to Reynaud, Duban and Vaudoyer are on pp. 57, 24 and 17 respectively.

7   C. R. Cockerell, who had wished to be an artist but was prevailed on by his architect father to follow him into the profession, wrote the following in his diary, during his excavations in Greece in April 1811: 'As we were sailing out of the port (of the Piraeus) in our open boat we overtook the ship with Lord Byron on board (on his return to England). Passing under her stern we sang a favourite song of his, on which he looked out of the windows and invited us in. There we drank a glass of port with him, Colonel Travers, and two of the English officers . . . We slept very well in the boat, and next morning reached Aegina'. Quoted in David Watkin, *The Life and Work of C. R. Cockerell*, London (Zwemmer), 1974, p. 9. Watkin also makes interesting comments on biological analogies used by Cockerell in his Royal Academy lectures, *ibid.*, p. 122.

8   Horatio Greenough, *Form and Function: Remarks on Art, Design and Architecture*, ed. Harold A. Small, with an introduction by Erle Loran, Berkeley and Los Angeles (University of California Press), 1969, p. 58.

9   Quoted by Narciso G. Menocal, *Architecture as Nature*, Madison, Wisconsin (University of Wisconsin Press), 1981, p. 64.

10 See Philip Steadman, *The Evolution of Designs: Biological Analogy in Architecture and the Applied Arts* (Cambridge University Press), 1979, ch. 3, pp. 23–32. Steadman's work is an essential guide to the relation of biology and architecture in the modern period. David Watkin, *Sir John Soane: Enlightenment Thought and the Royal Academy Lectures* (Cambridge University Press), 1996, p. 410, observes that Soane's observations on plant forms were close to those of Goethe.

11 Harry Francis Mallgrave, *Gottfried Semper: Architect of the Nineteenth Century*, New Haven and London (Yale University Press), 1996, p. 159.

12 Sylvia Lavin, *Quatremère de Quincy and the Invention of a Modern Language of Architecture*, Cambridge, Mass. (MIT Press), 1992, pp. 20–21.

13 See Neil Levine, 'The Competition for the Grand Prix in 1824', in Robin Middleton (ed.), *The Beaux-Arts and Nineteenth-Century French Architecture*, London (Thames and Hudson), 1982, p. 99.

14 Steadman, *Evolution of Designs*, p. 47.

15 See Ernst Mayr, *The Growth of Biological Thought*, Cambridge, Mass. (Belknap Press), 1982, p. 355.

16   See Steadman, *Evolution of Designs*, pp. 130–36.

17   Edward de Zurko, *Origins of Functionalist Theory*, New York 1957, ch. 5, pp. 75–124.

18   See Mayr, *Growth of Biological Thought*, pp. 51–52.

19   For further reflections on the biological analogy in architecture see Joseph Mashek, 'Textual Life of the Living-machine', *Building-Art: Modern Architecture under Cultural Construction* (Cambridge University Press), 1993, pp. 77–94.

20   Louis H. Sullivan, *The Autobiography of an Idea* (1925), New York (Dover), 1956, pp. 207 and 254–55. On Sullivan's significance in the development of modern architecture see also David S. Andrew, *Louis Sullivan and the Polemics of Modern Architecture*, Urbana and Chicago (University of Illinois Press), 1985; David Van Zanten, 'Sullivan to 1890', in Wim de Wit (ed.), *Louis Sullivan: The Function of Ornament*, New York (W. W. Norton), 1986, pp. 13–63. Extracts from Sullivan's important essay 'The Tall Office Building Artistically Considered' are reprinted in Tim and Charlotte Benton (eds), with Dennis Sharp, *Form and Function: A Source Book for the History of Architecture and Design 1890–1939*, London (Crosby Lockwood Staples), 1975, pp. 11–14.

21   Theosophy was founded in 1875 by Madame Helena Blavatsky and Colonel H. S. Olcott. Its doctrine was primarily derived from Buddhism. Rudolf Steiner, who had been the General Secretary of the German Section from 1902, split from the movement to form the Anthroposophical Society in 1913. The Steiner movement developed a distinctive view of architecture which still flourishes. Note, for example, the remark of the Steinerian architect Christopher Day that 'I believe in a sort of spiritual functionalism', in Tom Dyckhoff, *Perspectives on Architecture*, Issue 29 (June/July 1997), pp. 72–73.

22   See Joseph Rykwert, 'The Dark Side of the Bauhaus' in *The Necessity of Artifice*, London (Academy Editions), 1982, pp. 44–49; Allan Doig, *Theo van Doesburg: Painting into Architecture, Theory into Practice* (Cambridge University Press), 1986.

23   See Kenneth Frampton, *Modern Architecture: A Critical History*, 3rd edition, London and New York (Thames and Hudson), 1992, p. 135.

24   The issue and its many implications are discussed in Peter Collins, *Changing Ideals in Modern Architecture*, London (Faber and Faber), 1965; Nikolaus Pevsner, *Some Architectural Writers of the Nineteenth Century* (Oxford University Press), 1972; J. Mordaunt Crook, *The Dilemma of Style: Architectural Ideas from the Picturesque to the Post-modern*, London (John Murray), 1989; Heinrich Hubsch *et al.*, *In What Style Should We Build?*, ed. and trans. Wolfgang Herrmann, Santa Monica (Getty Center for the Arts and the Humanities), 1992; Richard A. Etlin, *Frank Lloyd Wright and Le Corbusier: The Romantic*

Legacy (Manchester University Press), 1994, ch. 4, 'The Spirit of the Age', pp. 165–99.

25 Robert Kerr, *The Newleafe Discourses on the Fine Art Architecture*, London (J. Weale), 1846.

26 Collins, *Changing Ideals*, p. 143.

27 See Pevsner, *Some Architectural Writers*, pp. 229 and 232.

28 Collins, *Changing Ideals*, p. 144.

29 Benton, Benton and Sharp, *Form and Function*, p. 39.

30 *Ibid.*, p. 194.

31 *Ibid.*, pp. 40–45.

32 *Ibid.*, p. 169.

33 *Ibid.*, p. 118.

34 See H. Allen Brooks, *Le Corbusier's Formative Years: Charles-Edouard Jeanneret at La Chaux-de-Fonds* (University of Chicago Press), 1997, pp. 172–75.

35 See K. Michael Hays, *Modernism and the Posthumanist Subject: The Architecture of Hannes Meyer and Ludwig Hilberseimer*, Cambridge, Mass. (MIT Press), 1992; for the opposite kind of view, which nevertheless shares a similar over-estimate of modernism's 'post-humanism', and which portrays Aalto as 'an exemplary resistance fighter' against it, see Colin St John Wilson, *Architectural Reflections: Studies in the Philosophy and Practice of Architecture*, London (Butterworth Architecture), 1992.

36 See, for example, HRH The Prince of Wales, *A Vision of Britain: A Personal View of Architecture*, London (Doubleday), 1989.

37 Roger Scruton, *The Aesthetics of Architecture*, London (Methuen), 1979, ch. 8, 'Expression and Abstraction', pp. 179–205.

38 John Summerson, 'The Case for a Theory of "Modern" Architecture' (1957) in *The Unromantic Castle and Other Essays*, London (Thames and Hudson), 1990, pp. 257–66.

39 Peter Eisenman, 'House I 1967', in *Five Architects: Eisenman, Graves, Gwathmey, Hejduk, Meier*, 2nd edition, New York (Oxford University Press), 1975. pp. 15–23.

40 Peter Eisenman, 'Misreading' in *House of Cards*, New York (Oxford University Press), 1987, p. 167.

41 Peter Eisenman, *Fin D'Ou T HouS*, with an introduction by Jeffrey Kipnis, London (Architectural Association), 1985; and *Moving Arrows and Other Errors: An Architecture of Absence. Box 3*, London (Architectural Association), 1986.

42 Kipnis in Eisenman, *Fin D'Ou T HouS*, p. 3.

43 Theodor Adorno, 'Functionalism Today', *Oppositions* 17 (Summer 1979), p. 39.

Photograph Credits

4: Edifice; 5: The Building of Bath Museum; 6: George Jackson and Sons; 7: The Trustees of Sir John Soane's Museum; 8: The Trustees of Sir John Soane's Museum; 9: The National Trust; 11: Sir John Soane's Museum; 13: Victoria and Albert Museum; 14: RIBA Drawings Collection; 16: Tim Ronalds; 17: Tim Ronalds; 18: © 1998 The Frank Lloyd Wright Foundation, Scottsdale, Arizona; 19: © 1998 The Frank Lloyd Wright Foundation, Scottsdale, Arizona; 20: The Walker Art Gallery, National Museums and Galleries on Merseyside; 22: Avoncroft Museum of Historic Buildings; 23: John Segal; 24: John Segal; 26: Grant Mudford; 28: Martin Charles; 31: By kind permission of Harvard University Press; 32: Hélène Binet; 33: Stephan Couturier, Archipress; 37: A. F. Kersting; 38: A. F. Kersting; 41: The Georgian Group; 42: The James Stirling Foundation, photo Richard Einzig; 43: The James Stirling Foundation; 44: Alinari; 45: Alinari; 46: Alinari; 47: The President, Fellows and Graduate Students of Clare Hall, Cambridge; 48: Swedish Museum of Architecture, Photographic Collections; 49: The President, Fellows and Graduate Students of Clare Hall, Cambridge; 50: Collection Philippe Garner; 51: Collection Philippe Garner; 52: Lucien Hervé; 53: Martin Charles; 54: Martin Charles; 55: Andrew Peckham; 56: Venturi, Rauch and Scott Brown, photo Tom Bernard; 58: Alinari; 59: Adrian Forty; 60: Fondation Le Corbusier; 61: Ian Pearson/Mexicolore; 63: A. F. Kersting; 64: The Architectural Association slide library; 67: Roger-Viollet; 68: Louise Campbell; 69: Victoria and Albert Museum Picture Library, photo Andrew Putler; 70: The Architectural Association slide library; 73: Timothy Soar; 74: RIBA Drawings Collection; 75: Edifice; 76: Venturi,

Index